WHATEVER
BECAME
OF . . . ?

Second Series

WHATEVER BECAME OF...?

Second Series

by
RICHARD LAMPARSKI

CROWN PUBLISHERS, INC., NEW YORK

Acknowledgments

The author would like to express thanks to the following people who helped in the preparation of this book: Alfred Monaco, Clifford May, Peter Hanson, John Robbins, Jon Virzi, Joe Riccuiti, Bob Stewart, Don Koll, Ian McGowan, and Danny Frank. And to the following organizations for their cooperation: A.F.T.R.A., *Movie Star News, The Sporting News,* and Cinemabilia.

The photographs contained in this book are from the author's own collection, or were kindly supplied by the personalities themselves, or are part of the collections of Jon Virzi, John Robbins, Diana Keyt, and Clifford May.

Individuals whose names carry an asterisk (*) in the text appear as separate segments in Volume One of *Whatever Became of . . . ?*

Published simultaneously in Canada by
General Publishing Company Limited
Fourth Printing, February, 1971

*For Mary Margaret McBride, The First Lady of Radio,
with many thanks for the help and encouragement she
gave me and the luck her friendship brought me.*

CONTENTS

In Alphabetical Order

The great artist in a 1933 publicity shot for one of his frequent radio appearances. *NBC*

PAUL ROBESON

One of the twentieth century's most talented and controversial men, who was to become best known as a great singing star, was born in Princeton, New Jersey, in 1898. His schoolteacher mother died when he was only six years old. His father was a poor but highly respected minister who early in his lifetime had escaped from slavery in North Carolina. Robeson worked hard to win a scholarship to Rutgers in 1915. He was the third member of his race to be admitted to what was then a private institution. He did sensationally well. He made Phi Beta Kappa in his junior year and as a senior was selected for Cap & Skull in 1919. He excelled at track, basketball, football, and baseball, winning twelve varsity letters. By the time he graduated, the expression "Robeson of Rutgers" was well known.

To support himself while going to Columbia Law School Paul Robeson played pro football. While attending the university he met and married Eslanda Cardozo Goode in 1921. She assisted and advised him in everything he did after that. It was she who in 1920 persuaded him to play a role in *Simon the Cyrenian* at the Harlem YMCA, against his better judgment. He was asked to join the Provincetown Players, a Greenwich Village theatre group which included the playwright Eugene O'Neill.

George Jean Nathan, the dean of theatre critics at the time, saw Robeson in *All God's Chillun Got Wings* in 1924 and again the same year in *Emperor Jones* and called him one of the most thoroughly eloquent and convincing actors he had ever seen.

The following year the famous singer gave his first of many concerts. Through radio and phonograph records the name of Paul Robeson soon became known throughout the world. In 1928 he sang "Ole Man River" in *Show Boat* in London and remained to play the role of Othello in 1930.

In England, where he spent most of his time until 1939, Robeson became intensely interested in economics and politics. When George Bernard Shaw first asked his opinion of Socialism, Robeson hardly knew what the word meant. He was to state years later, however, that a "socialist society represents an advance to a higher stage of life." In 1934 he made the first of many trips to the Soviet Union and expressed his admiration for their way of life, emphasizing the lack of racial discrimination he found there. During the Spanish Civil War he sang for the Loyalist troops.

One of the highlights of his career was when he first sang "Ballad for Americans" on radio in 1939. His greatest dramatic triumph was when he played the title role in *Othello* on Broadway in 1943.

Robeson was active in civil rights before it was popular and was a founder of the Progressive Party, which nominated Henry Wallace and Senator Glen Taylor (now manufacturing toupees in Millbrae, California) for President and Vice-President in 1948. In 1949, because of his frequent statements criticizing the United States and complimenting Russia, an outdoor concert in Peekskill, New York, was interrupted by violence. Held a week later, over twenty thousand fans turned out.

The Robeson's only child, Paul, Jr., married a white girl in 1949. A year later his father's passport was withdrawn and for eight years he engaged in a legal battle to regain it. In 1946 he had testified under oath that he was not a Communist Party member, but in hearings after that he refused to answer the question, stating that it infringed upon his constitutional rights.

In 1952 he was awarded the Stalin Peace Prize, but was unable to go to Russia to receive it until 1958 when the State Department was ordered by a federal court to return his passport. While in Europe on that trip he played *Othello* at Stratford-on-Avon. The bad press he had received in this country for years made his appearances here rare, but in Europe he was still regarded for his artistry alone. His concertizing on the Continent continued through the early sixties.

In 1963 Robeson took ill and underwent treatment in an East German hospital. That year he and Mrs. Robeson, who was acting as his manager at that time, returned to the United States. His wife, who in later years had also been his spokesman to the press, died in 1965. Robeson has never fully regained his health and ever since, has lived in their apartment on Jumal Place in Harlem— with frequent trips to Philadelphia where he also maintains a home. He no longer gives interviews and letters are answered by his son, stating that his father's health does not permit him to perform or answer questions.

A rare stroll near his Manhattan home. *UPI*

Entering a federal court in 1948.

"AXIS SALLY"

Very little is known about Mildred Gillars Sisk prior to her World War II emergence on Radio Berlin, which prompted the G.I. nickname "Axis Sally."

She grew up in Portland, Maine. After attending Ohio Wesleyan College during the thirties she spent several years knocking about as an actress in New York City with no success of any note. She did no better in Europe during her few years there before Pearl Harbor. Afterward, overnight, she became a radio personality of such fame that she was known on two continents. Although her voice was not heard in America except by those who might have picked up German radio on short wave, her countrymen were informed of her regular broadcasts by the American press and in letters written home by boys serving in the European Theatre of operations.

Mildred has maintained from the time she was arrested by the Allied Forces after the fall of Berlin that she was not "Axis Sally." She claims that she had broadcast under the name of "Midge." The nickname came about, according to Mildred, when the American boys confused her with another woman who did use the name "Axis Sally." This woman, says Mildred, broadcast from Rome, and it was she whose broadcasts gave "aid and comfort to the enemy." To this day Mildred Sisk swears that she was so upset at the time over what the Rome "Axis Sally" was saying on the air that she made several strong protests to the German Foreign Office, which were ignored.

Unlike Mildred, the Roman "Axis Sally" had renounced her United States citizenship. The Italian counterpart was born in New York City to Constantine Zucca, owner of an Italian restaurant in Manhattan's theatre district. Rita Louise Zucca was prevented from reentering the United States after the war and eventually served nine months in an Italian prison. Her present whereabouts are unknown.

The Allied Occupation Forces returned Mildred to the United States in 1947, and a year later she was made to stand trial in federal court. The prosecution's case against her was much weaker than most observers expected. While ten counts of treason were brought against her, she was convicted of only one. Still, treason is never treated lightly anywhere and the single count was enough to bring her a sentence of "from ten to thirty years."

Mildred was paroled in 1960 after serving ten years in the woman's federal prison at Alderson, West Virginia. Another inmate of the penitentiary at the same time was Mrs. Iva Toguri D'Aquino, better known to G.I.'s who fought in the Pacific Theatre as "Tokyo Rose." Mrs. D'Aquino, who was a Nisei Japanese, was last known to be living with her father, a Chicago pearl importer.

During her imprisonment Mildred was converted to the Roman Catholic faith by nuns who were doing social work among the prisoners.

Upon her release she visited for a time with her half sister who lives in Ashtabula, Ohio. The two had never been close, but were reconciled during Mildred's trial when her sister read the evidence against her and decided that she was being railroaded. The sisters are close friends today. Mrs. Nieminen is fifteen years younger than Mildred.

For the past seven years "Axis Sally" has been living quietly in a small apartment that is part of a convent. Although she has not taken her vows, Mildred lives and works with the Sisters of the Poor Child Jesus who run a girls' boarding school in Columbus, Ohio. She receives a salary as a music teacher and has apparently impressed both the faculty and student body. Parents of the children attending the school are aware that the notorious "Axis Sally" is teaching their children, but no one seems a bit disturbed. When asked about her employee recently, the Mother Superior said that Mildred has been "definitely a good influence on the students." A spokesman for the diocese was quoted as saying that "She has been living a very productive life since she came here."

"Axis Sally," still rather theatrical in manner, does not like to grant interviews or to be photographed. On the rare occasions she talks to a reporter she is reluctant to discuss the past except to say in a voice that would be instantly recognized by thousands of World War II veterans: "There is no doubt in my mind that I received an unfair trial. It all happened so long ago."

At work recently. *UPI*

With Howdy Doody in 1950.

BUFFALO BOB SMITH

The man who was to become the first—and the most popular—kiddie entertainer on television got his nickname from his home town.

His first job in show business was as a member of a singing trio known as the "Hi-Hatters." In 1933, the year of Repeal, they were heard over a local radio station sponsored by a brewery. The following year the late Ted Collins brought them to New York City where they were featured on the Hudson Terraplane Show, which starred Kate Smith. Six months later Smith was back in Buffalo as staff pianist and musical arranger at WBEN. He held various jobs in local radio until 1945 when the New York City NBC station, then called WEAF, hired him to do their morning show Monday through Saturday from 6 A.M. to 9 A.M.

For two years Smith pestered the network brass to try him on the technically primitive medium of television, without success. He developed the Howdy Doody character on his Saturday morning radio program, which was called "Triple B Ranch." It was basically a quiz show for children.

"Howdy Doody Time" finally made TV on December 27, 1947, the day after New York's famous blizzard. Its time slot was 5:30 to 6:00 P.M. Monday through Friday. It was the first offering of the day on TV at that time and was preceded by the well remembered test pattern of one geometric design or another. This was before the coaxial cable had linked the East and West coasts, and therefore seen only in six eastern cities.

A few weeks after the premiere Smith suggested to the sales department that he offer a free Howdy Doody pin to any boy or girl writing in. The mail pull would be an indication of his listenership since rating services had not at that point been developed for the new medium. All the National Broadcasting Company knew was that there were approximately forty thousand television sets within the viewing area. In three days eighty thousand requests were received. These were the days when a family with a television set with its seven-inch screen made larger by a thick glass bubble in front of it was watched by as many neighbors on the block as the living room could accommodate. Still, no one had guessed that the red-haired puppet and his friends, John J. Fadozle, America's No. 1 (Boing!) Private Eye, Cornelius J. Cobb, storekeeper in the town of Doodyville, and Flub-a-Dub, Howdy's pet, had gained such popularity in so short a time. It was a success that was to continue and even increase until Smith suffered a heart attack in 1957 and switched to one show a week on Saturday mornings from 10 to 10:30.

The same year he completely sold out his interest in Howdy Doody items— tee shirts, dolls, spoons, dishes, and comic books—to NBC and took a whopping capital gain.

The Saturday show went off the air on September 30, 1960. The original Clarabell, a clown who never spoke but was handy with a seltzer bottle, was played by Bob Keeshan, now CBS's Captain Kangaroo. Judy Tyler played Princess Summerfallwinterspring until she was killed in an automobile accident on July 4, 1956. And the puppet Howdy Doody, which had three different heads available, is kept by Rufus Rose, the show's chief puppeteer. (Perhaps Howdy Doody's chief competitor was Mr. I. Magination, played and created by Paul Tripp, now hosting a local NBC program called "Birthday House.")

Since 1960 Buffalo Bob has devoted most of his time to his family. Smith has been married since 1940 to his first grade classmate. His oldest son, Ron, is a stockbroker. The second, Robin, is in medical school, and teen-ager Chris is in high school. The Smiths spend their winters in Fort Lauderdale, Florida, where they build and sell condominium apartments. They summer in Calais, Maine. Smith owns the local radio station, WQDY, and just purchased stations WOU at Houlton, and WMKR at Millinocket. During the fall and spring their home is a nine-room apartment in New Rochelle, New York, a few blocks from Smith's Wykagyl Liquor Store.

During an interview by Author Richard Lamparski in Bob's New Rochelle apartment. *Peter Schaeffer*

A famous Vandamm Studios photograph in 1934.

KATHARINE CORNELL

The First Lady of the American Theatre was born in 1898 in Berlin, where her father was studying medicine, and raised in Buffalo, New York. Her father gave up his medical practice to manage the Star Theatre in that city. In her youth, Katharine leaned more toward athletics than acting. She excelled in swimming, tennis, and ice skating, although she did study drama at the Oaksmere School in Mamaroneck, New York.

She made her debut in 1916 with the Washington Square Players in *Bushido,* and then studied and toured for three seasons with the famous Jessie Bonstelle Players. It was because of her work there that she was chosen in 1919 to play in *Little Women,* in London. That year she was introduced to Guthrie McClintic in the office of producer William Brady.

McClintic was a director who once wanted to be an actor. Miss Cornell was an actress who lacked the ambition necessary to succeed in the theatre. Following their marriage in 1921, throughout her career he supplied the drive and guidance she needed. He directed all of her vehicles after 1921, when she captivated New York audiences in *A Bill of Divorcement.*

Mostly her roles were romantic and emotional. Because melodrama and love stories were the rage of her era, she soon became a major star.

On Broadway she starred in *The Enchanted Cottage* (1923), *Candida* (1924), which she was to revive many times, *The Green Hat* (1925), her most spectacular success during the twenties, *The Letter* (1927), and *The Age of Innocence* (1928).

Dean of Drama Critics George Jean Nathan once said of her, "I would give all the other young actresses put together for her—and three-quarters of the older ones."

Undoubtedly, her best remembered role was as Elizabeth Barrett Browning in *The Barretts of Wimpole Street,* which she first did in 1931. After a year on Broadway, she took it on the road. No other actress of her time was more popular with women. She is credited by many in the theatre as being responsible for reopening "the road"—by proving to producers that plays on tour

14

could be very profitable. Since Miss Cornell produced her own plays, under the banner of "Katharine Cornell Presents," she took all the chances but in return reaped huge profits. She revived *Barretts* over and over again. As late as 1956, she played it on television. Unfortunately, by this time the material was overly familiar, and she was too old for the role.

In 1934 she was in *Romeo and Juliet*. *St. Joan* (1936) was another personal triumph. In 1939 she played *No Time for Comedy* on Broadway and on tour. In 1941 she appeared in *The Doctor's Dilemma*, which she followed with an all-star revival of *Candida* in 1942. In 1943 she made her brief and only appearance in a movie, *Stage Door Canteen*, playing herself. In 1944 Miss Cornell talked the U.S.O. into sponsoring an overseas tour for servicemen. At first the officials thought the actress would be too "heavy" for war-weary G.I.'s, but she proved them quite wrong. Her *Antigone* was an artistic success, though it was a box-office failure in 1946. In 1947 she was in *Anthony and Cleopatra*.

During the thirties and forties she was heard occasionally on U.S. Steel's radio show, "Theatre Guild on the Air." In 1957 she headed the cast of a TV production of "There Shall Be No Night."

In 1959-60 "Kit," as her colleagues call her, made her farewell tour in *Dear Liar*. She traveled all over the nation in a trailer built especially for her.

In 1961 Guthrie McClintic died, and she has not acted since. Asked why recently, she replied: "I was nervous from the beginning, and it got worse as years went on. He always gave me the security I needed. I felt I couldn't do anything after that."

If she had any temptations to go back on her word, it became impossible after 1966 when she developed a heart condition. Her time is divided between her summer home in Martha's Vineyard and a brownstone in Manhattan's East Fifties. Miss Cornell keeps a huge dachshund named Kasper as a companion. Her only professional activities in the past few years have been some narrations she has done for National Educational Television and the recordings she has been doing for the blind for some time now.

"Kasper" and his mistress in their Manhattan home. *Larry Fried.*

Leopold (left) and Loeb (center) under arrest for their thrill killing. *UPI*

NATHAN LEOPOLD

The co-conspirator in what was perhaps the most vicious, most pointless murder on record was also the youngest student ever to graduate from the University of Chicago. He came from a wealthy family and was about to continue his education at Harvard when at the age of nineteen he and his friend, Richard Loeb, brutally murdered Bobby Franks, a fourteen-year-old distant cousin of Loeb's. Loeb was a great admirer of Nietzsche and fancied himself a "Superman." He was quite handsome and had been the youngest graduate in the history of the University of Michigan. Leopold admired Loeb's supreme confidence and intelligence and was strongly attracted to him sexually.

Their plan for the perfect crime was carried out on May 21, 1924, in a cold-blooded, awkward fashion. The victim was not even the one they had originally intended to kill. Their sole purpose in the murder was to prove that they were of superior intelligence and could not be caught. They further complicated matters by calling the victim's family and demanding ransom money, pretending that the child had been kidnapped and was still alive. They flaunted their cunning and audacity among themselves by actually aiding the police in the search for the missing boy and offering suggestions and theories to the authorities, whom they felt were bunglers and incompetents.

Bobby Frank's body was found the day after the murder and not far from it police picked up a pair of glasses, carelessly dropped by Leopold. He and Loeb denied they knew anything about the case. They claimed to have been driving all day in Leopold's Willys-Knight. They had no apparent motive. They knew the boy and had liked him. Not everyone, however, liked them. The family chauffeur, who had always found the boys insufferable, told police the car had never left the garage on May 21. Leopold said that he might have lost his glasses when he was in the area bird-watching several weeks before, yet they were spotless when found. The police separated the boys and played them against each other. Loeb, the "Superman," cracked first. Rather arrogantly they admitted what they had done.

They were young, rich, and privileged, with contemptible manners, and they had committed a heinous crime in a state that had capital punishment;

and being Jewish certainly didn't help. Their families obtained Clarence Darrow to represent them.

Darrow had them plead guilty and then for over one month the prosecution attempted to convince Judge John R. Caverly that the only possible penalty was the death sentence while the defense countered with testimony from doctors, psychiatrists, and neurologists. Darrow's summation lasted two full days. Since the boys had admitted guilt at the beginning, Darrow put capital punishment on trial. To the amazement of most and the disgust of many they received "life imprisonment, plus ninety-nine years each." The judge said that he kept them from hanging only because of their ages.

Darrow stated years later in his autobiography that the fees he received would not even have covered his office expenses. The Loebs and Leopolds at first made no effort to pay at all, and indicated that they felt the sentences were harsh.

In 1936 Richard Loeb was stabbed to death by a fellow inmate who claimed that Loeb had attempted to molest him sexually. Although the pair had been kept separate from the time they entered Joliet prison, there were outcries from the press about preferred treatment.

"Babe," as Loeb used to call his partner, was a model prisoner from the start. He allowed himself to be used as a test case for new drugs, and tutored other prisoners. However, when Nathan Leopold was paroled in 1958 more than a few voices of dissent were raised. He went immediately and quietly to Puerto Rico where he has been doing medical research. Although he still considers himself a Jew, he has been closely associated with the work of the Church of Brethren in curbing disease.

In 1961 he married the widow of a doctor in San Juan. Having served out his parole, Leopold is now a free man. He is the director of research for the Health Department of Puerto Rico, and is credited with helping combat tropical parasites and leprosy. Leopold is often offered as a model of rehabilitation. What spare time he has is spent writing scientific articles. When Meyer Levin's very successful book, play, and motion picture *Compulsion* appeared a few years ago Leopold filed suit claiming that he alone had literary rights to his own life. His autobiography, *99 Years Plus Life*, was published several years ago but did not do well.

A director of research today. *UPI*

The "King of Jazz" in 1928.

TED LEWIS

The High-hatted Tragedian of Song was born to an owner of a local department store in Circleville, Ohio, in 1891. His real name is Theodore Leopold Friedman. By 1906 he was featured in his home-town theatre playing the clarinet. Shortly afterward Ted ran away from home to join a carnival where he did spiels in front of the kooch-dancers, and became one of the exhibits of Dr. Cooper's Medicine Show, billed as "Wild Rosie." Ted was also the emcee.

Lewis claims it took him fifteen years to make it big in show business. In the interim he appeared in burlesque, dog and pony shows, vaudeville, and minstrels. He was once fired from Professor Oscar Ameringer's Symphony Band for jazzing up Beethoven's Fifth Symphony. At one point he teamed up with another musician named Al Lewis. Ted changed his name shortly afterward because Friedman could not be accommodated by the small marquee of a theatre. In 1911 he got his first break when he played the famous Hammerstein Theatre on West 42nd Street with his partners Duffy & Giser. Victor Moore and Will Rogers were on the same bill. By 1916 he had formed his own four-piece band and played the College Arms in Coney Island. From there he went to the fashionable Rector's on Broadway where Bonds clothing store stands today. He was a big hit and introduced his theme song, "When My Baby Smiles at Me." It was the Rector's engagement more than anything else that earned him the title many people associate with Paul Whiteman, "The King of Jazz." Lewis is the original. It was also at Rector's that he first wore the famous battered silk top hat which he won in a crap game from a cabbie. The first time he performed in it was as a joke but he has never been without it on stage since and considers it good luck. Saks Fifth Avenue once borrowed the hat to create a display around it in one of their windows.

Another big boost to his career was when John Murray Anderson asked him to fill in a five-minute spot at the Greenwich Theatre in Greenwich Village. It was supposed to be temporary until Anderson could get "a name," but Lewis was such a hit he was kept on for three years.

In 1922 he married Ada Baker, a toe dancer he had known more by correspondence than by their three or four meetings. His partners gave it six weeks. The Lewises were married first on stage in Rochester, New York, then by a city hall clerk, and again in a rabbi's home. It took. She has been his wife, friend, and manager ever since.

During the twenties he had the very successful Ted Lewis Club at 52nd Street and Seventh Avenue. The money he made there with a $3 cover charge more than offset his $150,000 loss—his *Ted Lewis Frolics* bombed in 1923 before it got to Broadway. He was also in Broadway shows such as *Artists and Models* in 1927 and played the Ziegfeld Roof. In one year he played in 150 different places in addition to his own club.

Lewis has for years enjoyed great popularity in England and has given a command performance for George V.

Some of the songs Ted popularized and introduced were "When My Baby Smiles At Me," "The Sunny Side of the Street," "Me and My Shadow," and "Cuddle Up a Little Closer."

His movies include *Is Everybody Happy?* (1929), *Show of Shows* (1929), *Here Comes the Band* (1935) with Virginia Bruce and *Manhattan Merry-Go-Round* (1937) with Ann Dvorak.

Some who were members of Lewis' band before they made it on their own are Kay Kyser (who lives with his wife the former Georgia Carroll in Chapel Hill, North Carolina, where he is a teacher and practitioner of Christian Science), George Raft, and the Dorsey brothers.

Lewis made a fortune over the years in radio, television, and nightclub appearances, right through the forties and sporadically through the fifties. He still plays several engagements a year and would have brought a show to Broadway in 1966 if Sophie Tucker, one of his co-stars, had not died before the opening. Miss Tucker was also one of his closest friends. His "shadow," dancer Eddie Chester, still works with Lewis whenever he has a booking.

The man who introduced the talking and laughing horns lives with his wife at the Majestic apartments on Manhattan's Central Park West for over thirty-five years now.

His famous top hat probably will be donated to the Ted Lewis Museum in Circleville, Ohio. The town also has a Ted Lewis Playground courtesy of the Lewises. He was voted a life member of their Chamber of Commerce in 1934 for the many plugs he has given it in his shows over the years.

In his Manhattan apartment. *Diana Keyt*

Starring in *Rose of the Rancho,* 1936.

GLADYS SWARTHOUT

The beautiful prima donna of the Metropolitan Opera and motion pictures was born in 1904 in Deepwater, Missouri, an Ozark mining town. She attended the Central High School in Kansas City and went on to Bush Conservatory of Music in Chicago from which she received a Doctorate of Music in 1923.

Gladys began singing as a very young girl at her local church. After Bush, she spent the summer of 1924 preparing for an operatic debut. She learned twenty-two roles for the 1924–1925 season of the Chicago Civic Opera Company. Gladys sang fifty performances, more than any other member of the company. After that she went to Europe for a rest and upon her return joined the Ravinia Park Opera Company and sang with them during the seasons of 1927, 1928, and 1929. By the time she left to join the Metropolitan she was considered among their top attractions.

Her debut with the Metropolitan came in 1929 as La Cieca in *La Gioconda.* She also sang the roles of Niejata in the United States premiere of *Sadko* and Cathos when Lattuada's *La Preziose Ridicole* made its bow in this country. She was very soon one of the company's leading mezzo-sopranos. Her most famous roles were in *Norma, Peter Ibbetson, La Gioconda, La Forza del Destino, Mignon,* and *Carmen.* Her repertoire contained twenty-five operas.

Paramount was anxious to have a star to compete with M-G-M's Jeanette MacDonald and Columbia's Grace Moore. They signed the singer to a lucrative contract and introduced her to the movie-going public in a barrage of publicity. Her film efforts, however, were not well received at the box office. She made *Rose of the Rancho* (1936) with John Boles, *Give Us This Night* (1936), which had a score by Erich Korngold, a book by Oscar Hammerstein II, and Jan Kiepura as her co-star, *Champagne Waltz* (1937), *To Have and to Hold* (1937) with Fred MacMurray, and *Romance in the Dark* (1938) with John Boles. Her last picture was a melodrama with Lloyd Nolan, *Ambush* (1939).

Radio, however, proved a boon to her career. She began in the medium in 1935 and appeared on such programs as the "Chase and Sanborn Hour," "Caravan," and the "Ford Sunday Evening." She also had her own program which was heard in New York City over WEAF, now WNBC, and sang everything from arias to pop songs and spirituals. For five successive years beginning in the late thirties she was named the Number One Female Singer of Classics on radio by the critics in the United States and Canada, outpolling even the popular Jessica Dragonette.* Her radio popularity made her concert tours and recordings among the most successful year after year.

Her Carnegie Hall appearance in 1942 caused critic-composer Robert Lawrence to write "a genuine mezzo-soprano, the best among present day American singers of this genre." Miss Swarthout was particularly effective in person. She was not only lovely to look at but had great chic and several times was named among the best dressed women in America.

In 1956 she underwent a very delicate and critical operation on her heart which had been damaged during a bout with rheumatic fever as a child. By 1957 she retired.

In 1958 the singer won the Heart of the Year award and became a member of the Mended Heart Club, which is made up of past major heart surgery patients.

After she left the music world, Gladys and her husband Frank Chapman divided their time between their Connecticut home and their villa set in an avocado grove in Florence, Italy. Chapman, who had given up his own singing career to manage his wife's, died in 1966. They had been married for thirty-five years. Miss Swarthout's first husband, Harry Richmond Kern, died in 1931 after six years of marriage. She has no children by either union and has never remarried.

She spends spring and summer at La Ragnaia in the suburbs of Florence "because my husband loved that place most." The fall and winters are spent in her New York Fifth Avenue apartment. She attends Metropolitan performances from time to time but never sings, "not even in the bathtub."

The former prima donna at a recent party in Florence. *Clifford May*

"The Citizen of the World" arrives in the country of his birth in 1950. N. Y. *Daily News*

GARRY DAVIS

The ex-GI who emerged from the shadow of his famous father to become known around the globe as "the citizen of the world," was born in Bar Harbor, Maine, in 1922. Until he joined the United States Air Force at the outbreak of World War II, he had spent most of his life in Philadelphia where he was known somewhat as a playboy. For awhile he was gainfully employed as understudy to Danny Kaye. The only reason for any public attention he may have received during those years was the fact that he was the son of society band leader Meyer Davis.

After mustering out of the service Davis stayed in Paris where he became interested in the World Federalist movement, which he left after becoming disenchanted.

At first the press treated him as little more than a nut with good intentions and bad taste when in 1948 he announced that he was giving up his United States citizenship and dramatized this by tearing up his passport. He would not, he said, apply for another from any country. He had formed the Association for the International Registry of World Citizens and People's Assembly and was now "a citizen of the world." He had fought one war and firmly believed that nationalism was the basis for all conflicts between nations. Through his canny sense of publicity Davis broke into the news over and over again. At one point he took refuge from authorities in Paris by retreating to the international grounds of the United Nations offices. On another occasion the gendarmes had to be called out to escort him from the grounds of the Palais de Chaillot where he had camped in a pup tent. His phrase "citizen of the world" had a ring to it and he began to attract huge crowds of war-weary young Frenchmen wherever he spoke. France's initial reaction was to give him twenty-four hours to leave the country. But it was not long before he was received in a private interview by French President Vincent Auriol. Not all his followers were starry-eyed peaceniks. His plan for the world government was endorsed publicly by such men as André Gide, Jean-Paul Sartre, Albert Camus, and Albert Einstein. The French press began referring to him affectionately as "le petit homme" and his mail reached four hundred letters per day from all over the world.

Throughout it all Davis wore his brown leather flyer's jacket with a faded decal of a pinup girl on the back.

Days of glory for Garry were short. His failure to forge his crusade into something resembling a political power is perhaps a proof of his sincerity. Had he lusted after power as he did after peace, he might have survived. By 1950 all of the steam had gone out of his movement as it broke off into countless fringe groups. The intensity of the Cold War at that time made the Davis dream seem like a wonderful but wistful bit of science fiction. In April of 1950 he returned to the United States where he was detained for four days of questioning on Ellis Island. He told reporters that he was still "a resident of the earth" and that he disagreed with United States intervention in Korea.

In Ellsworth, Maine, in 1950, Davis married the former Hollywood dancer Esther Peters in an original service he created, called "unification of love." It was announced shortly afterward by the State Department that Davis had made a formal request for reinstatement as a United States citizen. A spokesman for the government said that his application would be considered along with all others that were on file from French immigrants. Davis had entered this country on an immigration visa.

Davis and his wife drifted back and forth across the Atlantic and have now settled in Mulhouse, Alsace. In 1961 he published his book, *The World is My Country*, in which he states that the only real solution to the problems besetting the world is for the various countries to give up their sovereignty and accept a global government. Today he admits that his idea of world law is "way out" but remains firmly committed to it. "In other words," he said, "the brotherhood of man must be realized politically. I consider the problem to be essentially a spiritual one."

The firebrand of the forties supports his family—three boys and a girl ranging from one year old to fourteen years old—as the holder of a franchise for the Culligan water-softening process and a dry lubricant called Dri-Slide, which is used in industry.

The famous leather jacket that stood for many as a symbol of the hope for peace that Garry Davis instilled in his followers was given to a hobo nearly twenty years ago.

Esther and Garry pose on the land they purchased recently in Wettolsheim, Haut-Rhin, France. On the deed it is registered as "World Territory."

With Raymond Walburn (left) in *Professor Beware,* in 1938.

HAROLD LLOYD

The movie comedian whose films grossed over $30,000,000 was born in Burchard, Nebraska, in 1894.

Harold had some experience in amateur theatricals before the family moved to southern California where he attended San Diego High School. For awhile he entertained the notion of becoming a professional boxer. When the Edison Company came to town and announced that they would be hiring extras to appear in a film they were making, Harold's mother encouraged him to try out, hoping this would make him forget about the dangerous sport. It worked because immediately after graduation, his acting ambition fired by the one short job he got from Edison, Lloyd went north to Hollywood where he found occasional work as a walk-on or extra. He appeared with Jane Novak (who lives in Sherman Oaks, California, not far from her sister Eva Novak of Van Nuys). Like the characters he played later, Harold never gave up in the face of hard times or adversity. Director Ford Sterling told him that he had no talent whatever for comedy.

Then in 1915 a young man named Hal Roach, who had just inherited a few thousand dollars, thought Harold was funny and together they devised a character they called "Willie Work." Later it was changed considerably and renamed "Lonesome Luke." Their Rolin Film Company made one- and two-reelers featuring the awkward optimist who became popular the world over. In 1917 Lloyd added the now famous horn-rimmed glasses and developed the character still further for his first feature picture, *Grandma's Boy* (1917), which was a howling success.

When Lloyd and Roach amicably parted company in 1923 Harold went to Pathé where, as his own producer, he had even greater success. His revised character, always named Harold, had been refined and developed into a clean-cut, honest, very likable young man whom bullies and the world in general conspired against. Lloyd played down his natural handsome features and thereby had as many men as women rooting for him when he tried to win the campus sweetheart or free himself from some of the complicated and dangerous situations that developed in all of his pictures.

His features such as *Why Worry?* (1923), *Hot Water* (1924), *The Freshman* (1925), and *For Heaven's Sake* (1926) were full of sight gags, all on Harold and usually as suspenseful as they were funny. He hung from ledges of skyscrapers, braved live lions and fierce revolutionaries. He always fought clean and he always won both the fight and the girl. His leading ladies were Bebe Daniels,* Jobyna Ralston, and Mildred Davis, whom he married in 1923.

Harold Lloyd made his talkie debut in *Welcome Danger* (1929). His films were fewer after sound came in but still very successful. A few were *Feet First* (1930), *Movie Crazy* (1932), *The Cat's Paw* (1934), *The Milky Way* (1936) with Lionel Stander (who lives with his wife in the Park Lane section of London), and *Professor, Beware* (1938) with Raymond Walburn (who still does an occasional Broadway role, and lives with his wife in Gramercy Park in Manhattan), his last until *Mad Wednesday,* which he made for the late Preston Sturges in 1947.

In 1952 the Motion Picture Academy presented Lloyd with a special Oscar engraved "Master Comedian and Good Citizen." In 1962 a compilation of clips from his pictures brought raves at the Cannes Film Festival. It has been released in the United States under the title *Harold Lloyd's World of Comedy.*

One of the richest stars in Hollywood, Lloyd is still married to Mildred Davis. They have one son, Harold, Jr., who is a singer, and two daughters. Their Italian Renaissance mansion in Beverly Hills is on twenty acres of some of the world's most expensive real estate and includes a nine hole golf course, two swimming pools, a tennis court, and a bowling alley. Harold keeps in good condition by spending time at each of the sports every day. He is an expert photographer and has had articles published in trade journals on color stereo photography.

Like the character he played on the screen, Lloyd is a most friendly and unpretentious man. Much of his huge wealth is diverted to charity and a great deal of his spare time is spent working for the Shriners, which he headed for some years. When he senses that visitors to his estate are overwhelmed by the lavish surroundings, he usually points out some priceless rug or piece of antique furniture that his Great Danes have ruined.

In his Beverly Hills home. *Jon Virzi*

The Governor in 1944 . . .

THOMAS E. DEWEY

The twice defeated Republican presidential candidate was born in Owosso, Michigan, in 1902 over the general store that belonged to his maternal grandfather. His paternal grandfather was for many years the G.O.P. county chairman and had been a charter member of the party when it was founded. Thomas E. was also a cousin of Admiral George Dewey, hero of Manila Bay.

During his campaigns much was made of the fact that he had worked his way through the University of Michigan, from which he was graduated in 1923. Actually, Tom had a group of local boys selling magazines for him in a clever and profitable arrangement whereby he held the franchise and the boys did the selling. To hear Dewey's public relations people tell it he was a poor newsboy on a windy street corner. Quite otherwise. His father was the publisher of the Owosso *Times*.

Dewey's study of law was second to his ambition to be an opera singer. He was an exceptional baritone and when he came to New York in 1923, it was to study singing as well as to attend Columbia's Law School. While training he sang regularly in churches in and around Manhattan. He says that he also sang in a synagogue, but when questioned where, his memory fails him. His voice could not be counted on. When he developed laryngitis before a recital, Tom decided to devote all of his time and energy to law and politics.

In 1928 he married a girl who always amazed those who met her by the contrast she provided to her husband. Frances E. Hutt, grandniece of Jefferson Davis, is warm and friendly with a delightful sense of humor.

From private practice, in which he did very well after his admission to the bar in 1926, he was appointed chief assistant United States Attorney for the Southern District of New York. By this time his local politicking had been rewarded with a district captainship. Two days after F.D.R. was elected President in 1932, Dewey's superior resigned. Dewey took full charge of the prosecution of Irving "Waxey Gordon" Wechsler, a beer baron, and to the surprise of everyone, most of all the racketeers, won a conviction on charges of tax evasion. It was the first of many guilty verdicts. Dewey left the punks to his assistants. The big boys he reserved for his special skill which was not always noticeably considerate of the defendants' civil liberties. Following a return to private practice in 1933, he accepted an appointment in 1935 as a special prosecutor against organized crime. In a nearly perfect score as a prosecutor, Dewey obtained convictions against Tammany district leader James J. Hines, stockbroker-socialite Richard Whitney, Bundist Fritz Kuhn, and Louis "Lepke" Buchalter. Dewey was credited with breaking up the notorious "Murder, Inc.," and by the late thirties his reputation as a racket smasher was nationwide. He achieved his biggest courtroom victory when Charles "Lucky" Luciano was found guilty and deported to Italy.

From 1937 to 1941, Dewey was serving as District Attorney in New York City under Fiorello H. La Guardia. In his first try for the governorship in 1938 he was narrowly defeated by incumbent Herbert Lehman. His *Case Against the New Deal* in 1940 was a best seller, and he came to the G.O.P. convention of 1940 as a favorite for the nomination but lost to the gallery demands of "We want Willkie."

Dewey's basic principles seemed to change with the times and the opinion polls. Prior to World War II there were warm words from the isolationists; in his last years in public life he was generally regarded as an internationalist. As Governor from 1943 to 1954 he won badly needed reapportionment, liberalized unemployment insurance, built highways, and sponsored public housing. His heart may have been to the right but his eye was dead center on the White House.

His defeat by Roosevelt in 1944 was no surprise since the war was still on, but when he received 189 electoral votes to Harry S. Truman's 303 in the 1948 election the entire Western world shook its head in wonderment. The late Dorothy Parker cost him not a few votes when she summed up his humorlessness and conservative image in one quip—"He looks like the little man on the wedding cake."

What fooled the professionals as well as Dewey was his remarkable ability to persuade a jury or a board of directors. In small groups he exuded confidence. To the masses he appeared pompous, and in a man so young it must have seemed even more distasteful.

Dewey and his wife now keep a large apartment in Manhattan's Seventies, and a country estate in Pawling, New York. His Wall Street law firm of Dewey, Ballantine, Bushby, Palmer & Wood, in which he is still active, is one of the most prestigious and lucrative in the country.

. . . and addressing the G.O.P. Convention, 1968. *UPI*

A typical publicity pose, 1952. *UPI*

"GORGEOUS GUSSIE" MORAN

Gertrude Augusta Moran was born of Irish and German parents in Santa Monica, California, in 1924. She began playing tennis when she was twelve years old. By thirteen she had earned the name "tomboy." Ever since a boy in her class spotted her middle name on a report card, and teased her about it long and hard, she became known as Gussie. "Gorgeous" was added by *Life* magazine in the late forties when the pretty athlete began copping titles around the country.

At sixteen she was playing well enough to be considered among the more important young prospects in southern California. She had some coaching from the late Bill Tilden and Eleanor Tennant who had coached Alice Marble. But Gussie's interest slackened after Charlie Chaplin, who played with her regularly, warned her that if she continued her game as often and as hard as she customarily did, she would develop large muscles. She continued playing but less frequently, until her enthusiasm revived in 1945.

Gussie had two things against her. She had a rather late start and the rather stuffy Southern California Tennis Association gave her little help or encouragement since it frowned on her colorful clothes and flamboyant behavior.

In 1946 at the Nationals, which were held at Forest Hills, New York, a practically unknown Gussie fought her way to the quarterfinals and took a set from Pauline Betz, the only one Miss Betz lost in the whole tournament; in 1947 she and Mary Arnold Prentiss won the National Clay Court Doubles. Gussie and Pancho Segura won the Seabright mixed doubles crown in 1946, and got to the final round of the National Mixed Doubles where they lost to an Australian team of Bromwich and Brough. On the way to that final they licked defending champs Billy Talbert and Margaret Osborne Du Pont. The next year Gussie made the Top Ten of Tennis list for the first time. In the spring of 1949 she came to tackle the National Indoor Tennis Championships. She wound up on March 26 with three titles: Mixed Doubles, Women's Doubles, and the coveted Women's Singles. At Wimbledon in 1949 she was beaten after the third round by Gem Hoahing.

Gussie was a press agent's dream. She had a commercial airplane named for her. She dated just about everyone and posed for publicity pictures in every conceivable costume and position. On the front of magazines she appeared as a cover girl, and on the back, as an endorsement for cigarettes. In 1950 the American Fashion Academy named her the "best dressed woman in sports." She made up her own list of the most attractive men in sports. Wherever there was an open microphone or shutter, Gussie was there. Her really big break came when Colonel Teddy Tindling designed an outfit for her to wear at Wimbledon in 1949, which did not include panties. Gussie says she wanted something to make her look more feminine and added panties trimmed in lace. The photographers went wild and people who never saw a tennis match knew who "Gorgeous Gussie" was after that. And Gussie was pretty good at reminding them every chance she got. She has since worn leopard skin panties.

On October 26, 1950, she made her pro debut in Madison Square Garden. She also played exhibition matches and gave tennis lessons (one of her pupils was Ron Ely, star of TV's "Tarzan" series). There was talk of her going into movies but the only part she ever played was herself in *Pat and Mike* (1952) with two of her friends, Katharine Hepburn and the late Spencer Tracy. For a while she designed and manufactured a line of tennis apparel which did not include lace panties.

Gussie had a hard serve, and a good ground stroke and forehand. Her favorite partners are Pancho Segura and Pancho Gonzales (who has a tennis club and school in Malibu. He and Gussie still play). She plays at least four or five times a week. Next to tennis her favorite sport is swimming and she does plenty of it.

According to "Gorgeous Gussie," she has been married "2½ times." The "½" was annulled. In 1966, single, she moved to Manhattan and accepted a position as an advertising consultant for World Tennis and a job with Eastman-Kodel for whom she arranges fashion shows and does commercials. In 1968 she covered the Wimbledon games for Westinghouse Radio.

Gussie today, in her Manhattan apartment. *Diana Keyt*

At the height of her career. *NBC-TV*

FAYE EMERSON

The unofficial First Lady of Television was born in Elizabeth, Lousiana, in 1917. Faye Margaret lived with her father, who held jobs as varied as rancher and court stenographer, and mother in Texas, Illinois, and, finally, California where her parents were divorced when she was thirteen years old. Her mother remarried and settled in San Diego, while Faye was placed in a convent boarding school in Oceanside, California. After high school graduation, she attended San Diego State College, and appeared in several productions of the Community Players.

In 1941 she married William Crawford, a San Diego automobile dealer. They had one child "Scoop." The Crawfords were divorced in 1942.

Faye was appearing in *Here Today* in 1941 at San Diego's Municipal Theatre when she was offered contracts by both Paramount Pictures and Warner Brothers. She chose Warners and remained with them for five-and-a-half years during which time she made such pictures as *Murder in the Big House* (1942) with Van Johnson, *Mask for Demetrious* (1944) with the late Peter Lorre, *Destination Tokyo* (1944), *Between Two Worlds* (1944), her personal favorite, *The Very Thought of You* (1944) with Dennis Morgan, *Hotel Berlin* (1945) with Helmut Dantine (who resides in Beverly Hills with his wife, the daughter of movie mogul Joe Schenk), and *Danger Signal* (1945) with the late Zachary Scott.

Faye never really became a star in movies but was one of the more interesting leading ladies at a time when most films were essentially men's pictures. While at Warners her close friend, the late Ann Sheridan, induced her to bleach her brunette hair blonde. She wore her hair pulled back tightly which became her trademark.

Her first real fame came as the wife of Elliott Roosevelt whom she first met at a Hollywood dinner party. The couple were married on the rim of Grand Canyon in 1944. During part of their marriage Faye lived at the White House, with F.D.R. baby-sitting with "Scoop" and Mrs. Roosevelt reading him bedtime stories. Until she died Mrs. Roosevelt always asked Faye and her son to spend

30

New Year's Eve with her. After the war Faye and her husband were the first journalists to be permitted to enter the Soviet Union where they interviewed Stalin for a national magazine. They were divorced in 1950.

Faye Emerson truly came into her own on television. She was first seen on May 11, 1948, in "Tonight on Broadway." She was making her Broadway debut at the time in *The Play's the Thing*. For the next fifteen years she was probably the busiest woman in the business. She was the femcee on "Cavalcade of Fashion," a panelist on "Leave it to the Girls," and for five years beginning in 1953, on "I've Got a Secret." She wrote a thrice weekly TV column which was syndicated by United Press, and substituted for Arlene Francis (on "Home"), Garry Moore, Dave Garroway, and Edward R. Murrow (on "Person to Person") shows. Faye even had a show with her third husband Skitch Henderson on the New York NBC station in 1953 and 1954. They were divorced in 1957 after seven years of marriage.

During those years, Faye was on Broadway in such plays as *Parisienne* (1950), *Heavenly Twins* (1955), *Protective Custody* (1956), and *Back to Methuselah* (1958) opposite the late Tyrone Power. In the following summer months she toured the straw-hat circuit in *Goodbye, My Fancy, Dangerous Corner,* and *State of the Union.*

In 1963 the lady who had been chosen the best-dressed woman on TV, for no apparent reason announced that she was going to take a year's leave of absence and would travel extensively in Europe. To the surprise of everyone she never returned. Until a few years ago she lived in Klosters, Switzerland, and in 1965 bought her present four-bedroom home in the suburbs of Palma, Majorca. Faye has never remarried. No month goes by that she does not refuse a TV or movie offer. Since 1963 she has been in the United States only once for a few days on business. Her Manhattan town house is rented through her son, a real estate broker, who doubts she will ever come back to work on TV and the stage again.

At a bar in Majorca recently. *John Howard*

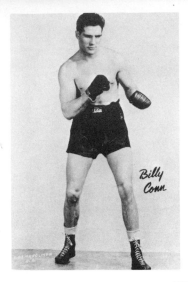

Battling Billy in 1941.

BILLY CONN

The man who nearly took the heavyweight championship away from Joe Louis was born in the tough East Liberty section of Pittsburgh, Pennsylvania, in 1917.

At fourteen he began to be a regular face around the East Liberty Gymnasium which was run by Johnny Ray who later became Billy's manager. At first Conn only ran errands but he soon began going a round or two invariably with older and bigger boys.

Billy flunked several times in grade school, tried the industrial school, and left for good. In a short time he was back at the gym full time.

He began to fight professionally in 1935, losing his very first encounter. It only goaded him on and in the next two years he made an important record for himself. In 1937 alone he whipped one former middleweight and four former welterweight champions. He fought the formidable ex-champion, Fred Apostoli, twice. The second time around Conn and the Italian exchanged some verbal unpleasantries which were heard over the overhead microphone of which neither was aware. Their language not only was profane but contained more than a few racial slurs. If anything, it only served to further endear Conn to Irish-Americans. He had become their hope of regaining the crown the much loved James Braddock* lost to Joe Louis not long before. Billy won both Apostoli fights and went on to take a close decision against Melio Bettina, thus winning the light-heavyweight championship.

Billy began to put on weight, with an eye on the heavyweight title held by Louis. He impressed the pros when his merciless body attack flattened Bob Pastor. Conn and promoter Mike Jacobs were determined to put the twenty-three-year-old Billy against the Brown Bomber. In November of 1940 Billy disposed of Lee Savold, a heavyweight who was then considered Louis' closest threat. Billy took a terrible beating in the process but outboxed his challenger and won on points. This was the plan he had in mind for Louis.

The famous match took place in the Polo Grounds on June 18, 1941. Everything went according to Billy's plan with the exception of the third round when Louis got in his best punch. But Billy survived it and the crowd roared.

Billy was smaller and lighter, all the odds were against him, and yet he was boxing circles around the champion. Conn went to the ring with his usual cockiness and was growing bolder with each round. Even when Joe was able to hit him Billy showed no signs of weakening. What's more he had so confused Louis and tired him that he was able to get in some very good punches of his own. By the twelfth round Billy was way ahead on points and the crowd was hysterical. He came out of his corner for the thirteenth round with all the confidence in the world. He jabbed Louis and hooked him and for a minute it looked like the Bomber was going to go down. Then, while his handlers screamed to Billy to "move," Conn went in for the kill. Billy got greedy. Louis caught him with an uppercut and while 60,071 fans watched with their mouths open Billy Conn fell to the canvas, knocked out. Had the punch come just three seconds later, the bell would have saved him. After the war they were rematched again but Billy was no longer the quick young man. Louis KO'd him in the seventh round on June 19, 1946.

Years later the two were discussing the legendary scrap and Billy said to the ex-champion, "Joe, why didn't you let me win that one? You could have sort of loaned me the crown for six months." "Billy," said Louis, looking straight at his old foe, "you *had* that title for twelve rounds."

Billy went back to the Steel capital but not to East Liberty. The Conns, four children and his wife Mary, live in a $60,000 home on Dennison Avenue in the Squirrel Hill section. Most of Billy's earnings went into a very lucky oil speculation, and was reinvested in Pittsburgh real estate, which he has since managed. Until 1967 he was the greeter at the Stardust Hotel in Las Vegas, Nevada. From time to time Billy referees a big fight. In 1967 he stopped the Carlos Ortiz-Sugar Ramos battle in the fifth round in Mexico City and proclaimed Ortiz the winner. He is not an unfamiliar face at ringside for an important fight, but swears that he really isn't very interested in the sport any longer—"there just aren't any more fighters." In the past several years he has been in the papers on occasions involving brawls with relatives and strangers. In all cases Billy was the victor.

Today he is Billy the Businessman.
UPI

Head Technocrat Scott, 1934. *UPI*

HOWARD SCOTT

Howard Scott, the leader of the bizarre economic movement that bemused and amused most of the United States during the Great Depression, was born in Virginia before 1900. Facts about his personal life and background, like a clear explanation of his scheme, were never divulged.

He has stated that on July 1, 1918, he opened his first Technology office at 107 Waverly Place in Greenwich Village, and remained through the twenties. It was not until Depression days that the Technocrats came into their own. Scott's plan promised that every workingman who labored for 4 hours per day, 4 days per week, 165 days per year would be paid $20,000 annually for his efforts. Nor would those efforts be strenuous, as Technocracy would reduce all toil to the barest minimum.

In 1932 several Columbia University professors discussed Technocracy with Scott in a formal symposium held on school grounds. As soon as the meetings were publicized the University asked Scott to leave and disavowed the Technocrats.

Explanations of how the Technate State of North America would function were few and vague. One capsule of the plan from Scott's own literature said: ". . . if sufficient energy-consuming devices are installed and total amount of extraneous energy consumer per capita reaches or exceeds 200,000 kilogram calories per capita per day, toil and workers alike will be eliminated."

During the Depression era, when they were going strong, Scott made many appearances on radio and was in the papers constantly. Chapters of Technocracy were all over the country, with an Institute of Technocracy in California. Those who took them seriously listed the Technocrats as Rightists and yet Scott has been quoted as saying that, "Marxian Communism is so far to the right it is bourgeois" when compared to his philosophy.

Although Scott has always maintained that his movement was not a political party and had no desire for political power, those who remember the gray uniforms and automobiles complete with their emblem of a circle separated by a curved line felt it had all the trappings, including a military salute, of a Fascist organization.

Walter Lippmann dismissed Scott's plans for replacing currency with energy units of "ergs" and "joules" as, "nothing but the pretentious ignorance of a crank."

Engineers, who would be the elite of the country under Technocracy, and economists have suggested that many of Scott's plans were similar to those set forth by William Henry Smyth and Thorstein Veblen, but the founder states that "We derive most of our concepts of thermodynamics and energy germinants from the works of J. Willard Gibbs."

By 1942 interest in the movement, which had dwindled greatly as the Depression subsided, was revived briefly when full page advertisements appeared in newspapers throughout the United States asking President Roosevelt to make Howard Scott the "Director General of Defense." These, said Scott recently, were placed by overenthusiastic members of his West Coast branches.

In 1948 Scott was again in the news when a former official asked the courts for an accounting of the monies Scott received for uniform sales and membership dues (at that time $6 yearly). The fallen-away Technocrat stated that there were then 8,900 members. This is the only figure ever divulged and even today Scott refuses to say how many members he has or has had.

Scott has always managed to keep something resembling an office over the last twenty years to testify that Technocracy is not dead, as many people thought he was. The last few years he has maintained some kind of a project in Rushland, Pennsylvania, which houses Technocracy's publishing enterprises. Their magazine, *The Technocrat*, is still sent out monthly to the faithful.

He boasts chapters in the Northwest, Canada, and California. In the past year ads have begun to appear in Greenwich Village newspapers promoting meetings and literature. Although over seventy years old, Scott still runs the whole show. Most of the movement's writings are by him and nothing is decided without his approval. Their slogan, after fifty years, is unchanged— "Something New Under the Sun." His followers, whose dues are now $9 a year, who would run the North American continent on the principles of engineering, do not seem troubled that their leader still has no degree in either economics or engineering.

The director in chief at his headquarters in Rushland, Pennsylvania. *The Technocrat*

At one of her regular guest appearances on network variety shows, 1933.

ETHEL WATERS

The first Negro woman to receive star billing in America was born in Chester, Pennsylvania, in 1900. At five Ethel was singing in churches. When she was sixteen she was working as a laundress and chambermaid in a Philadelphia hotel for $4.75 a week. On her seventeenth birthday, which was Halloween, two boys took her to a nightclub on Juniper Street, and encouraged her to sing; a mask she was wearing helped overcome her initial shyness. She sang two songs which went over so well that the boys convinced her to turn professional. They got her a job for $9 a week at the Lincoln Theatre in Baltimore. The money seemed fine until she learned that they each were getting $25 a week as her managers.

Throughout much of the twenties she performed in theatres, cabarets, and vaudeville. Much of her work was in the South and all of it in the Negro circuit of show business. Her material was usually "blue," but always deeply religious; she sang spirituals off stage. In 1927 she debuted on Broadway in *Africana* and in 1929 made *On With the Show*, her first movie, with Sally O'Neil, in which Ethel sang "Am I Blue?"

In 1930 she opened on Broadway in *Lew Leslie's Blackbirds* and in 1931 starred in *Rhapsody in Black*, which was so successful that versions appeared in 1932 and 1933.

When she was appearing in *As Thousands Cheer* during the 1933–1934 season, the authors Moss Hart and Irving Berlin invited her to the weekly cast parties. She agreed to attend though only as a performer.

Two of her titles were "the tawny Yvette Guilbert," and "the bronze Raquel Miller." In 1935 she was featured with Bea Lillie in *At Home Abroad*. All through the thirties Ethel was a frequent guest star on network radio programs where her color was no problem. In 1938 she had a highly successful one-woman concert at Carnegie Hall.

36

Perhaps Miss Waters' greatest hit was her role in *Mamba's Daughters* which opened on Broadway in January, 1939. It is also her personal favorite. She is also closely associated with *Cabin in the Sky* in which she introduced the standard "Takin' a Chance on Love" in 1940 and repeated her role in the movie version in 1943.

In 1942 Ethel and Count Basie packed them in at the Palace. In 1949 she headed the bill at the Roxy. She made such films as *Tales of Manhattan* (1941), *Stage Door Canteen* (1943), and *Pinky* (1949), a highly controversial movie on race relations at a time when the subject was considered taboo by Hollywood. For her performance Ethel was nominated for an Academy Award.

In 1950 Ethel Waters was back on Broadway in the memorable Carson McCullers play, *The Member of the Wedding,* which she also played on the road. The movie version, which was a box office failure, brought her a second Academy Award nomination. At a fade-out Miss Waters is seen in a rocking chair singing "His Eye Is on the Sparrow" which was the title of her autobiography, a 1951 best seller.

On TV she was the original "Beulah" but left the role after one season in 1950. In 1956 she made *The Heart Is a Rebel* and in 1959 was seen in *The Sound and the Fury,* her last movie. In 1960 her great weight (at times as much as 250 pounds) and worry over money brought on a heart attack. She has lived quietly ever since.

The lady who popularized such hits as "Supper Time," "Heat Wave," and "Stormy Weather" has an apartment on Orange Drive in Los Angeles. She has been married and divorced three times, but has no children. There were bad investments and tax troubles and now all her money is gone. Her few public appearances are with Billy Graham's Crusades. After attending one of the evangelist's Madison Square Garden rallies, she sang in the choir every night afterward. Says Ethel: "I heard them singing "This is My Song" and I thought I'd come home. That was the turning point in my life.

On a recent rare night out. *Jon Virzi*

Heavyweight Champion of the World
in 1950. *Ring Magazine*

EZZARD CHARLES

Boxing's most colorless champion was born in the crossroads town of Law-renceville, Georgia, in 1921, though he has always considered Cincinnati his home. Ezzard began fighting as a boy in the streets and in the ring. For three years he was an amateur and for nineteen years a professional. It was instinctive with him. He has said that for years he did not really understand the difference in the categories. "I just thought you went in and fought, and they gave you something, or not."

Charles was by no means a second-rate fighter. He simply had the misfortune of being the World's Heavyweight Champion between Joe Louis, probably the sport's most loved, and Rocky Marciano, a very popular and colorful champion. (Ezzard always admired the comic strip character Joe Palooka, who was basically a gentleman.) Charles had few enemies, but the sport promoters knew that people bought tickets to see a fighter lose as well as win; Ezzard just didn't draw crowds. He lacked the killer instinct which makes for both excitement and victories. Sports writers called him "Snooks" to distinguish him from the "bombers" and the "maulers."

Charles fought 122 times as a pro and won 96. He first came to national attention in 1948 when the twenty-year-old Sam Baroudi died of a brain hemorrhage after hitting the canvas from Charles' slugging in the fourth round in Chicago. And in December of that year he whipped Joe Baksi, which put him in the challenger class for the heavyweight crown.

Even the fight that brought him the title was dull. He outpointed Jersey Joe Walcott in June, 1949, to win the National Boxing Association's crown (not recognized in New York or London). The crowd booed both fighters in the match that had been promoted by Joe Louis. In August of 1949 he won with a T-K.O. The following August Charles and Freddie Beshore drew the lowest gate in the history of heavyweight championship fights, $28,666.00, at the

Buffalo Memorial Stadium. While 6,298 fans watched, the referee stopped the scrap in the fourteenth round, with Ezzard winning.

He held the title only two years. Even after he beat Joe Louis in September, 1950, when the former champion tried to come back in Yankee Stadium, Charles seemed to gather no glamour. Louis was much older, and tired, and it went the full fifteen rounds for a decision in Ezzard's favor. Then on July 18, 1951, he was rematched with Jersey Joe Walcott,* and the former champion KO'd him in the seventh round.

Charles fought for a few years and then returned to Cincinnati, the city that had showered him in chrysanthemums when he had come home a hero, where he became a salesman for a wholesale wine firm.

After collecting purses totaling $1,500,000, Ezzard is now working for a salary which he is very glad to get each week. He has a job with Mayor Daley's Commission on Youth Welfare. From a small office on Chicago's South Side, the former champion tries to steer Negro youths on the right path. He arranges block parties and runs films which are made for rehabilitation and self-improvement. "I jive around with the kids mostly. I try to pick the worst kid, and jive him. Sometimes it works, sometimes not." None of the boys remember him as world champion, but they all know that he was one. Even when he was on top Charles liked young people. He used to load up his big convertible and take as many boys and girls as it would hold out for a drive and a rare visit to a restaurant where they were told to order anything they wanted. For a while after leaving the ring Charles was a wholesale wine salesman, but his health has been greatly impaired by lateral sclerosis, and he really prefers what he is doing now. His financial condition he philosophically attributes to "bad investments." He still likes boxing and says that in spite of his present situation he thinks the game gave him "a wonderful life."

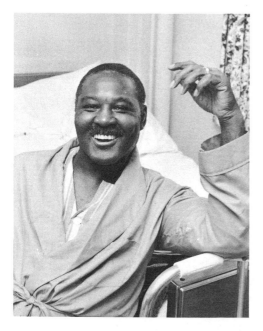

Recuperating from a recent illness.
Chicago Daily News

As Gilda in *Rigoletto* in 1940. *De Bellis*

LILY PONS

Lily Pons was born in Draguignan, France, in 1904 of French-Italian parents. The family was musical, the father a fine violinist, the mother a singer, and Lily and her two sisters pianists.

Lily first discovered her singing talents during World War I when she entertained soldiers but it wasn't until after a stint with the Paris Theatre des Varieties, for which she undertook ingenue roles, that she seriously considered singing as a career. Her first husband August Mesritz encouraged her to study singing. At twenty-one she began studying with the great master Alberti de Gorostiaga, who was to remain her only teacher. Within three years she made her operatic debut singing the title role in *Lakmé* at Mulhouse, Alsace. Other engagements in provincial opera houses followed in quick succession.

She was heard by Giovanni Zenatello, then scouting for the New York Metropolitan Opera, and he recommended her for an audition. Her Met debut was made in 1931 singing what was to become her most famous role, *Lucia di Lammermoor.* Also in the cast were Benjamino Gigli and Ezio Pinza. Olin Downes, then critic of *The New York Times,* said of her performance, "Her mad scene was a foretaste of full-fledged virtuosity." The public concurred apparently, for she received sixteen curtain calls. Madame Pons has always sung the mad scene a full key higher (F) than the key in which Donizetti wrote it (E Flat).

From 1931 to 1938 she sang at the Metropolitan and the Colón in Buenos Aires. In addition, she made appearances with the San Francisco, Chicago, St. Louis, and Philadelphia opera companies. She toured South America, Canada, Australia, Europe, and the British Isles.

Lakmé was revived at the Met especially for her as was *La Sonnambula.* Her repertoire also includes Gilda in *Rigoletto,* Rosina in *The Barber of Seville,* Olympia in *The Tales of Hoffman,* and Philine in *Mignon,* in addition to other coloratura parts.

She made such films as *I Dream Too Much* (1935) with Henry Fonda (one critic said it should have been called *I Scream Too Much*), *That Girl From Paris* (1936) with Jack Oakie and Gene Raymond, and *Hitting a New High* (1937), again with Fonda. During these years she appeared weekly on radio, singing with the forty-piece orchestra that her new husband André Kostelanetz conducted. They were married in 1938, just five years after her divorce from her first husband. Together they were to become the highest paid musical duet in history. Her activity at the Met during the first ten postwar years had included only thirty-four performances during that time.

Throughout the fifties Madame Pons made countless television appearances, having been on "The Perry Como Show," "What's My Line?," "The Ed Sullivan Show," and "The Show of Shows." She was once the subject of "This is Your Life," and has sung occasionally during the sixties.

In 1965 the Met feted her on the twenty-five years of her continuous activity at the house. No other soprano has ever sustained such a time span at the Met. The Met presented the famed coloratura in an assemblage of familiar arias and songs, including, of course, the mad scene from *Lucia*. Among the audience were Leopold Stokowski, Gladys Swarthout, and David Oistrakh.

Lily had no sentimental attachments to the old house. When it was being razed she was one of the few former stars not passionately in favor of saving it. She told an interviewer that the dressing rooms were impossible and that the house was hopelessly antiquated.

Lily Pons has in the course of her public career received many honors, ranging from being made an officer of the French Legion of Honor to the naming of a town after her, in Maryland, Lilypons, previously Lily Pond.

Madame Pons maintains residences in Dallas, Palm Springs, New York, and the south of France. She was divorced from Kostelanetz in 1958 and has never remarried. She has had no children. Although her engagements are scarce and have been rather poorly received in the last few years, she continues to sing. It is most unfortunate because her voice is nowhere near the lovely thing it was.

Former Metropolitan Opera stars (left to right) Bidu Sayao, Giovanni Martinelli, and Lily Pons on a TV discussion show.

Beck in 1936. *UPI*

DAVE BECK

The precursor of Jimmy Hoffa was born in 1894 in Stockton, California. His father, Lemuel, was a carpet cleaner and his mother took in washing to help support the family. In 1898 the Becks moved to Seattle. Dave left school when he was sixteen and went from one job to another. In 1914 he began driving a laundry truck. During World War I, while a member of the United States Navy, Dave flew on anti-zeppelin missions over the North Sea. After the Armistice he married Dorothy Leschender, and went back to his old job. This was during the early days of organized labor in America. Dave joined Local 566 of the Teamsters as its secretary, and in 1923 became president of the Joint Council of Teamsters. In 1927, he was made general organizer for the Pacific North West and British Columbia. Ten years later he formed the Western Conference of Teamsters. In a short time it also included the Midwest and East. In 1940 he became vice-president. He was made executive vice-president in 1947 and elected president in 1952.

Beck was the old style union leader who never avoided a fight. When Harry Bridges challenged the Teamsters for representation of the warehouse workers on the West Coast in the late thirties the formidable longshoremen battled their competition in the streets, repeatedly, but to no avail. The Teamsters won both the battles and the jurisdiction.

Since Beck ran the Teamsters as his personal fief, most of the credit for their rise must be given to him. He also had to take the blame for its faults when the legal troubles began. Four years after he assumed the presidency, the union treasury had increased by $9,000,000 and the membership by 250,000. He prided himself on the claim that his union lived up to its contracts and kept strikes to a minimum. His critics, even some within the Teamsters, attributed this to the fact that Beck was also a businessman and employer. It was an open secret that he had large holdings in such things as gas stations and bowling alleys.

By the time his serious woes with the government began, Beck had achieved respectability and was considered by many to be a perfect example of what a poor boy in America could achieve if he really tried. He was on the Washington State Parole Board and a member of the Seattle Civic Service Commission. Other status positions he had obtained were membership in the Board of Regents of Washington State University and officership in the American Legion and the Elks. Politically he was on the conservative side. His worst enemy never accused the Teamsters of any Communist infiltration.

No one seemed to question how he had become a millionaire on a union official's salary. Then a Senate investigating committee began to inquire into the sources of his personal fortune and the workings of his giant union. It was revealed that Beck had been running the Teamsters like one of his private holdings. Very few decisions on matters of contracts and investments of union funds were delegated. (When he became president, Beck turned over all organizing chores to his protégé Jimmy Hoffa, who was later to succeed him.) There was a report that Teamster money had been used to build a huge mansion in the suburbs of Seattle. This house was later sold to the union for $163,000 but Beck continued to live in it rent free, with the union paying the taxes on the property. When in 1955 the Teamsters opened their new $5,000,000 headquarters in Washington, D.C., Dave moved into a lavishly furnished office in the penthouse which had a view of the Capitol dome. Although he favored handmade suits and expensive cars, he did not drink, smoke, or gamble.

In 1961 Beck was sentenced to five years in prison for filing false income-tax returns. He was paroled after serving two-and-a-half years at the United States penitentiary on McNeil Island, near Tacoma, Washington. During his trial and subsequent appeals Beck never lost his cool. The roly-poly unionist became a model prisoner and when he was released in 1964 went right back to Seattle where he oversees his business and real estate holdings estimated by more than one source to be worth over $2,000,000. All the time he was in jail he continued to draw his yearly $50,000 salary from the Teamsters.

In 1967 Dave Beck married his second wife Helen and honeymooned in Hawaii. Beck will talk with newsmen but refuses to get into anything controversial. During the Hoffa trials and upon his imprisonment, for instance, Beck had no comment. He still refuses to discuss the matter.

With wife, Helen, on a recent vacation. *UPI*

Something to write home about in the 1940's.

ESTHER WILLIAMS

"The Queen of the Surf," as the M-G-M press agents dubbed her, was born in Los Angeles in 1923.

She attended the University of Southern California for awhile and did some modeling until Billy Rose hired her in 1939 to appear in his Aquacade at the Golden Gate International Exposition in San Francisco. Esther probably would have competed in the Olympics but they were not held due to the outbreak of World War II.

Metro-Goldwyn-Mayer put her under contract and gave her a few small roles such as in *Andy Hardy's Double Life* (1942) and *A Guy Named Joe* (1943), in which she supported Irene Dunne* and the late Spencer Tracy.

The Esther Williams moviegoers remember from the forties and fifties emerged in *Bathing Beauty* with Red Skelton and organist Ethel Smith (who resides in Manhattan's Parc Vendome apartments) in 1944. She never developed into much of an actress and try as she did her singing was never more than mediocre, but her pictures were loaded with catchy tunes and talented people. Esther did little more than swim or pose in a bathing suit. As it happened she did both very well. Her figure was curvaceous and in Technicolor her luscious complexion came over very well. There was not another girl in the movies who could swim so well—and could she kiss underwater!

Most of Esther's notices were terrible but they seemed to have no affect on her fans. In 1950 exhibitors named her one of the world's biggest box office draws.

Most of her pictures were musicals shot in Technicolor. They had big names, handsome leading men, and some fine underwater photography. The Culver City lot spared no expense when they put her in such vehicles as *Thrill of a Romance* (1945) with Van Johnson, *Ziegfeld Follies* (1945) with Lucille Bremmer, *Easy to Wed* (1946) with Lucille Ball, *Fiesta* (1947) with Ricardo

Montalban, *This Time for Keeps* (1947) with Lauritz Melchior, *On An Island With You* (1948) with Peter Lawford and Jimmy Durante, *Take Me Out to the Ball Game* (1949) with Frank Sinatra and Betty Garrett (living in Los Angeles with her husband Larry Parks*), *Neptune's Daughter* (1949) with Red Skelton, *Pagan Love Song* (1950) with Howard Keel, *The Duchess of Idaho* (1950), *Texas Carnival* (1951), *Million Dollar Mermaid* (1952) with Victor Mature, *Dangerous When Wet* (1953) with Fernando Lamas, *Easy to Love* (1953), and *Jupiter's Darling* (1955) with Marge and Gower Champion.

Toward the end of her career Esther made a valiant but unsuccessful attempt to climb out of the water and into dramatic roles. In 1957 NBC television presented her in the "Aqua Spectacular," the last of her bathing suit appearances. After that she did *The Unguarded Moment* (1956), in which she was sexually molested by John Saxon; with the late Jeff Chandler, she made *Raw Wind in Eden* (1958) in Italy; and after the rather tacky *The Big Show* (1961) with Robert Vaughn, she quit.

In 1957 Esther ended her thirteen year marriage to actor-producer Ben Gage. She was awarded custody of their children—two girls, Benjie, eighteen, and Susan, fourteen, and a boy, Kim, who at seventeen stands 6 feet 7 inches tall.

Fortunately, for Esther, not all her savings were invested in the ill-fated Esther Williams Swimming Pools—she can still afford to turn down movie and TV roles. She expresses very little interest in working again, but does not close the door completely to offers. "I'm perfectly content to sit in my Santa Monica home watching my kids grow up," she said recently.

When in 1967 she was inducted into the Swimming Pool Hall of Fame, Esther was accompanied by her close friend and constant companion, Fernando Lamas. As the cameras clicked and fans gawked everyone commented on how well she looked. Yes, she swims every day.

With 1928 Oympic gold medal winner Arne Borg from Sweden after induction together into the Swimming Pool Hall of Fame in Fort Lauderdale, Florida. *Ed Plummer*

Glenn (left) congratulates Ben Eastman who won the half-mile on the
same day Cuningham broke the mile
record, June 16, 1934. *Acme*

GLENN CUNNINGHAM

The Master Miler of the thirties was born in Atlanta, Kansas, in 1912. When
he was seven years old Glenn was caught in a schoolhouse fire. His legs were
so badly burned that at first doctors doubted the boy would live. For seven
months he had to lie in bed while the burns turned to ugly scars. Once he
was permitted to walk there was no stopping him. Each day he walked a little
more around his father's farm and little by little he was walking faster. Once
he had proved to himself that he could walk long distances, he began running.
A little at first, and then more and more.

Cunningham's leg trouble did not end when he started running and winning
races. The burns ate away the flesh and left delicate scar tissue in its stead.
He was unable to limber up like most athletes. Instead, he had to prance. He
was immediately labeled a show-off and was soundly booed at some meets
even before they began. Once the warm-up periods were over, however, the
crowds' attitude was somewhat different. Cunningham piled up a staggering
record of wins during his career. On June 16, 1934, at Princeton, New Jersey,
Glenn, representing the University of Kansas, broke the world record for the
mile. His time was 4:06.8. The race, which was sponsored by the university,
saw another record shattered. Ben Eastman of Stanford set 1:49.8 as the new
standard for the half-mile.

At the 1936 Olympics, held in Berlin, he romped in second in a sensational
1,500-meter race in which Jack Lovelock of New Zealand set the world's
record of 3:47.8. Two years later Glenn picked up a trophy for the mile run
in New York at the Seventh Regiment Games on February 11. He was clocked
at 4:15.2, breaking the 4:18.2 meet record which had stood for twenty-five
years. Then in April of 1938 Archie San Romani forged ahead of him at the
last minute and broke the tape at 4:23 on the Kansas University track.

Galloping Glenn was the model athlete. He never broke training in or out
of season. He did not drink or smoke, and never has. But he had a great deal
going for him when he was out on the track. His hearing was so sensitive that

not only could he detect his opponents approaching from behind but could distinguish among them just by the sound of their feet on the cinder path. In 1936 he was admittedly out of condition when he was matched with Joe Mangan and Gene Venske. Mangan broke on top and decided to yield the lead. No one would pass him. He slowed down to a walk until the last 220 yards when all at once Glenn took off and bolted past both his opponents to win. The race has been called the Typographical Error Mile because he was clocked at 4.46.8, which looked more like a typist's mistake than a time.

Glenn hasn't run in competition since he was stationed at the Great Lakes Naval Base during World War II. Following the war, he and his first wife, a fellow student at Kansas University whom he married in 1934, were divorced. They had two children. In 1946 he married again, and has ten children by this marriage.

After graduating from Kansas University he continued his studies at New York University, and received his Ph.D. in June, 1938. Afterward he accepted a job with Cornell College in Mount Vernon, Iowa, as Director of Student Health.

Since 1946 Glenn has been a farmer. The Cunninghams have a large spread on Route 2 just outside Augusta, Kansas. The farm is very well known in those parts, but not so much for the fact that its owner is one of the all-time sport greats. Along with their herd of livestock the family has collected wild and exotic animals from all over the world. Tourists often stop to see children playing with yaks and llamas, but more often than not the children are not Cunninghams. Glenn and his wife have turned their home into a place for children from "troubled homes." They have had as many as eighty-eight boys and girls living with them at one time. The great runner is justly proud of the remarkable results the healthy atmosphere of his farm and family have produced in kids who would otherwise be kept in institutions.

In June of 1968 Cunningham appeared on "The Joey Bishop Show" and announced that not only was he broke but deeply in debt because of the great expense he has been undergoing in supporting so many children. He asked for contributions.

At home today. *Augusta Daily Gazette*

In *Polo Joe*, 1936.

JOE E. BROWN

Joe Evans Brown, the famous big-mouthed comedian, was born in 1892 in Holgate, Ohio, one of seven children of a poor family. As a boy he knew cold, hunger, and hard work. Joe taught himself acrobatics, and when he was ten years old he was accepted as a member of the Five Marvelous Ashtons, traveling with Sells and Downs Circus. His salary was $2.50 a week.

In 1906 the Ashtons broke up after their appearance at a honky-tonk house, the Haymarket Music Hall, which was destroyed by the San Francisco earthquake. Joe went into baseball, a game he has always loved and which was the background for several of his movies. He played off-seasons and summers for such semipro teams as Crowley's All Stars. He was such a cutup that the other players encouraged him to return to show business, but as a comic this time. He joined the Bell-Prevost Trio in 1914. They specialized in acrobatics at the Henderson Music Hall at Coney Island. On the bill with them was a sketch called "Change Your Act" with Victor Moore. On the same bill was a man named W. C. Fields. The trio remained together for eleven years and played just about every burlesque house and vaudeville circuit in the country. Along the way Bell dropped out and they became known as Prevost and Brown.

Joe E. was never a favorite of the intelligentsia. His comedy was rather obvious and without much subtlety, but at least it was not pretentious. He was a natural comic who needed neither gags nor gimmicks to get a laugh. He had what might be called the humor of reaction—a frustration of purpose or a confrontation with some unlooked-for situation. His face was marvellously expressive and his mouth was huge.

Joe made his Broadway debut in 1918 in *Listen Lester* which starred the late Clifton Webb. This was followed by *Jim Jam Jems* (1920), in which he co-starred with the late Frank Fay. He was in the third edition of the *Greenwich Village Follies* in 1921 along with the late Harry Langdon and Ned Sparks. The show introduced the song "Three O'Clock in the Morning." He was also in *Shore Leave* (1922) and *Betty Lee* (1925).

While he worked on Broadway he made countless screen tests at the old studios in Fort Lee, New Jersey, none of which prompted a studio to sign him. Then he came to Los Angeles with the late Ona Munson in *Twinkle, Twinkle*. An agent saw him, considered him a "natural," and talked director Ralph Ince into seeing Brown perform in the show. He was placed under contract to F.B.O.

Studios (later to become R.K.O.) and appeared in *Crooks Can't Win,* his first film, in 1922. Joe bombed in each of his first six pictures, playing dramatic parts. He clicked first in *Hold Everything* (1930) and received star billing afterward for many years. Of his seventy-five movies twenty-nine were made during his nine-year contract with Warner Brothers. Some of them were: *Circus Kid* (1928), *Sally* (1929) with Marilyn Miller, *The Tenderfoot* (1932), *Elmer the Great* (1933), his favorite role, *A Midsummer Night's Dream* (1935), in which he played the role of Flute. His pictures were the biggest money-makers the studio had for 1932, 1935, and 1936.

During World War II he set a record entertaining troops in 742 overseas shows. Congress awarded him the Bronze Star for his efforts, one of the very few times a civilian has been so honored. Joe wrote a book about his wartime experiences, *Your Kids and Mine.* His son, Don, was killed in action.

After the war he starred on the stage in the Mary Chase (who lives in Denver, Colorado) comedy, *Harvey,* for 1,680 performances in the national company and then in Australia and England. In 1951 he had a short run in *Courtin' Time,* a musical version of *The Farmer's Wife.*

During the fifties he was quite active in television. He emceed "Talent Scouts," when Arthur Godfrey was away, and "Strike It Rich," and he starred on "Circus Hour."

In 1956 his autobiography *Laughter Is a Wonderful Thing* was published. It revealed him as a man not too dissimilar from the character he had been playing for so many years.

In 1959 he re-created Cap'n Andy in *Show Boat* in the City Center production, a part he played a decade earlier on the screen. In 1959 he had the last and most outrageous line in the Billy Wilder picture *Some Like It Hot.* Jack Lemmon is seated next to him in drag. Joe E. has just asked Lemmon to marry him and Lemmon tells him that there is something he should know, that he, Lemmon, is actually a man. "Well," replies Joe, "no one's perfect." He has rarely worked since and there is no financial need for him to do so.

Always a close family man, Joe lives in Los Angeles with his wife, the former Kathryn McGraw, whom he married in 1915 at New York's City Hall after courting her by mail for months. They have a son, two adopted daughters, and a number of grandchildren with whom he spends much time. He is an avid, skilled golfer.

At the Los Angeles Country Club.

The Girl of the Year, 1938. N. Y. *Daily News*

BRENDA FRAZIER

The Girl of the Year 1938 was born in 1921. Her parents, who were socially prominent Bostonians, separated shortly after her birth. Like Brenda's beaus, friends, husbands, and relatives, they were very, very rich. It was old, quite respectable money. Or at least until 1938.

Brenda lived part of the year with her father and part with her mother. Her parents lived in different cities, moved in different circles, and called Brenda by different names. Her father, who spent most of his time in Palm Beach, called her Diana—her full maiden name is Brenda Diana Duff Frazier.

When Miss Frazier's father died in 1933 his will stated that on her twenty-first birthday she was to receive the $4,000,000 he had left her only if she did not continue to live with her mother. "Mummy," who didn't care much for him either, had the will invalidated so that Brenda got the money and Mrs. Frazier got Brenda—whom she took to live with her at the Ritz in Manhattan. As the only child of a wealthy, socially ambitious woman, Brenda was schooled at Miss Porter's and Miss Hewitt's before being sent to Munich where she attended a very chichi finishing school. Mummy chose her clothes, her dates, and her friends. When in 1937 Mummy decided that Brenda was to "come out," no amount of the girl's pleading against a debut could dissuade Mrs. Frazier.

The year was 1938. Spain was in flames and the rest of Europe was a tinder-box; Chamberlain appeased Hitler at Munich; Japanese armies swept across China; and at home continued labor unrest made Americans wonder whether the Great Depression would ever end. But the Girl of the Year was Brenda Frazier. Her pictures were in all the papers, and her name was in the columns. *Life* magazine featured her on the cover. The press saw only the waxen skin, and vivid red lips and nails of a girl whose mother had the naïveté to spend a fortune on a single party while many of her countrymen considered themselves lucky if they had enough to eat. Some readers were infuriated while others were simply amused to read of Cafe Society's antics. The important thing was that Brenda sold papers. She became a household name in homes that had never read the Cholly Knickerbocker column. The El Morocco's Jerome Zerbee photographed her against the famous zebra skin upholstery of the club's banquettes, and no one did more to make the Stork Club "in" than Brenda Frazier—whose friendship with proprietor Sherman Billingsley lasted until he died in 1967. The club's press agent, Chick Farmer (now the P.R. man for the Garden City Hotel on Long Island) made sure she got the right table and lots of attention.

The only other deb who came close to Brenda in prominence was Cobina Wright, Jr. Millions of radio listeners tuned to the "Bob Hope Show" laughed weekly at the merciless parody by Blanche Stewart and Eliva Allman playing "Brenda and Cobina."

At a time when $50 per week was considered a living wage by millions of American families, Brenda turned down a $500,000 offer to star in M-G-M films. But endorsed Woodbury soap.

After her marriage in 1941 to John Simms Kelly (known to football fans as "Shipwreck" Kelly) Brenda settled down to a quiet life on Long Island. In 1945 the Kellys had a daughter, Victoria; the marriage ended in 1956. The next year Brenda married Robert F. Chatfield-Taylor, a distant relative.

Brenda no longer lives with her second husband. The last few years of her life have been spent in a large secluded house in Medfield, outside of Boston. Although she does very little entertaining and is seldom seen in nightclubs, her life in past years has not been without incident. There was a long bout with ill health, which was the result of years spent on a near-starvation diet to avoid gaining weight; she has survived a complete nervous breakdown; and in 1961 she attempted suicide.

In 1967 Brenda and her daughter, a tall blonde girl who is very attentive to her mother, returned to Boston and took an apartment. Brenda continues to see her analyst who has been working with her for five years now almost every day.

It is doubtful that many people personally disliked Brenda—it was inevitable that a girl so rich and pretty would be envied and even laughed at during such a time in America's history. Her ways were no more extravagant nor her antics more ludicrous than those who succeed her today. Probably the worst thing that can be said about such people is that they are completely nonessential.

Brenda today. *UPI*

"Hoppy" in 1935.

WILLIAM BOYD

"Hopalong Cassidy," as he is known around the world, was born in Cambridge, Ohio, in 1895. When his parents died he left school and home in Tulsa, Oklahoma, and set out for Hollywood, spending his last nickel on a ticket to Granfe, California, where he worked as an orange packer for a year before he could save enough money to reach his destination. Arriving at the movie capital, he worked as a laborer in a steel mill and as a policeman nights while he spent his days trying to break into pictures. Bill worked as an extra for several years before he managed to get any featured roles. In 1919 he had a very small part in the Cecil B. De Mille production of *Why Change Your Wife?* It was De Mille who also gave him his two best parts in the silent *Volga Boatman* (1926) and *King of Kings* (1927) in which he played Simon of Cyrene.

During the twenties, Boyd was a popular leading man with the audiences and directors for his straightforward performances as well as with his co-stars for his easygoing manner. His greatest drawback was a famous stage actor by the same name who had played Sergeant Quirt in *What Price Glory?* Boyd tried calling himself Bill instead of William, but there was still a lot of confusion between the two. In 1931 the stage actor was arrested at a party at which there was illegal liquor and gambling. Many of the nation's newspapers ran Bill's photograph by mistake, which certainly did his career no good. When the stage actor died Boyd reverted to William.

Some of the silent pictures he made were *Road to Yesterday* (1925), and *The Last Frontier* (1926), *Dress Parade* (1927), *Night Flyer* (1928), and the D. W. Griffith production *Lady of the Pavements* (1929) with Jetta Goudal (who lives in Los Angeles with her husband, designer Harold Grieve). He might have achieved full star status had Gary Cooper not been able to make *The Plainsman*—De Mille admitted that Boyd was his second choice. Many years later he seriously considered him for the role of Moses in the remake of *The Ten Commandments*.

Boyd's talkie career limped along with such mediocre films as *The Painted Desert* (1931) with the late Helen Twelvetrees, *Lucky Devils* (1933) with William Gargan (who has retired since a throat operation left him with a mechanical voice box), and *The Storm* (1934).

In 1939 Boyd won the title role in *Hopalong Cassidy,* originally intended for James Gleason. Bill changed the character from a hard-drinking old reprobate to a westerner who was practically gallant. He took the role quite seriously and within a short time developed a huge audience of adult men who identified with the man in the black cowboy suit who could handle any trouble that arose. The Saturday matinee crowd liked him because the action was never delayed for a song or two nor did their hero have much truck with the sheriff's daughter or her like. To his friends, what was most surprising of all was that Bill actually learned to ride well; until then he had not only been a wretched horseman but disliked horses.

When Harry "Pop" Sherman stepped down after producing fifty-four features, Boyd took over in 1943 and made another twelve. He economized on them until the productions suffered in quality, and at the box office. At one point he was on the brink of bankruptcy. Then along came television and Boyd saw a chance to make a fortune. He sold his ranch, borrowed every penny he could, and bought all rights to the character. His gamble paid off handsomely. In 1951 alone the gross sales of "Hoppy" products and commercials tie-ins were $25,000,000. He made new pictures expressly for TV and took great care to keep violence at a minimum. He also toured the country with his own circus. Sixty-three TV stations carried the series, 155 newspapers ran the "Hoppy" comic strip, 152 radio stations broadcast the audio version, and 108 manufacturers turned out products bearing the Hopalong Cassidy name. The character, the products, and the films grossed $70,000,000 in 1952, the height of the boom.

In the late 1950's Boyd sold out all his interests for a staggering profit, which he could treat as a capital gain on his income tax return. He has made several appearances since, but has a policy against kids being charged to see him. For more than a decade he and his fourth wife, actress Grace Bradley, whom he married in 1937, have lived quietly in their Palm Desert home.

In his desert home. *Jon Virzi*

Billings (left) and Tom Mooney meet in prison in 1935. *UPI*

WARREN K. BILLINGS

The co-defendant in what has been referred to as the "American Dreyfus Case" was born in Middletown, New York, in 1894.

On July 22, 1916, a bomb exploded during a Preparedness Day Parade in San Francisco, killing nine and maiming many others. Tom Mooney, a powerful and articulate labor organizer, and his twenty-two-year-old protégé, Warren Billings, were arrested and brought to trial. Mooney was sentenced to death (after Woodrow Wilson interceded this was reduced to a life term) and Billings got life imprisonment.

Some of the most influential men in the country objected strongly to the trial and the sentences. Upton Sinclair (living the past few years in ill health in Monrovia, California) and the late Theodore Dreiser were among the many who joined organizations to secure the release of the men they believed to be innocent. A Presidential commission was set up to investigate the matter and when its report was filed it stated that "The utilities sought to get Mooney and Billings." It was also found that the district attorney who prosecuted the two had knowingly destroyed evidence and that major testimony had been perjured.

Billings and Mooney, while symbols of a cause, were also victims of the era as well. Shortly after the bombing, the United States entered World War I and public attention was focused on defense and victory. During the ensuing Roaring Twenties the nation underwent a "Red Scare" second only to the McCarthyism of the fifties. In the thirties people were preoccupied with the Great Depression, but by that time the two had become so famous that many felt they might lead a workers' revolt if they were released. The press often referred to them as "radical labor leaders" which suggested to many that while they might not be guilty as charged the country was safer with them behind bars. "Believe me, it took a hell of a lot more money to keep us there than it did to put us there to begin with," said Billings recently.

Finally, California's first Democratic governor of the century, Culbert Olson, honoring an election pledge, pardoned Mooney on January 7, 1939. Mooney at once began a campaign to free Billings. However, because of expenditures and

Mooney's association with the Communists the two old friends soon fell out. When Mooney died in 1942 he had already lost much of the respect he had gained during his years in prison.

While politicans argued among themselves over the case, prisoner #10699 languished for another ten months in Folsom Prison in California. After reading the pile of evidence that should have proved his innocence, the state's Attorney General said he saw "no justification for release" and voted against it as a member of the Prison Advisory Board. He was later elected governor and then appointed Chief Justice of the Supreme Court. His name—Earl Warren.

Billings was released in October, 1939, after having spent twenty-three years, two months, and twenty-three days incarcerated for a crime he did not commit. Even then he was not given a full pardon, but only a commutation of his sentence, with the result that he could not vote or own property. It was not until 1962 when Governor Edmund "Pat" Brown granted him a full pardon that he was completely freed of the stigma of guilt. He has yet to receive a penny from the state in compensation for the years of his life that were taken away.

In October of 1940 Billings married Josephine Rudolph with whom he had corresponded for seventeen years. He opened a watch repair shop at Seventh and Market streets in San Francisco only blocks from where the bombing took place. He ran his business until 1958 when he became eligible for Social Security. The Billingses now live in San Mateo where he works two days a week in a jewelry shop to supplement the $89 a month he gets from the government. Still a strong union man, Billings is a member of the executive board of the Watchmakers' Local No. 101.

His semiretirement has allowed him to renovate the sixty-year-old house in which they live and to begin his book of personal recollections about the Mooney-Billings case. The working title is *Bum Beef*, a prison expression for an unjust conviction. In the meantime he sells autographed copies of *Frame-up*, a 1967 book on the case, making about $3 per book—an arrangement he worked out with the book's author in return for his cooperation when the book was being written.

The former cause célèbre at a recent union meeting. *Los Angeles Citizen*

One of the top-rated weekly radio shows, 1939. *NBC*

EDGAR BERGEN

The perfect stooge for his wisecracking cheeky, world-weary teen-ager dummy was rated Number One in every radio popularity poll of his day. Edgar Bergen was making $6,400 a week for his weekly radio appearance, $75,000 a year from movies, and $100,000 a year from dolls, gadgets, and so forth. And all this just one year after his radio debut!

He has rightly been called the Noel Coward of ventriloquists.

While attending Lakeview High School in Chicago, Illinois (where he was born in 1903 of Swedish immigrant parents), Bergen conceived the idea for a dummy, having long since discovered in himself a flare for ventriloquism. Theodore Mack, a master craftsman, carved a dummy to his specifications, copying the facial features of a newsboy whom Bergen knew, named Charlie. He named his dummy Charlie Mack. He changed it to McCarthy purely for the sake of euphony. The cost of the dummy, made of basswood, paint, string, and springs, was $35.

As an afterschool usher at the old Victoria Theatre, he was able to entertain at Saturday matinees. Upon graduation he attended Northwestern University, and entertained at campus functions.

After leaving college, he quickly found work since his act was virtually unique, eventually playing in almost every state. He played London, opening at the Grosvenor House, and was very well received. Following London he went to Sweden, playing before the Crown Prince in his native language.

By the time he returned to the United States vaudeville was dead, and he adapted his act for nightclubs. He was soon playing the Casanova Club in Hollywood, the Chez Paree in Chicago, and the Rainbow Room in New York City. At an Elsa Maxwell party Rudy Vallee caught his act and signed him to appear several times on his radio program, finally permanently in 1937. That same year Chase and Sanborn gave them a program on Sunday nights, with Don Ameche as emcee, and singer Dorothy Lamour. W. C. Fields joined them later.

Although Bergen and McCarthy made twelve shorts for the old Vitaphone Company between 1933 and 1935, they now went to Hollywood as full-fledged stars, appearing in such films as *The Goldwyn Follies* (1938) with Zorina, Bobby Clark, and the Ritz Brothers, *Charlie McCarthy, Detective* (1939), *You Can't Cheat an Honest Man* (1939) with W. C. Fields, and *Look Who's Laughing* (1941) with Lucille Ball, Fibber McGee and Molly, and Neil Hamilton.

In 1939 Bergen introduced another dummy, Mortimer Snerd, a country bumpkin, and sometime later another dummy, Effie, a sort of hip old maid.

Although Hollywood circles considered Bergen a sort of man-about-town, often escorting stars at various functions, he lived a quiet private life with his mother until her death in 1945. The same year he married Frances Westerman, a former Powers' model and actress. Their daughter Candice was born in 1946 and their son Kris Edgar in 1961.

Since World War II, throughout which he traveled extensively entertaining troops, Bergen was restricted to nightclubs, although he appeared on TV, sometimes without his little friends, as in the 1948 movie version of *I Remember Mama*. His last movie appearance was also a solo venture *Don't Make Waves,* with Tony Curtis and Claudia Cardinale. Beginning in 1956 Bergen and his wooden friend hosted the daytime quiz show "Do You Trust Your Wife?" for a few years.

His beautiful daughter Candice has become a star in her own right. And in 1967, she and Bergen made their legitimate stage debut at the Westbury Music Fair in Long Island in *Sabrina Fair,* playing father and daughter.

That he never made it as a straight actor disappointed him. He is somewhat resentful that the dummy became more famous and recognizable than its creator. The millionaire can well afford to nurse his grievances. Much of his money is in Hollywood real estate. He owns an entire block on Sunset Boulevard, in which his magic shop is located. He often wanders in. Even at the height of his career he was able to walk in and mingle with the customers who did not recognize him without his toupee and "Charlie McCarthy."

A family portrait: Edgar and daughter Candice.

A studio publicity still, 1938.

ELEANOR HOLM

The girl whose divorce-plaintiff fame nearly overshadowed her success as a swimmer was born in Brooklyn in 1914.

When she was only fourteen Eleanor won the the three hundred yard medley in the Olympics in four minutes and twenty-five seconds. In 1932 she set a new world's record in the Olympics with her fifty-yard backstroke. The same year she won the three hundred yard medley. Altogether Eleanor held fourteen titles in domestic and Olympic swimming meets. She won the National Indoor Junior Championship in three different categories, the National Women's Indoor Championships in five different categories, and the outdoor Junior Medley Championship. She is the only American female swimmer to have competed in three Olympic games.

In 1933 Eleanor became the wife of singer Arthur Jarrett, who traveled with her much of the time and managed her career. In 1936 the swimmer moved from the sport pages to the headlines when she was removed from the United States Olympic team of that year for breaking the strict training rules. There was a great deal of jealousy among her teammates as well as the Olympic board over the fact that she was so well known. They seemed to feel that her notoriety came close to violating the sacred amateur standing that is so closely guarded in this country. What caused the crisis was when Eleanor attended a party where she was the only team member. In plain view of the Olympic officers and their wives she drank champagne. No one accused her of being drunk but the incident was enough to have her dumped.

The press was on Eleanor's side and for awhile it looked like she might be reinstated. When confronted with the signatures of one hundred Olympic contenders from different countries asking that Eleanor be allowed to compete, the board grew even more adamant. Eleanor's amateur days were over.

In 1932 Eleanor had been named one of the Wampus Baby Stars of that year along with Ginger Rogers, the late Boots Mallory, and Mary Carlisle (now manager of the Elizabeth Arden Salon in Beverly Hills). Her movie career, however, never caught fire—she received terrible notices for her starring role in *Tarzan's Revenge* in 1938.

In 1938 she and Jarrett were divorced and a year later Eleanor married the pint-sized impresario, Billy Rose, who starred her in his Aquacade at the 1939–1940 World's Fair. The two seemed to get along beautifully for the next twelve years, during which time she hosted his frequent parties at their lavish Mount Kisco estate. In his autobiography Rose praised her to the sky in a chapter entitled "Holm, sweet, Holm." Her marriage ended her career.

In 1951 Joyce Mathews, who had been married to Milton Berle, slashed her wrists in Rose's apartment. Eleanor dropped by about that time and the "War of the Roses," as the press dubbed it, began. Eleanor, with the true instincts of a champion, retained attorney Louis Nizer. Billy locked her out of his town house. She threatened to produce a list of six of his playmates. He stated that he had a list of his own and that not all of Eleanor's trangressions had been with men. The tabloids played up the lesbian angle and ran quotes from some of the Broadway notables who knew and disliked Rose, which included just about everyone who had ever done business with him.

Just when it looked like the two parties were going to come to court, where names would be named, Rose capitulated. After three years of well reported antics and insults back and forth they settled—a Beekman Place town house, $200,000 cash, and an annual allowance of $30,000 for his former wife.

Eleanor was seen around town at nightclubs and parties for a few years and then in 1960 she quietly moved to Miami Beach where she has lived ever since. She likes the climate and finds it very conducive to the outdoor sports she still participates in regularly. Recently she wrote a booklet on swimming for beginners, which is distributed to youngsters as a public service by the Pepsi Cola Company. She has not remarried and has no children. Along with occasional traveling Eleanor works on a few committees for charities and does an interior decorating job from time to time, a knack she found she had during her Mount Kisco days.

In 1967 Eleanor filed suit against the already entangled Billy Rose estate, claiming that $20,000,000 was due her for several phony Renoirs the late producer had given her as part of their settlement.

From left to right: Johnny Weissmuller, Eleanor Holm, sportscaster Jack Whittaker, and Buster Crabbe when the three swimmers were installed in the Swimming Pool Hall of Fame in Fort Lauderdale, Florida. *Ed Plummer*

Between her two terms in Congress, she spoke at pacifist rallies throughout the nation, this one in New York in 1933. N. Y. *Daily News*

JEANNETTE RANKIN

The first woman to be elected to the United States Congress was born in 1880 in the territory of Montana (Montana was not admitted to the Union until 1889).

A feminist, Miss Rankin was active in suffragette movements from her early years when the idea of women having the right to vote was either ludicrous or anathema to many men. Coming from a well-to-do family she was able to devote all of her time and energy to advancing the cause of suffrage. Before she was able to cast a ballot in a polling booth she won the right to vote and debate in the House of Representatives.

In 1916 Miss Rankin was elected to Congress from Montana on a woman's suffrage ticket, despite the Democratic landslide that year. Her first term in the House was distinguished by her determined efforts to keep America out of World War I. Even after the sinking of the Lusitania she opposed our entry and joined with forty-nine congressmen and six senators on April 16, 1917, to vote against the declaration of war against Germany. "I want to stand by my country, but I cannot vote for war," she stated. The vote, which was in the minority, did not increase her popularity and when she was up for reelection in 1918 her district was gerrymandered. Undaunted, Miss Rankin ran instead for the senate seat, but was defeated.

Throughout the 1920's and 1930's Jeannette Rankin appeared on countless platforms speaking for disarmament and peace. When she was not in office she lobbied against increased military appropriations, claiming it was the generals who had caused all the wars to justify their own existence. She has opposed United States intervention into any conflict, however small, anywhere in the world. "America," she has said, "has the war habit. It is a habit we must break before we are broken by it."

When World War II broke out Miss Rankin again ran for Congress from the state of Montana and was elected on the Republican ticket. "I've always been a Republican," she says, "for the same reason that most people are either Democrats or Republicans—because their fathers were one or the other. Frankly, I cannot see a particle of difference between the two." Her second term which began in 1940 was ended for all practical purposes on December 9, 1941. That was the day that Jeannette Rankin became the sole member of either house to vote "nay" on America's declaration of war against Japan. Three days later she simply said "present" when her name was called in the vote to go to war against Germany and Italy. "What good would it have done to vote 'no,'" she said recently. "We were already at war against Japan. F.D.R. had what he wanted—war. He wanted to be a war President. Everything he did from the day he first took office pointed to the fact that he wanted to fight Germany." Few members of government have been treated as Jeannette Rankin was treated after those votes. Her congressional colleagues shunned her, the press ignored her, and she was publicly booed and hissed. Even many who had stood on America First platforms with her were caught up in the patriotic spirit that prevailed in the country after Pearl Harbor, and had no sympathy with her stand. "They all said that would be the last anyone would hear of me. Well, they were wrong. I have never stopped working for peace and I never will," said Miss Rankin the day after she lead a group of five thousand women in Washington, D.C. under the banner of the Jeannette Rankin Brigade to protest the war in Vietnam. That was January 15, 1968.

Miss Rankin divides her time between a ranch in Montana where she summers and her winter home in Watkinsville, Georgia. She is still available for lectures and rallies and enjoys them thoroughly. To those who find the energy and spirit of the eighty-eight-year-old spinster remarkable she says: "But you see I have to keep going. No one can let up in this effort to bring about peace. Real peace. A lasting peace. We have got to get it into our heads once and for all that we cannot settle disputes by eliminating human beings."

The Honorable Jeannette Rankin at eighty-eight. *Ben Fernandez*

Once the biggest moneymaking team in show business, circa 1945, with Bud on the right.

"BUD" ABBOTT

The straight man of one of the most popular comedy duos in show business was born in Asbury Park, New Jersey, in 1895. He was named William. His father was the advance man of a circus in which his mother performed as a bareback rider. Bud's childhood was spent in the Coney Island section of Brooklyn.

There are several versions of how and why the team originally got together. One has it that Lou Costello's straight man didn't show up one night and Abbott, who had been working in the box office, was asked to pinch hit in a burlesque theatre in upstate New York where the act was booked. Another story tells of Costello, who was a compulsive gambler all his life, losing his shirt in a poker game and Abbott bailing him out. Both agreed that they first met in a burlesque house in upstate New York, but as with most references to their private lives, Abbott and Costello could never get together on the origin of their famous partnership.

On stage few twosomes ever had the smooth rapport they developed. From the time they joined forces in 1925 until they broke into the big time in 1938, the boys moved around the country in tab shows, vaudeville and mainly burlesque. In a short time Abbott and Costello were "top bananas" on the bump and grind circuits, and worked fairly steadily. There were many disagreements between them, but no one watching their comedy routines would ever know it. Costello was short, fat and mad. Abbott was thin, dour, and easily exasperated.

In 1938 they were booked into a New York vaudeville house, where the late Ted Collins spotted them and put them on the "Kate Smith Show," which at the time was one of the most popular radio programs in America. People who would never think of entering a burlesque theatre heard them that night. The material they had developed and used over the years was completely fresh to this audience, and the reaction was national convulsions. Other top shows signed them to appear and the following year they were seen in *Streets of Paris* on Broadway. The movies grabbed them and they debuted in *One Night in the Tropics*.

Through the forties and into the fifties Abbott and Costello were the comedy kings of America on their own radio programs and in feature film after feature film. A few that helped keep Universal-International Pictures out of bankruptcy during very lean years were *Buck Privates* (1941), *Pardon My Sarong* (1942), *Lost in a Harem* (1944), *Abbott and Costello in Hollywood* (1945), *Abbott and Costello Meet Frankenstein* (1948), *Abbott and Costello in the Foreign Legion* (1950), and *Abbott and Costello Meet Captain Kidd* (1952). They were included every year from 1941 until 1951 among the top ten box office favorites in the country. Typical of how financially successful they were are the figures reported on one of their starrers: cost of production—$90,000, grossed—over $10,000,000.

In 1957, after a great success on television, they finally split. Costello was being offered as a single. Abbott, ten years older than his partner, said that he would retire to his ranch in Ojai, California.

In 1958 Abbott filed suit against Costello for $222,465.19 he claimed was owed him for a TV series they had done together. It was still in litigation a year later when on March 3, 1959, Costello died of a heart attack.

Then the Internal Revenue claimed that he owed them several hundred thousand dollars in past taxes. Within weeks Abbott, who thought he was set financially for the rest of his life, was forced to sell his ranch, the property surrounding his Encino home, and the residual rights to his TV films. Had he sold everything he owned, he could not pay the principal and interest.

About then, Abbott and Eddie Foy, Jr., announced they would team as a comedy act, but nothing came of it.

In 1964 the comedian suffered a mild stroke. In his few statements to the press these past years, he seems free of any bitterness. He seems proud of the fact that he and Costello had sold over $80,000,000 worth of war bonds in the forties, and that despite his home in Woodland Hills having become less sumptuous than he had been used to, he did not seek bankruptcy as a way out of his troubles.

What final settlement he made with Uncle Sam is not known, but he and Betty Abbott, his wife of many years, live comfortably not far from the Motion Picture Country Hospital.

Bud spents most of his time in Western attire. *Jon Virzi*

The songbird in a publicity shot from 1939.

GERTRUDE NIESEN

The musical comedy and radio star of the thirties was born to Colonel and Mrs. Monte Niesen in 1910 while her parents were returning by ship to New York from a summer in Europe. She began her vocal exercises early, crying all the way to the docks. Gertrude attended the Brooklyn Heights Seminary School between road tours of *The Vagabond King, Sonny, Good News,* and others. While in high school, she went to see a performance of *You Said It* and left the theatre determined to become a big star like the late Lyda Roberti. She began to do imitations of the Polish comedienne, becoming so good that her friends encouraged her to try out in Broadway auditions. (Some time much later, she replaced Miss Roberti as Lou Holtz's partner.) She made the rounds of booking agents who turned thumbs down on her. However, one agent's office boy tipped her off that "Feet" Edson was looking for a girl for Joe Taylor's vaudeville act. She got the job, which paid $100 a week. The year was 1931. Shortly afterward she was signed by the 300 Club in New York City.

Gertrude's big boost came when Rudy Vallee signed her to appear on radio on his Fleischmann Hour. At the time, Vallee was the hottest name on the air waves and the guest spots gave her excellent exposure. Almost immediately she landed a job singing a commercial. Since in those days all commercials were done live, Gertrude had to go from one radio station to another. This gave her a chance to meet most of the important people in the business as well as becoming a familiar voice to listeners all over America. More guest spots were offered by other top radio personalities and she was signed to a steady spot on a program featuring the late Lulu McConnell and the Isham Jones Orchestra. She gained great popularity in the medium. In one national poll, she ranked after Ruth Etting and Kate Smith.

Her popularity on radio soon made her a draw at presentation houses. As early as 1933 she received top billing at the Palace Theatre. The second attraction to play the Radio City Music Hall was Roger Wolfe Kahn's band with Gertrude Niesen.

She was known as a vocalist who could get lost in a torch song and turn right around and belt out something big and brassy. It made her a natural for musical comedy. Her first show was *Take a Chance* in 1933 but she was seen only in one performance—she was understudy to a lady with notoriously good health, Ethel Merman. In 1934 she did *Calling All Stars* and in 1936 was with Josephine Baker, Eve Arden, Bob Hope, and Judy Canova* in *The Ziegfeld Follies*. In 1937 she made her only movie, for Universal, heading the cast of *Top of the Town*. She was supported by the late Mischa Auer, Ella Logan,* and Peggy Ryan (the proprietress of an ice skating and dancing school in Honolulu). A year later she headed the London cast of *No Sky So Blue*. Her biggest success was in *Follow the Girls* in 1945 with an unknown comic named Jackie Gleason. One critic said she delivered the big number "I Wanna Get Married" with "a combination of hungry appeal and desperate determination." She was with the show for 882 performances on Broadway and then took it on the road.

Gertrude played just about every top supper club in New York and quite a few around the country during her heyday. She headlined the show at such spots as the St. Regis Roof, the Versailles, and Casino de Paree. In 1947 the Zanzibar paid her $4,700 a week to star in a revue entitled *The Affairs of Vanity Fair*. She was supported by Hal Le Roy (living in Maywood, New Jersey).

The star had a way with real estate like she had with a song. Her heavy investing proved profitable even when she was still working and did not need the money. At one point, she bought a $2,500,000 Newport, Rhode Island, mansion for $21,000.

During the fifties her appearances began to fall off. When she starred for the last time in 1958 at the Copacabana, columnist Louis Sobol who had been one of her most ardent fans right from the beginning asked, "Why has she dropped out of show business?" The question remains unanswered. Sobol mused recently, "I guess she just made a happy marriage and called it quits."

Gertrude has been married for some time to the owner of the now defunct Black Orchid Club in Chicago. Several years ago she sold her island off Port Chester, Connecticut. She and her husband live on Hollywood's famed Mulholland Drive, though none of her show business contemporaries hear a word from her.

At a recent Hollywood premiere. *Jon Virzi*

During the 1940's, Mrs. Nussbaum
was a household name. *NBC Radio*

"MRS. NUSSBAUM"

The most famous dialect comedienne from the Golden Age of Radio was born
Minerva Pious in Odessa, Russia, in 1909. She came to this country when
she was three years old and settled with her parents in Bridgeport, Connecticut.
Minerva did not grow up in a neighborhood of mixed ethnic backgrounds;
the only accents she remembers during her early years were those of her
Russian-Jewish parents. The woman who has been called the "Ruth Draper
of Radio" attributes her unique ability to keen powers of observation. "I am
an inveterate eavesdropper in crowded places," she says, "and am benefited
by what I hear through the aid of a sharp musical ear, plus absolute pitch."

Minerva is one of the few performers to be discovered and developed completely by radio. When she came to Fred Allen in 1933 through one of his
writers, she was in her own words, "a complete amateur." She used her "Nussbaum" voice on the show for some time before "Allen's Alley" was formed
and the character got a name, Pansy Nussbaum, bestowed by Allen himself.
She stayed with the program until 1949, doing all the female voices. The
other inhabitants of the famous Alley were Ajax Cassidy, the drunken Irishman
who drew the most complaints from listeners, Senator Claghorn, and Titus
Moody. But it was Mrs. Nussbaum with her absurd stories about her husband
Pierre, who never appeared, that brought the most applause each week. One
of her other popular characters was a woman called Blossom Rappaport.

Though Minerva Pious never became known to the general public, in
the trade, she developed a reputation for being able to do any accent
or dialect. The actress who can sound like a Park Avenue matron, cockney
fishwife, or midwestern schoolgirl claims that the most sensitive nationalities are
the Irish and Scotch. Her natural voice is so clear that she once received an

award for having diction completely free of regional influences or affectations.

Radio performers, of course, were not seen and received scanty billing unless they were stars. Few listeners, therefore, realized that the lady who convulsed much of America as Pansy Nussbaum was also being heard on most of the other shows as well, playing totally different roles. On the "Kate Smith Show" Minerva was a debutante with a broad New York accent. For Al Jolson she was paired in sketches with Monty Woolley. Sammy Kaye's audiences heard her as Gypsy Rose Rabinowitz. Her straight man in those skits was Red Barber. Once she played a Jewish Camille to Charles Boyer's Armand. A few of the other programs of the day on which she was a frequent guest were "Easy Aces," the "Philip Morris Playhouse," and "Duffy's Tavern." She worked with the biggest names in the profession—W. C. Fields, Robert Benchley, Bob Hope, Bing Crosby, and Tallulah Bankhead.

Her motion pictures include *It's in the Bag* (1945) with Jack Benny and Fred Allen, *The Ambassador's Daughter* (1956), and *Love in the Afternoon* with Gary Cooper and Audrey Hepburn in 1957. During the fifties she spent most of her time living and working in France and England. She made *Joe Macbeth* (1956) while living in London.

She has been seen on Broadway in *Love in Our Time* (1941), *Dear Me, the Sky Is Falling* (1963) with the late Gertrude Berg, and *The Last Analysis* (1964).

Minerva was married briefly, in the forties, to Bernie Hanighen, the songwriter and lyricist. She has a foster son who was orphaned during World War II. One of the first things she did for him was to have the twelve-year-old Italian fitted with an articulated artificial leg. She lives in a hotel in Manhattan's theatrical district and appears from time to time on such TV shows as "Merv Griffin" and "Les Crane." She has also done character parts on "Edge of Night" and "Another World." She is currently to be seen with Louis Jacobi in a TV commercial for Traveler's Insurance.

Minerva in her hotel room in Manhattan.
Diana Keyt

In 1930 Charles Farrell and Janet Gaynor were the most popular movie pair in the world.

CHARLES FARRELL

The male half of talkies' first "screen lovers" was the only son of an old New England family. He was born on Cape Cod in 1902, and matriculated at Boston University where he majored in business administration. Before he could receive his diploma the school required one year of vocational training. He was assigned the position of business manager for a prominent actor of the day who was touring the Orpheum circuit. The glamour of the theatre got to him in a short time, and he was hooked. From then on it was an actor's life for Charles.

His first job in movies was an extra in the Pola Negri* film *The Cheat* (1923). He did bit parts in six more pictures before Paramount took a chance on him as "the boy" in *Old Ironsides* (1926). In 1927 he starred in *Street Angel.*

Farrell heard that Frank Borzage was slated to direct the movie version of the stage play *Seventh Heaven.* Since he knew the director personally, he went to see him. He hoped to put in a good word for a friend he thought would be ideal for the lead. To his surprise, Borzage gave him the role instead. The part of Chico was considered a plum even before shooting began, but no one guessed that the 1927 production would be the phenomenal success it turned out to be. (That was the first year of the Academy Awards which were not called "Oscars" until Bette Davis named the statuettes for one of her husbands, who is now a Los Angeles advertising executive.) Awards were won by co-star Janet Gaynor for Best Actress, Borzage for direction, and Benjamin Glazer for screen adaptation.

Miss Gaynor had been his leading lady before, in *Street Angel,* but when they were paired in *Heaven* as the appealing waif and the young street cleaner who fell in love in Paris, audiences around the world wept. The film's theme music, "Diane," which accompanied the silent feature was a great addition. Not until Jeanette MacDonald and Nelson Eddy appeared in the mid-thirties was the popularity of Farrell and Gaynor equaled.

Charles and Janet continued as a duo in a series of features which enjoyed great popularity, but never equaled *Seventh Heaven.* Some of their vehicles were *The First Year* (1932), *Tess of the Storm Country* (1932), and *Change of Heart* (1934). Farrell made some on his own, such as *City Girl* (1930), *After Tomorrow* (1932) opposite Marion Nixon, *Girl Without a Room* (1933), *The Big Shakedown* (1934) with Bette Davis, and *Fighting Youth* (1935). His popularity began to slip in the mid-thirties, and he began to take lesser roles in such pictures as *Moonlight Sonata* (1937) with Ignace Paderewski, *Just Around the Corner* (1938) with Shirley Temple, and *The Sun Never Sets* (1939) with the late Basil Rathbone. By 1941 he was working for Monogram, the "B" studio, in *Deadly Game*. Two years earlier he had re-created his role of Chico on Broadway, with Milli Monti as Diane, but it failed to revitalize his career.

Since 1934 Charles had gone regularly to Palm Springs. The climate was good for his hay fever, and he was an avid tennis player. He and Ralph Bellamy built a few bungalows and tennis courts which eventually became *the* chic private club in the resort town. They called it the Racquet Club. Bellamy sold out early, before it mushroomed into a project that netted as much as $500,000 a year for Farrell.

In 1952 Farrell made a comeback on TV in "My Little Margie," which began June 16, 1952, as a summer replacement for the "I Love Lucy" series. Despite bad reviews it proved so popular it was continued for 128 segments, and was in syndication for many years after it went off the CBS network. Farrell and his co-star, Gale Storm, even did a radio version of the show for a couple of seasons. Charles had a series of his own after "Margie" went into reruns, called "The Charlie Farrell Show." He played himself, the manager of the Palm Springs Racquet Club.

Although Farrell has not been active on television or in pictures for a number of years, his whereabouts are well known to the movie colony. During the fifties, for seven years Farrell was the mayor of the town. In 1959 he sold his interest in the Club for $1,000,000, but continues to manage it. In 1931 he was married to silent star Virginia Valli, who was a devout Catholic. They had no children. Charles gave up polo a few years ago, but he is still one of the best tennis players on his courts.

At the Racquet Club in Palm Springs, California. *Jon Virzi*

With Jean Gabin in *The Human Beast,* directed by Jean Renoir.

SIMONE SIMON

The girl with the most redundant name in movies was born in Marseilles, France, in 1914. Although it was rumored that she was the daughter of Marion Davies by William Randolph Hearst, her early life seems well documented to prove otherwise. Simon with her mother and stepfather, moved to Madagascar when she was three years old. Before settling in Paris in her teens she attended schools in Berlin, Budapest, and Turin.

In June of 1931 Mlle. Simon was sipping coffee on the terrace of the Café de la Paix one afternoon when she was noticed by the exiled Russian director Tourjansky, who offered her a part in a movie he was about to make in Paris. She debuted opposite the opera singer, Muratore, in the picture *Le Chanteur Inconnu* that year. Continental audiences took an immediate liking to the girl with a kittenish quality that made her seem very feminine, and that made men act very masculine. In her French films *Un Fils d' Amerique* (1932), *Le Petite Chocolatiere,* and *Les Yeux Noirs* (1933) her directors, Tourjansky and Marc Allegret, made the most of her impish appeal. By the time Hollywood took notice, La Simon had become known as "la sauvage tendre," which Twentieth Century-Fox press agents translated as "Europe's Sweetheart."

Simone was one of Hollywood's most spectacular failures. There are two versions of how she accomplished that dubious distinction. According to her studio who brought her over in 1935, she was uncooperative, temperamental, and refused to master English. She was replaced by Claudette Colbert in *Under Two Flags* (1936), a role which would probably have made her an American star overnight. According to Simone, it was the fault of the studio. Darryl Zanuck, she said, cast her in unsuitable roles and Ernie Westmore attempted to change her coiffure and makeup in order to "glamorize her." She quarreled constantly with her directors. In spite of her disfavor with the front office she managed to turn a small part in *Girls' Dormitory* (1936) which starred the late Herbert Marshall and Ruth Chatterton to such good account that the studio was deluged with fan mail for her. She registered again the next year in *Seventh Heaven* in dramatic scenes with Jimmy Stewart and Gale

Sondergaard.* In 1938 she was seen in *Josette* with Don Ameche and then in *Love and Hisses* with Walter Winchell and the late Ben Bernie. That year she brought charges against her former private secretary who had forged her name on more than $10,000 in checks. The defendant took the stand and told how Miss Simon had arranged for gold-plated keys to the front door of her houses as gifts to her "particular friends." While all America guessed, only one name appeared in print, George Gershwin.

History would seem to belie her being a failure as an actress because after her $2,000 per week contract ended and she returned to France, she made a number of good pictures. *The Human Beast* (1940) was such a hit that Holly-wood offered her another chance. She returned in 1940 and made *All That Money Can Buy* (1941), a screen version of *The Devil and Daniel Webster* which starred Walter Huston, and followed that with *Tahiti Honey* (1943). Two of her United States films made during her second visit, *Cat People* (1942) and *Curse of the Cat People* (1943), have become minor classics among horror-film buffs. In 1944 she and Kurt Kreuger made *Mademoiselle Fifi* (1944).

Her attempted American comeback during the early forties included a few vaudeville appearances and a legitimate musical, *Three After Three,* with Stepin Fetchit,* which never made it to Broadway.

While she never regained the status she had enjoyed in Europe during the 1930's, the actress continued to make movies. In England she appeared in *Temptation Harbor* (1947) and *Extra Dry Day* (1956). In Italy she did *Donna Senza None* (1949). In France she has been seen in *La Ronde* (1950), *Le Plaisir* (1951), and *Pit of Loneliness* (1954) in which she played a lesbian.

She is still a Parisian, and has yet to manage a change of name by marriage, although her friendship with a Frenchman with several million dollars and a wife is well known in theatrical and social circles. Her favorite pastime is playing gin rummy. She appeared in Paris in 1966 in the play *La Courte Paille* opposite Jean Meyer, but friends say it is only an exercise in ego. She wanted to prove that she was still attractive and as good an actress as people remember. She was.

Leaving her Paris apartment. *Jon Virzi*

Detroit's top Tiger in 1938. *UPI*

HANK GREENBERG

The right-handed hitter who overcame extreme awkwardness as an athlete to be twice voted the most valuable player in the American League was born in 1911 in Greenwich Village. He moved to the Bronx when he was seven where he attended public schools. In 1927 he played first base with the James Monroe High School team but had a reputation as a "tanglefoot," one who gets in his own way. Classmates remember him as being much better on a basketball court or a soccer field than on the baseball diamond. After high school graduation in 1929, he studied at New York University for a year.

Greenberg's first contract with the major leagues was signed in 1930, and he became a Tiger. There had been a bid from the Yankees but the Detroit team, according to *The New York Times,* offered a bonus of $9,000. During his entire first season he played in only one game and failed to hit. The Tigers farmed Hank to Hartford in the Eastern League, then to Raleigh in the Piedmont League where he batted .314. In 1932 he batted .318 for Evansville in the Three-I League and .290 for Beaumont in the Texas League.

In 1933 Greenberg was back with the Tigers. That year he played first base and batted .301. In 1934 he was batting .339. By 1936 he was at .348. They shifted him to the outfield in 1940, and he batted .340. The reason for the change was that the team wanted to get Rudy York's bat into the lineup.

In 1941 he became Private Henry Greenberg in the United States Army. In 1945 he was discharged as a captain in the Army Air Corps and went back to Detroit as an outfielder. He batted .311 that season. In 1946 he was moved back to first base and his hitting dropped to .277.

The Tigers sold Hank to Pittsburgh in the National League in 1947. He played first base and batted .249 for a salary of $60,000.

On August 23, 1947, the Polo Grounds held a "Greenberg Day" with all cash gifts going to the Rehabilitation Institute of New York University, one of Hank's favorite charities. He retired the following year when he became the general manager of the Cleveland Indians at the same salary he had been drawing on the playing field in Pittsburgh. He already had large holdings in the ball team.

During his career he played in 1,394 major league games and hit safely 1,628 times. His lifetime batting average was .313 with 331 home runs to his credit. In 1938 he came within two of tying Babe Ruth's record of sixty in a season. Greenberg was a player in two all-star games and four World Series.

After being chosen the most valuable player in the American League in 1935 and again in 1939, Hank was elected to the Baseball Hall of Fame in 1956.

Although he never became a batting champion for his league, Greenberg led at different times in home runs, triples, doubles, runs batted in, runs scored, and total bases.

Hank left his post with the Indians after the 1957 season. From 1959 to 1961 he served as vice-president of the Chicago White Sox. Since that time he has served on the board of directors of several large corporations. His money was well invested and there will never be any need for a benefit for Hank Greenberg.

In 1946 he was married to the daughter of the department store mogul, Bernard J. Gimbel. They were divorced in 1959. Hank, who has not remarried, lives in a beautiful home in the exclusive Cleveland suburb of Shaker Heights.

Two of Hank's three children are students at Yale. Neither is very enthusiastic about baseball, although both play. The oldest boy excels at football and is considering playing pro-ball after graduation. The younger Yalie is a fine soccer player.

After Greenberg gave up the national pastime he took up tennis and plays as much as four times a week. One of his frequent partners when he is on the West Coast is Pancho Segura. He rates himself "a B player. I can't beat the good guys but I'm good enough to play with them."

Steve Greenberg takes a little professional advice from his dad. Falmouth won. *UPI*

A publicity portrait taken in 1937, shortly after Madeleine came to the United States.

MADELEINE CARROLL

The beautiful and talented blonde movie star was born Madeleine Bernadette O'Carroll in 1906 in West Bromwich, England.

For a brief time she was a teacher before making her debut on the London stage in *The Lash* in 1927. The following year she made her first film, *The Guns at Loos,* and did *The Constant Nymph* in the West End. In 1929 and 1930, respectively, she was seen by Londoners in *Beau Geste* and *French Leave.*

Madeleine Carroll had a rare and valued quality depicting affluence and breeding. On a close-up, just from the eyes, everyone knew here was an intelligent woman of great composure. In the clumsy costume of an early settler in C. B. De Mille's *North West Mounted Police* (1940) or a sarong in *Bahama Passage* (1941) she still looked like what she was—a lady.

Her early movies included *Young Woodley* (1930), *Sleeping Car* (1933) with the late Ivor Novello, and *The World Moves On* (1934), in which her co-star was Franchot Tone. In 1935 Alfred Hitchcock picked her for the lead in the great suspense film *The 39 Steps.* The late Robert Donat was male lead. Hitchcock used her again, in 1936, for another successful thriller, *Secret Agent* which co-featured the late Peter Lorre. Both films were made in England.

In Hollywood Madeleine followed up her rave notices from the Hitchcock pictures with meaty roles in Ronald Colman's version of *The Prisoner of Zenda* (1937) and *The General Died at Dawn* (1937) opposite Gary Cooper. That next year she and a young contract player named Tyrone Power starred in *Lloyds of London* with Freddie Bartholomew.*

In 1938 the late David O. Selznick cast her opposite Henry Fonda in the highly controversial *Blockade,* a film about the Spanish Civil War which was sympathetic to the Loyalist cause, thus earning the condemnation of the Roman Catholic Church.

Before leaving Hollywood for London where she spent most of the World War II years Madeleine made *My Son, My Son* (1940), *Virginia* (1941), and

My Favorite Blonde (1942) with Bob Hope. At the height of her fame a group of American servicemen voted Madeleine Carroll as the girl they would most like to be marooned on a desert island with. When informed of the honor Madeleine replied in that soft English accent, "I'm very flattered but if I'm ever cast away I hope the man is a good obstetrician."

Although she became a United States citizen in 1943, following the death of her sister in the blitz, Madeleine always remained loyal to England. She was very active in the Allied Relief Fund and worked tirelessly for the American Red Cross. For her efforts she has been honored by the American Legion and French government, and in 1948 the National Conference of Christians and Jews named Madeleine Carroll the "Woman of the Year."

Her only appearance on Broadway was for the very successful run of *Goodbye, My Fancy* in 1948. To the disappointment of many, the role in the motion picture version went to Joan Crawford.

Unfortunately, her pictures after the war were for the most part disappointing. She made *An Innocent Affair* (1949) and *Lady Windermere's Fan* (1949). Because of her beautifully modulated voice she was welcomed back to radio drama where she had always been very effective. In 1950 on TV's "Robert Montgomery Presents" she turned in a stunning performance in Somerset Maugham's *The Letter*.

Madeleine has been married and divorced four times. She married her first husband, Philip Astley, in 1931. In 1942 she divorced the producer, Henri Lavorel, to marry Sterling Hayden. They were divorced in 1946. Her marriage in 1950 to Andrew Heiskell, the publisher of *Life* magazine, lasted over a decade. During their marriage they maintained a town house in Manhattan and an estate on Long Island.

During the past six years Miss Carroll has spent most of her time in Paris and London, and is only an occasional visitor to New York.

In 1964 Miss Carroll was replaced by Arlene Francis in the play *Beekman Place* during its pre-Broadway road tour. Her agent maintains that her comeback needs only a script that meets with her approval.

With shipmate Ferdinand Gravet, fellow Parisian and former film star, on a recent visit to the United States. N. Y. *Daily News*

In 1939, at the height of his fame.

BILLY GILBERT

The world's most famous sneezer was born in 1894 in a dressing room of the Hopkins Theatre in Louisville, Kentucky. His father was a leading tenor with the Metropolitan Opera and his mother was also a member of the company. The family settled in Los Angeles until Billy was ten and then moved to San Francisco. At the age of twelve Billy went on his first road tour with a show. At eighteen he left home for good to become an actor.

He does not recall the first time he used his famous sneezing act on stage, but his reputation for the bit began many years ago when he was playing a theatre in Wilkes Barre, Pennsylvania. There were only thirty people in the audience and none of them seemed interested in what was happening on stage. Then Gilbert went into his sneezing routine and milked more laughter than had been heard all evening. The next day the local critic ignored the play completely and gave Billy's sneezes a rave notice.

Although he is best known for his years as one of Hollywood's great funnymen, Billy was a headliner in both burlesque and vaudeville before he began making movies.

His first picture was *Noisy Neighbors* (1929) and he has made over three hundred since. At the beginning he worked as both an actor and writer in comedy shorts. Two of his best remembered are the Laurel and Hardy starrers *Their First Mistake* (1932) and *Them Thar Hills* (1934). Co-starring in both was "the ever popular" and late Mae Busch. During the thirties and forties he was one of the most popular and highest paid character actors in Hollywood. He played with W. C. Fields in *Million Dollar Legs* (1932). Some of his other credits are: *Flying Down to Rio* (1933), *Here Comes the Band* (1935) with Ted Lewis, *One Hundred Men and a Girl* (1937) which introduced Deanna Durbin, *Happy Landing* (1938), a Sonja Henie* vehicle,

Outcasts of Poker Flats (1937) with Jean Muir, *His Girl Friday* (1940), and *Anchors Aweigh* (1945) and *The Kissing Bandit* (1949) both starring Frank Sinatra.

Had he made no other films Billy Gilbert would be a movie immortal for his off-screen sneezes in the Walt Disney classic of 1937, *Snow White and the Seven Dwarfs*. The dwarf whose sounds he dubbed were, of course, "Sneezy." The other gem of his career was his portrayal of "Herring," a thinly disguised imitation of Field Marshal Hermann Göring, in the Charles Chaplin masterpiece, *The Great Dictator* (1940).

Most of Billy's professional efforts were devoted to television and the stage during the fifties. In 1952 he starred in the musical *Buttrio Square* which was fated to close before it reached Broadway. Later, however, the producers of *Fanny,* who had heard of his fine performance, put him into the role of Panisse, originated by Walter Slezak. The critics wrote glowing notices. The same year, 1956, Billy played on TV in the spectacular "Jack and the Beanstalk" and followed that in 1957 with many appearances on Shirley Temple's "Fairytales." He has guest starred on "Arthur Godfrey Time," "My Little Margie," the "Ed Sullivan Show," and "The Gary Moore Show."

In 1963 Billy suffered a slight stroke and for over a year could not speak at all. Now, he says, "I talk as much as ever. Maybe more." His last picture was *Three Weeks in a Balloon* (1964).

Over the years Gilbert has bought several apartment buildings in Beverly Hills and a small factory in Los Angeles. He and his wife, the former actress Ella McKensie, whom he met in 1937 when they made a picture together at RKO, entertain such friends as Robert Cummings, Rudy Vallee, and Ken Murray in their North Hollywood home. Ella McKensie appeared in the famous *Our Gang* comedies. Billy points out that although she is many years his junior, "We have the happiest of marriages. I live the life everyone hopes they will lead when they reach my age."

At home with wife and young friend, Clifford May.

"The Great Dane" under contract to M-G-M in the forties.

LAURITZ MELCHIOR

The foremost heldentenor (heroic tenor) of his day began his phenomenal career as a baritone. He made his operatic debut in 1913 with the Royal Copenhagen Opera Company, singing the role of Silvio in *Pagliacci*. His teacher at the time, the American singer, Mme. Charles Cahier (who also coached Marian Anderson), aware of her pupil's extraordinary range and detecting a certain restraint in his singing, urged him to become a tenor and thereby give fuller vent to his voice.

From his birth in 1890, Lauritz Melchior, who has been called The Great Dane, was slated for the traditional family vocation of educator, but the family was also musical, and because the boy showed unusual promise (he was a soprano in the English church at Copenhagen), his father encouraged him. However, money was lacking. The family housekeeper offered to finance his musical education. She had in effect taken the place of the children's mother ever since the mother's death in Lauritz's infancy. This lady, Miss Kristine Jensen, had recently written a cookbook which became a best seller of its day.

Lauritz was eighteen when he began to study music seriously. Four years later he was admitted to the School of the Royal Opera, and the following year he made his aforementioned debut.

Melchior's first appearance as a tenor was in 1918, singing the role of Tannhäuser, which resulted in an appearance at Covent Garden, in London. There he met and became close friends with the British novelist, Hugh Walpole, who later helped him with money, advice, and encouragement. Then, too, Marconi, the inventor, invited the young singer to appear on the first worldwide radio broadcast—from the Marconi Experimental Station in Chelmford, England, on July 30, 1920. Singing with him was the famed late Dame Nellie Melba. His English sojourn also won him a coveted invitation from Siegfried and Cosima Wagner to study Wagnerian roles at Bayreuth, where he made his first appearance as Siegfried in 1925.

Melchior's American debut was in 1926 when he sang Tannhäuser at the Metropolitan Opera. He was to remain with the company until 1950, when he quit over a dispute with manager Rudolf Bing. His last performance at the famed opera house was his seventy-first Lohengrin and his five hundred and thirteenth appearance in the twenty-four-year affiliation. Other roles included Tristan, the two Siegfrieds, Parsifal, together with non-Wagnerian parts, his favorite among these being Othello, Le Prophet, and Canio in *Pagliacci*. During these years he also appeared in the capitals of Europe and cities in the United States. He worked with dramatic sopranos Freida Leider, Kirsten Flagstad (with whom during the Depression era he consistently set box office records), Marjorie Lawrence, Lotte Lehmann, and Helen Traubel, among others.

After an appearance on the "Fred Allen Show," he was signed to a Hollywood contract. His pictures include *Thrill of Romance* (1945), *Two Sisters from Boston* (1946), *Luxury Liner* (1947), *This Time for Keeps* (1947), and *The Stars Are Singing* (1953).

In 1952 he made his vaudeville debut with an appearance at the Palace Theatre. Shortly after that he was featured in Guy Lombardo's Jones Beach extravaganza, *The Arabian Nights*. Since then he has done mostly concert work, occasionally appearing on TV or in nightclubs.

His first wife was Inger Nathansen, with whom he had two children. She died in 1924. The following year he married the German actress Maria Hacker, with whom he also had two children. Miss Hacker specialized in stunt pictures and they met when she literally fell out of the sky and at his feet in a parachute jump. Their marriage was a long and happy one. He always referred to her as "Kleinchen" (little one), and she took care of all his financial affairs. "I make the noise," he used to say, "she make the business." A year after her death in 1963, Melchior married Mary Markham, whom he had known for eighteen years. She had been his secretary and is thirty-four years his junior.

Today Melchior is as robust as ever, his 6 foot 4 inch frame still suits his 240 pounds. However, he is slightly deaf "from having listened to too much Wagner." He has only lately gone on safaris to such places as Mozambique to indulge another passion of his—big game hunting. Having become an American citizen in 1947, Melchior resides permanently in California. He is not retired completely from music, for he is continually giving auditions to prospective heldentenors. Those showing promise receive a scholarship grant from the greatest of them all, Lauritz Melchior.

During a recent interview. *New York Times*

Under contract to Columbia Pictures
during the forties.

EVELYN KEYES

No less an authority than Cecil B. De Mille said of Evelyn Keyes that she was "natural and unspoiled." It was this quality that the blonde beauty with the large moist eyes conveyed on the screen in countless wholesome roles.

Evelyn, when yet a child, was taken, along with her brother and three sisters, by her widowed mother from Port Arthur, Texas (where she was born in 1917), to Atlanta, Georgia. There she was brought up and educated, learning to play the piano and going to dancing school at an early age.

She had hoped for a career in ballet, but circumstances found her in the chorus line of a second-rate nightclub. A year later, in 1935, in a beauty contest sponsored by Universal Studios, she won a free Hollywood trip, including a screen test. She returned home to the chorus lines.

One night, she worked with the bandleader Ted Fiorito, who wrote a glowing letter of introduction to a top Hollywood agent, and off she went once again and got nowhere with the letter. Nevertheless, she soon got her break when she connected with Jeanie MacPherson one of De Mille's former top writers for over thirty years. Through her, Evelyn was signed to a personal contract.

Her first film was a small role in De Mille's 1938 version of *The Buccaneer* starring Fredric March. That same year she did *Union Pacific* (also for De Mille), *Dangerous to Know, Men With Wings, Artists and Models Abroad,* and *Sudden Money.* In addition, she landed the role of Suellen, Scarlett's sister in *Gone with the Wind,* which was responsible for a long-term contract at Columbia. Her first picture for them was a Rita Hayworth starrer, *The*

Lady in Question (1940). The following year she won her first real recognition in the leading feminine role in *Here Comes Mr. Jordan,* which starred Robert Montgomery. Then followed such films as *The Adventures of Martin Eden* (1942) with Glenn Ford, *Nine Girls* (1944), *The Jolson Story* (1946), the part that she is best remembered for as the wife of Larry Parks, *Johnny O'Clock* (1947) with Dick Powell, and *The Mating of Millie* (1948) with Glenn Ford. In 1949 she made her most dramatic picture *Mrs. Mike* with Dick Powell. The following year she did *The Prowler* with Van Heflin, and, in 1951, *The Killer that Stalked New York.*

Of her husbands, two were top movie directors, Charles Vidor and John Huston. She also had a long and very intense relationship with the late Michael Todd who gave her a cameo part in his modern classic *Around the World in 80 Days* (1956). Her last marital venture, at the time of her last film appearance, seems to have been a spectacular success in that she accomplished what neither Lana Turner, Ava Gardner, or Kathleen Winsor could do. She managed to stay married to Artie Shaw for over a decade.

Not long ago she told an interviewer that she doesn't miss Hollywood a bit. During the McCarthy era she had become thoroughly disgusted with a system she never had much respect for. The interest by fans in her pictures amuses more than flatters her. The other day one phoned her and asked if he was speaking to Evelyn Keyes. "My God," she replied, "I haven't seen her in years!"

Much of Evelyn's time is spent in their country home where she works on a mystery novel with a Hollywood background. They also keep an apartment in Manhattan.

With her husband, Artie Shaw, at a recent New York premiere. *Metro-Goldwyn-Mayer*

The photograph of George Weyerhauser circulated throughout North America by law-enforcement agents. *UPI*

THE WEYERHAUSER BABY

The Weyhausers were an immensely wealthy family, operators of the country's largest lumber company in the area of Tacoma, Washington. The company manager was John Phillip Weyerhauser, Jr., father of four children, the third of whom was to become the victim of one of the more sensational kidnappings of the thirties, the era of the big snatch, as it has been called.

On Friday, May 24, 1935, nine-year-old George Weyerhauser left school to have lunch at home, as usual. He did not make it home nor did he return to school.

That evening a special delivery letter arrived at the Weyerhauser house. It was a demand for $200,000 in small bills for the safe return of the boy. There were also instructions to place an advertisement in the personal columns of a local paper if the family meant to comply. The letter was signed Egoist. Weyerhauser told the police, already summoned when the boy failed to show up at home that noon, that he would pay the money. The tragic Lindbergh case was fresh in everyone's mind. Within the next four days Mr. Weyerhauser followed a series of intricate instructions delivered via telephone by a woman from various prearranged stations. On the fifth day a farmer and his wife answered the knock at their door and were confronted with a little boy who was by that time the most famous child in America. Said George to the startled pair, "I'm George Weyerhauser, the boy who was kidnapped."

To the police and F.B.I. agents (who had by then also been summoned on the case), the boy related an eerie story. Upon his way home that Friday noon he had been seized by a man and made to get into the trunk of a car. He spent the next four days of his life variously in two covered pits shackled to a stake, chained to a tree, and locked in a closet. He told of two men who fed and cared for him during the ordeal, but he had seen nothing of the woman who had called his father.

Two days after the boy's release, one of the bills (the serial numbers had been listed and distributed throughout the country by the F.B.I.) showed up in Portland, Oregon. Three days later several more were passed in Salt Lake City. Agents were then placed in all big stores to check all paper money taken in.

Before long in one of the stores where they were staked out a bill showed up. It had been offered by a young lady of nineteen who gave her name as Margaret Von Metz of Ogden, Utah. Upon checking the address the police found a man named Julius Thulin who claimed to have a granddaughter who had recently been married to one Harfon Von Metz Waley. This man proved to be an ex-convict with various prison records for burglary and robbery. Upon checking another local address, which had been given them by the girl, the agents found Waley. In the store of the furnished room was a partially burned roll of bills amounting to $3,700. Waley said the money had been given to him by a man who had driven him and his wife from Denver to Salt Lake City. He had thought the money was counterfeit, he added, and had no idea it was part of a ransom.

Meanwhile, in Butte, Montana, a detective recognized a man wanted for bank robbery. His name was William Dainard Mahan. Mahan escaped but left behind $15,500 of the ransom money in the car he abandoned.

In the meantime, Waley and his wife confessed to the crime and took authorities to a wooded area outside Salt Lake City where they dug up $97,000 in an oilcloth sack. The F.B.I. caught Mahan in San Francisco with $7,300 of the money with him. At the trial it was revealed that Waley had been born near Tacoma, knew the Weyerhausers were very wealthy, and plotted the snatch with Mahan while in prison. Waley pleaded guilty and was sentenced to forty-five years is prison. Mahan pleaded guilty, and was sentenced to sixty years in prison. Margaret, whose defense was that she had been unware of the crime until after it had been committed, did not convince the jury and she got twenty years. Her whereabouts since her release in 1948 are unknown.

During the Second World War George Weyerhauser served in the United States Navy and attended Yale afterward. He is the manager of the Springfield, Oregon, branch of the family business. George lives in Springfield with his wife and two children, neither of whom ever talk to strange men. He has vivid recollections of the four-day nightmare.

There still remains a big mystery. Approximately $74,000 of the ransom money has never turned up.

A businessman now. *UPI*

In 1927, salary: $3,500 a week.

BETTY COMPSON

Born in 1897 in Beaver City, Utah, with a name of Eleanor Luicime Compson, the future film star made her debut in Salt Lake City playing the violin in the orchestra of a local vaudeville house for $15 a week. When the manager gave her a chance to do a solo the family didn't have money for a costume. She went on in the rags of a street urchin. She billed herself as the "Vagabond Violinist." The audience loved it and mother and daughter were hooked.

Though still in her teens, Betty and her mother traveled up and down the West Coast playing a theatre one week and working as domestics the next until in 1915 she landed a job with Al Christie, the comedy director-producer of silent one-reelers, for $40 a week. Slapstick was in but Betty wisely avoided doing it, and although she had made twenty-eight Christie comedies when other offers came to her, she had not been typecast. The offers were welcome because Christie fired her in 1918 when she refused to make a personal appearance.

In 1919 she made *The Terror of the Range,* a serial. It was the last minor effort for many years. The same year she was cast with two other relatively unknown players in *The Miracle Man.* When the film was released Betty emerged along with Thomas Meighan and Lon Chaney as a major star. Three years later she made another blockbuster, *The Little Minister.*

Her silent films include: *Rustle of Silk* (1923) with Anna Q. Nilsson and *The White Flower* (1923) with Arline Pretty. Betty then made several films in England. On three of them Alfred Hitchcock was assistant director. In 1926 she came back to Hollywood where she made *Wise Guy* with Mary Astor. Eileen Percy was with Betty in *Twelve Miles Out* (1927). A very young Loretta Young supported the blonde star in *Scarlet Seas* (1928). The same year she made one of her best silents, *Docks of New York,* which had Olga Baclanova as its other star and Josef von Sternberg as its director.

On October 25, 1927, Betty married one of Hollywood's all-time greats, director James Cruze, who made *The Covered Wagon* (1923). Their palatial home, Flintridge, was the scene of some of the most lavish parties the movie capital has ever seen. After seven years they separated, reconciled, separated again, and after a few more years were divorced.

She made talkies when other silent stars were terrified over their voices. *The Barker,* in 1928, with Dorothy Mackaill was a smashing success. She had a whole new career ahead of her. In 1929 she and Sally O'Neil sang "Let Me Have My Dreams" in *On with the Show.* While her contemporaries starved in the new medium, Betty flourished—for awhile. She was indiscriminate about the roles she accepted. If a studio met her salary demands she would make the picture. Although she worked steadily through the thirties and into the forties, her billing soon slipped from star to bit player. Some of the cheapies that were her downfall were *Virtuous Husband* (1931) with Elliott Nugent (living on Manhattan's East 57th Street), *West of Singapore* (1933) with Margaret Lindsay (living in West Los Angeles), *Laughing Irish Eyes* (1936) with Evalyn Knapp, *Torchy Blane in Panama* (1938) with Lola Lane (a real estate dealer in Pacific Palisades, California), and *Cowboys from Texas* (1939) with Duncan Renaldo (semiretired to his estate on the Hope Ranch in Santa Barbara). In 1940 she had a meaty role in *Strange Cargo* but most of her part was cut out in the final print. Her old friend Alfred Hitchcock gave her a part in *Mr. and Mrs. Smith* (1941) and in 1946 Betty made her final movie, *Claudia and David.*

During the thirties she married producer Irving Wineberg who took her on a successful vaudeville tour of the Far East. Shortly after returning to the States, they were divorced. Betty tried to sell her own line of cosmetics for awhile and was briefly the manager of a woman's apparel shop in Beverly Hills. During World War II she met and married an ex-boxer, Silvious Jack Gall, who began a successful business of manufacturing ashtrays for hotels, clubs, and so on, which still prospers today. They lived in a large home which had belonged to her late mother in the foothills of Glendale, California. Since her husband's death in 1962, she lives there alone.

In Glendale, California, today. *Jon Virzi*

Putting the audience on in 1945.

JACK OAKIE

The master of the doubletake was born in Sedalia, Missouri, in 1903 with the name Lewis Delaney Offield. When he decided to go on the stage he took the name Oakie for Oklahoma where he had gone to school.

Jack bummed around vaudeville before he made it to Broadway in *Innocent Eyes* (1924) which starred the legendary Mistinguette. Its chorus line included the late Nancy Carroll and a girl named Lucille le Sueur, later to become Joan Crawford. Jack had a habit of playing practical jokes which the management found impractical. He was fired. In 1925 he got a job in *Artists and Models* and in 1926 was in *Peggy Ann*. The late Lulu McConnell was in both.

Paramount Pictures signed him to a long-term contract after he made *Finders Keepers* in 1927. Wesley Ruggles, a top director of the day, thought highly of Oakie's comic ability and put him into campus comedies. When sound came, these turned into musical comedies. Jack fitted perfectly as the round-faced young man who seldom got the girl but always got the laughs. He co-starred with the late Helen Kane (whose husband Dan Healy, "The Night Mayor of Broadway," lives in Jackson Heights, New York) in *Sweetie* in 1929. In a short time Oakie was one of the studio's most popular players. Others of the more than one-hundred features he made during the thirties and forties are *Million Dollar Legs* (1932), *Too Much Harmony* (1933) with Bing Crosby, *Alice in Wonderland* (1933) with Charlotte Henry, *Looking For Trouble* (1934) with the late Spencer Tracy, *If I Had a Million* (1932) with Wynne Gibson, *Big Broadcast of 1936*, *Florida Special* (1936) with Sally Eilers, *Thanks for Everything* (1938) with Jack Haley, *Tin Pan Alley* (1940) with John Payne, *Footlight Serenade* (1942), *On Stage Everybody* (1945) with Peggy Ryan, and *When My Baby Smiles at Me* (1948) with Betty Grable.

He was a guest on many of the network radio variety shows of the era, and in the late thirties had a program of his own for a while called "Jack Oakie's College."

Undoubtedly, his greatest plum came in the role of Mussolini in *The Great Dictator*. Bosley Crowther said of his performance in the acidic satire on Fascism, "Oakie ranks alongside Chaplin." Chaplin was the star and director but it was Jack who was nominated that year (1940) as the Best Supporting Actor.

Oakie was noted for his superb mugging and smooth delivery of wisecracks. Off the screen he was also pretty good at making caustic comments that did not always provoke laughter. He was also known in the business as an inveterate scene stealer. His best remembered bit was his famous "triple fade" which was actually a double take with one more take thrown in to milk the laughs. His timing was perfection.

Director Ernst Lubitsch called him "the best comedian in Hollywood." His first wife, actress Venita Varden, called him "jealous, quarrelsome, and abusive," when they were divorced on grounds of mental cruelty in 1938 after only two years of marriage.

His appearances in pictures dwindled greatly from the mid-forties on. He showed up in *Wonderful Country* in 1959 and *The Rat Race* in 1960 after an absence of eight years. The semicomeback was spurred by his part in the TV drama "The Battle for Wednesday Night" for which he received rave notices. His sole appearance previous to that was in a cameo part in *Around the World in 80 Days* (1956).

In 1960 his home town honored him with a parade and the dedication of a plaque. Senator Stuart Symington was one of the eulogists.

In 1963 he reportedly turned down $1,000,000 to play an ex-vaudevillian in a TV series. In spite of the enormous sum, most who know Jack believe the story. He has shown little interest in working hard for many years and has long been known to be one of the richest actors around. He was quoted sometime ago as saying that he bought A.T.&T. stock and General Electric when they were "American Smoke Signals and General Candle." He has lost his hearing almost completely, and a hearing aid does not help him.

For over twenty years he has been married to the former actress Victoria Horne. They live in a large home on Devonshire Drive in Northridge which Jack bought from Barbara Stanwyck after she divorced the late Frank Fay. Like Andy Devine, he has long been active in San Fernando Valley affairs and, also like Devine, has done very well in real estate in that area.

The white-haired comedian today. *Jon Virzi*

When she became a blonde in the late thirties. *NBC*

FRANCES LANGFORD

The blonde who was voted America's number one female singer in 1938 was born in Lakeland, Florida, in 1914 with a dark complexion and raven hair. Her mother Annie Newbern was a concert pianist. Frances majored in music at Southern College and sang in the Glee Club and school plays. She aspired to an operatic career but a tonsillectomy in 1930 changed her voice from a lyric soprano to a contralto.

In 1932 she was signed for thirteen weeks on a Tampa radio station by a cigar manufacturer after he heard her at an American Legion party. Rudy Vallee gave her a guest spot on one of his shows originating from New Orleans which was her first coast to coast program. Shortly afterward she was signed for the Phillips Magnesia program. On November 7, 1933, she opened on Broadway in the Peter Arno musical *Here Goes the Bride,* which ran for all of seven performances.

Shortly after making her legit debut, Frances was asked to perform at a party honoring Cole Porter. She sang "Night and Day" and was signed to a movie contract by Walter Wanger without even being tested.

Included in her film credits are *Every Night at Eight* (1935), which was her debut with Alice Faye and George Raft, *Collegiate* (1936) with Jack Oakie and the late Joe Penner, *Broadway Melody of 1936, Hollywood Hotel* (1937) with the Lane Sisters (Lola is a realtor in Pacific Palisades, California, and a neighbor of sister Rosemary; Priscilla is married to Joseph A. Howard, a building contractor, and lives in Andover, Massachusetts); *Too Many Girls* (1940) with Lucille Ball and Richard Carlson, *Hit Parade of 1941, Campus Rhythm of 1941* with Johnny Downs, *Girl Rush* (1944), *Bamboo Blonde* (1946), and *The Glenn Miller Story* (1954).

Frances was much bigger in radio than in movies. In 1939 she was the singing star of the Texaco Star Theatre with Ken Murray and Kenny Baker, and radio editors picked her as the "All-American Girl." In 1941 she began her long and very successful association with Bob Hope. She was the vocalist on his Pepsodent radio series and toured all the theatres of war with his famous troupe, from Cape Bon to Algiers to Bizerte, and Kairouan and Leyte. The singer was chosen by G.I.'s as the "No. 1 Girl of World War II," civilians picked her as Queen of the Campus City College of New York and Annapolis made her an honorary midshipman. At the end of the war she wrote a national news column, *Purple Heart Diary,* covering some of her experiences interviewing injured servicemen in hospitals around the world. Her most treasured award was a citation reading, "To Miss Frances Langford, with appreciation, for a grand job in North Africa. [signed] Dwight D. Eisenhower."

After the war she played nightclubs and had great success with the radio and TV series she did with Don Ameche entitled "The Bickersons." She was the star and hostess of two spectaculars, the first in 1959 with Bob Hope and Julie London, and the second the following year featuring Johnny Mathis and Don Ameche.

The singer who began her career as the "Moonglow Girl" and was once described by critic George Jean Nathan as "my dream girl" alternates her retirement years in Milwaukee, Wisconsin, and Jensen Beach, Florida, with her second husband Ralph Evinrude, Chairman of the Board of Evinrude Outboard Motor Company. They spend their winters in their Florida resort where Frances is sometimes coaxed to come on stage at "The Outrigger," their nightclub, to sing a few of the songs she has been closely associated with during her career: "You Are My Lucky Star," "I'm In the Mood For Love," and "Music, Maestro, Please."

Frances was divorced from actor Jon Hall (who lives in Malibu Beach, California) in 1955 after seventeen years of marriage. She married Evinrude the same year. She has no children.

Frances doesn't consider herself completely retired and occasionally she and Ameche get together on a TV guest spot to do their "Bickerson" skits. In 1952 she entertained U.S. troops in Korea and last year sang for the boys in Vietnam. When at home the Evinrudes do a lot of deep-sea fishing and traveling about on their yacht, the Chanticleer. Audiences are still amazed by her figure which she attributes to considerable exercise in her gym, and daily swimming.

Aboard the Evinrude yacht the *Chanticleer,* formerly Adolf Hitler's.

One of the world's great voices in 1930. *RCA Records*

LOTTE LEHMANN

The great soprano from the Golden Age of opera was born in 1888 in Perlberg, Germany, where she and her brother spent their early years. Her father was secretary to the Ritterschaft, a benevolent society, and eventually he was transferred to Berlin where Lotte attended Ulrich High School to train for a teaching career. A friend of Lotte's mother noticed the girl's voice and suggested that she be given vocal coaching. Her teacher was the renowned Emma Tiedke. Later she studied at the Gerster School and the Berlin Conservatory of Music.

In 1909 she was engaged for the Hamburg Opera at the same time that Otto Klemperer was making a name for himself as its conductor. Lotte debuted as the third boy in *The Magic Flute*. She was promoted to larger parts and then went to the Vienna State Opera where she was to achieve a singular success in the company of Leo Slezak (father of Walter), Maria Jeritza, and Richard Mayr. Her first role in Vienna was Agathe in *Freischütz*. Some of her other roles were Octavian in *Der Rosenkavalier, Manon*, and *Il Trittico*. Puccini signed a photograph to her after her performance in *Il Trittico*, addressing it "to the incomparable Angelica," which she played in his opera.

In 1922 Lotte went to England and appeared at Covent Garden where she sang the role of Marschallin in *Der Rosenkavalier*. Years later *The New York Times* music critic Harold Schonberg said, "One of the authentic 20th century operatic myths is Madame Lehmann in the role of Marschallin." She returned to Vienna and sang Christine in Strauss's *Intermezzo* in its premiere in 1924 and sang *Fidelio* for the first time in her career. In 1928 she made her first appearance in the Salzburg Festival.

After the death of her husband whom she had married during her days in

Hamburg, she came to the United States and made her debut at the Civic Opera House in Chicago in 1930 singing Sieglinde in *Die Walküre*. She then embarked on a highly successful American concert tour.

In 1934 she signed with the Metropolitan and debuted again as Sieglinde with Lauritz Melchior as Siegmund. Her most popular Wagnerian roles were Eva, Elizabeth, and Else, but Marschallin was always her greatest. She continued as one of the Met's leading prima donnas until 1945, after which she limited herself almost exclusively to concert work.

In 1951 at the age of sixty-three Madame Lehmann ended a singing career that had spanned forty-one years. During the intermission of a New York Town Hall recital she announced her retirement amid cries from the audience of "No! No!" Her final song of the evening was Schubert's "To Music," after which she broke down in sobs. The audience climbed onto the stage to bid the artist a tearful, emotion-packed farewell.

Madame Lehmann has written four books: *Eternal Flight* (1938), a novel; *Midway in My Song* (1938) an autobiography; *More than Singing* (1945), on interpretation, and *My Many Lines* (1948), a study of her roles.

She returned to the Metropolitan in 1962 to direct a new production of *Der Rosenkavalier*, but she has not sung publicly since her retirement. Even for friends she declines to sing anymore. "My voice is a shadow of myself," she says, "and I hate to have shadows around me." Since 1964, "just to keep up," she has devoted her time to teaching a few pupils at Santa Barbara, California, where she makes her home on the Hope Ranch. During the summer months she produces operas at Santa Barbara's Music Academy.

A young soprano once said to her, "It must be awful for such a great singer as you to realize that you've lost your voice." "No," she replied, "What would be awful is if I *didn't* realize it."

Madame Lehmann in her garden.
Santa Barbara News Press

The pudgy Crown Prince with his father just after Carol was restored to the throne in 1932. *UPI*

KING MICHAEL I OF RUMANIA

The former boy king was born in Sinaia, Rumania, in 1921. Shortly after his birth his father Carol II who had had one morganatic marriage before he wed Michael's mother, was banished from the country by Ferdinand I, Michael's grandfather. Carol's cavortings with his mistress, Magda Lupescu, * had become too flagrant even for the jaded society of Bucharest. In 1928 Queen Helen divorced Carol. The year before, Michael became king upon the death of Ferdinand. Because of his age a regency was established which lasted until 1930, when Carol and the Lupescu returned to Rumania to take the throne from Michael who was demoted to crown prince. To a great extent due to the influence of Lupescu, Carol aligned his country with France just as war clouds were gathering over Europe. His chief opponent was the Fascist Iron Guard who hated his mistress in part because she was Jewish.

In 1940 Michael, now nineteen, was returned to the throne via a coup d'etat engineered by Marshal Ion Antonescu. Carol and the Lupescu fled the country and never returned. Although Michael had a passionate dislike for the Lupescu he also wanted no part of Hitler, whose troops now occupied Rumania. Officially his country was now fighting with the Axis but Michael was careful to remain aloof from politics during this time. Although he was only a figurehead anyway while Nazis governed the country, the young king took great pains to avoid any involvement with the Germans, hoping his people would draw the correct conclusion. Hitler needed the king as a front and Michael felt relatively safe. In August of 1944 when the German armies were being driven from Russia, Michael's forces made their move and by another coup d'etat overthrew Antonescu and declared alliance with the Allies. After the war, however, the Communists were able to force Michael's abdication and in 1947 the king went into exile in England, assuming the title of Prince of Hohenzollern. He was able to take very little money with him and it was only through the help of the English Royal family that he and

Princess Anne of Bourbon-Parma, whom he married in 1948, were able to get by until Michael was able to establish himself. For a time they had to live in a haunted house, but the former king proved an excellent flyer and became a test pilot for one of the large aircraft manufacturers. They lived decently but hardly in a kingly manner. Queen Helen, who lives in Italy, was able to send her five grandchildren, all girls, to good schools, although she too, is not really wealthy.

In recent years Michael has done rather well from his inventions in the aeronautical field. In 1963 the New York firm of Droulia and Company announced that Michael would be their Swiss representative. He has avoided any association with Rumanians in exile, thus being able to stand above their constant squabbling among themselves, and will not take any Rumanian investment accounts.

Michael was subjected to a great deal of criticism when he did not attend the funeral of his father in 1952. Although he was genuinely fond of Carol he felt that he could not appear without becoming involved with the Lupescu, who had married Carol three years before and now insisted on being addressed as Princess Elena. Aside from a rather run-down castle on the Riviera, his father left him nothing. His fortune, which was in the millions, went to the Lupescu.

While his life as a stockbroker living in Versoix with offices in Geneva is far removed from the court of Bucharest, his interest in the internal politics of Rumania has remained keen. His employer emphasizes that Michael insists his associates address him by his first name but royalists who visit him regularly call him "Your Majesty" and have never been corrected.

The man who harbors dreams of a restoration to the throne of a country in which he has not set foot for over two decades, is the son of a German by a Princess of Greece. Perhaps he hopes that he might be crowned during his third reign. Something neither he nor his father ever managed.

With Greek Princesses Irene (left) and Sophie on a recent trip to Athens. *UPI*

In *The Glass Menagerie,* on Broadway, in 1945.

EDDIE DOWLING

The dean of the American theatre has been prominent as a songwriter, vaudevillian, musical comedy star, director, playwright, producer and dramatic actor.

He was born Joseph Nelson Goucher in 1894 in Woonsocket, Rhode Island, of a French-Canadian father and an Irish mother, whose maiden name he adopted for professional use. One of seventeen children, he learned to shift for himself at the age of eight, singing Irish ballads for pennies in front of bar rooms. His first job, at ten, was as a cabin boy on a coast steamer, then going to a similar position on a transatlantic ship, the Mauritania. In addition to his regular duties, he sang for the passengers. At the advice of an English vaudeville producer he joined the St. Paul's Cathedral Choir in London, and for some years, until his voice changed, toured with the group throughout the British Isles and the Continent.

Returning to America, he broke into vaudeville as a handy man at the old Keith Theatre in Providence, and eventually did a single song and dance routine. Within three years he was a headliner.

In the circuits he met and married Ray Dooley (of the famous British music hall family). After their marriage in 1911, they toured together, though not as a team.

In 1917 Dowling made his Broadway debut in an Erlanger production of Victor Herbert's operetta, *The Velvet Lady.* He helped rewrite it, including the composition of two songs. He was featured in 1917 in *The Ziegfeld Follies,* as was his wife—and Eddie Cantor.

In 1922 he had the first of a long string of successes, the musical comedy *Sally, Irene, and Mary,* in which he directed, produced, co-authored, and starred. It ran for three seasons on Broadway and, continued on the road. In 1926, performing all the same functions, he did the musical *Honeymoon Lane,* in which he introduced a manicurist he met in a Washington barber shop—Kate Smith. And Dowling's understudy was Bob Hope.

Dowling followed with *Sidewalks of New York* (1927), *Thumbs Up* (1934), and *At Home Abroad* (1935). Following *Thumbs Up* Dowling's wife retired from the stage.

In 1936 with Margaret Webster he co-produced Shakespeare's *Richard II,* a first in this country since the days of Edwin Booth. The star was Maurice Evans.

In 1938 Dowling did his first dramatic play, Philip Barry's *Here Come the Clowns,* co-starring with Madge Evans. In 1938 he introduced Paul Vincent Carroll to Broadway when he produced *Shadow and Substance,* starring Cedric Hardwicke and Julie Haydon. He followed this with Carroll's *The White Steed* with Barry Fitzgerald. Both these plays won the New York Drama Critics' Circle Award as the best foreign plays of their respective seasons.

In 1939 he did Saroyan's *The Time of Your Life,* starring with Julie Haydon. Newcomers in the cast were Celeste Holm, William Bendix, and Gene Kelly. This was the first play to win both the Drama Critics' Award and the Pulitzer Prize. Two years later he did two short plays, Chesterton's *Magic* and Saroyan's *Hello Out There.*

In 1945 he did *The Glass Menagerie,* thereby introducing Tennessee Williams to Broadway, and brought Laurette Taylor out of retirement to co-star with him and Julie Haydon. The play won the Drama Critics' Award.

In 1951 he did the unsuccessful *Angel in the Pawnshop,* co-starring Joan McCracken. The following year Dowling returned to the musical stage and took over the lead in the musical *Paint Your Wagon.*

Dowling was active in early radio, introducing to the air such stars as Jack Pearl,* Al Goodman and his Orchestra, Paul Robeson, Will Rogers, and Helen Morgan. And in the 1940's he emceed "We The People." He appeared on television as early as 1944 when he piloted the WOR series "Wide Horizons," an aviation program.

Dowling was the founder of the U.S.O. camp shows. Today he is deeply involved in the Eddie Dowling University Theatre Foundation, which produces plays at schools throughout the country.

The Dowlings have been living quietly in East Hampton, Long Island. Eddie produces an occasional industrial show, taking part in summer stock occasionally when roles appeal to him. He seldom comes into Manhattan but when he does there is usually a visit to the Lambs Club. Rae Dooley comes to town even less frequently. They had two children, one married daughter and a son killed in Argentina on assignment for Time-Life.

The famous showman today. *Howie Price*

Butterfly with the late Vivien Leigh in a scene from *Gone with the Wind,* 1939.

BUTTERFLY McQUEEN

The Negro pixie who achieved movie immortality through her role in *Gone with the Wind* (1939), was born in Tampa, Florida, in 1911. Her father was a stevedore on the Tampa docks and her mother worked as a domestic. The slight British tinge to her high-pitched voice comes from the neighbors. They were from Nassau. Her mother sent her to Augusta, where she received her early education from Catholic nuns at St. Benedict's Convent.

Deciding to go on the stage, Butterfly moved north to Harlem and joined Venezuela Jones' Negro Youth Group in Harlem in 1935. After she danced in the "Butterfly Ballet" in a production of *A Midsummer Night's Dream* people began calling her "Butterfly." She has never used Thelma, her real name, since.

She debuted on Broadway in December of 1937 in George Abbott's *Brown Sugar* which ran for only four performances. The critics, however, were impressed. And so was Abbott. In his next production the following year he tailored a part in it just with Butterfly in mind. *What a Life* was a smash hit and she played it on Broadway and on the road.

When the late David O. Selznick acquired the screen rights to Margaret Mitchell's *Gone with the Wind* Butterfly asked for the role of Prissy, and was told that she was wrong for the part, and too old. Two years later her agent presented her with a contract. Butterfly had serious misgivings about the way the book treated Negroes. She considers it her best work, but wonders whether it was a backward step; in one scene, Rhett Butler refers to her as "a simple-minded darkie."

Butterfly's performance in the civil war epic made a big impression on audiences as well as the studios but she never capitalized on it. Over the years she has turned down a succession of what she calls "handkerchief head" parts. Selznick used her two more times in *Since You Went Away* (1944) and *Duel in the Sun* (1946). She played Joan Crawford's cook in *Mildred Pierce* (1945). Her memories of *Cabin in the Sky* (1943) are mostly unhappy ones. Rochester

96

teased her unmercifully, Lena Horne treated her with contempt, and director Vincente Minnelli was nice to her face but cutting when she was not present.

She began to drift from job to job. She was for a time a paid companion to an old lady on Long Island, sold toys in Macy's Department Store, was a cab dispatcher in the Bronx, an operator of a little restaurant, and manager of a little theatre group at the Y.M.C.A. She has attended U.C.L.A., Los Angeles City College, and Southern Illinois University.

Much of the money she saved from her movie roles went into a one-woman concert she produced at Carnegie Hall in 1951. It was a financial disaster.

In 1957 Butterfly moved back to Augusta where she gave music lessons for awhile and had her own radio program. She returned to Manhattan briefly in 1964 to appear in the musical *The Athenian Touch* which had a short run off Broadway. Her big song was called "No Garlic Tonight." She went back to Georgia as a hostess at the Stone Mountain Memorial which is a complex of museums whose statuary honors the Confederacy. After that she guided tourists on strolls through a plantation mansion for several years. She is currently suing the owners, claiming that she was not paid for the photographs of her they used for publicity purposes.

She returned to Harlem in 1967 and waited tables awhile. M-G-M asked her to tour with their revival of *Gone with the Wind* in return for expenses. When the reissue premiered in New York, Butterfly was not in attendance.

In 1968 the producers of *Curley McDimple,* a musical spoof of Hollywood in the thirties, had a part written into the off-Broadway production especially for her.

Miss McQueen, who has never married, says she would like to be able to live in Africa six months of the year, although she has never traveled farther than Mexico. She works in her spare time helping with cleanup projects in her neighborhood and coaching young Negroes at a community theatre on West 125th Street.

Interviewed by the author at WBAI-FM, in New York City. *Frank Altman*

"Blondie" and "Dagwood" in 1941.

PENNY SINGLETON

The actress who became known the world over as "Blondie" was born in Philadelphia, Pennsylvania. Her uncle is former Postmaster General James A. Farley. Her real name is Mariana Dorothy McNulty and her real hair coloring is brunette.

After attending the Alex McClue School and Columbia University she performed as a singer and acrobat in Broadway in *Good News* (1928), *Follow Through* (1929), *Walk a Little Faster* (1932) with Bea Lillie, and *Hey Nonny, Nonny* (1932) before Hunt Stromberg, Sr., brought her to Hollywood. Although she had contracts with both Warners and M-G-M, her only significant part before that of Blondie was in *After the Thin Man* (1936), in which she played a nightclub dancer. Throughout the tenure of both contracts she fought continually against being cast either as the "other woman" or as a menace.

Her name, hair, and luck were all changed in 1937 when she married a dentist, Dr. Lawrence Singleton. She had a book of childrens' verse published that year under the name Penny Singleton, and decided to use it professionally as well. And the girl originally signed for the part of Blondie, Shirley Deane, took ill.

Blondie (1938), the original feature film, was made by Columbia Pictures on a low budget and released as a programmer. The radio serial which went on the air in 1939 as a summer replacement was called "silly" by *Variety*, which also remarked, "It is impossible to predict anything but a minimum audience to a minimum engagement." The public thought otherwise. Penny in the meantime divorced Dr. Singleton in 1939, and in 1941 married her present husband, Bob Sparks, who was for a time the producer of *Blondie* movies.

The Bumsteads became one of America's favorite families. The show included a little boy, Baby Dumpling, who became Alexander during the war, about the same time their cartoon daughter Cookie was born. The radio shows lasted over seven years.

Theatres around the country reported excellent audience reaction, and

98

some advertised the pictures as the featured attraction. A few of the films that endeared the efficient young housewife and her bungling hubby to America were *Blondie Brings Up Baby* (1939), *Blondie Has Servant Trouble* (1940), *Blondie Goes to College* (1942), *Blondie Knows Best* (1946), *Blondie's Secret* (1948), and *Blondie's Hero* (1950). The series was dropped in 1943 but the public complained and the studio revived it in 1945.

Although Penny made a few other features such as *Go West, Young Lady* (1941) with Glenn Ford, *Swing Your Partner* (1943) with the Late Louise Fazenda, and *Young Widow* (1946), the Blondie image eventually prevented her from continuing her career after the radio series and movies were discontinued. In the early fifties she worked in nightclubs and presentation houses doing songs and patter to good reviews but audiences kept waiting for Arthur Lake to come onstage. In 1952 she headlined the show at the Thunderbird Hotel in Las Vegas.

Since playing Blondie, Penny has been active in the American Guild of Variety Artists, the theatrical union representing dancers, singers, and so on, in nightclubs and on stage in ice shows and presentation houses. She served two terms as president in the fifties but by the early sixties was battling AGVA's officials at board meetings and finally in the courts. In 1962 she testified before a house committee on union activities that AGVA was writing "sweetheart contracts" which compelled girls working in strip bars to mingle with the customers, thus encouraging prostitution. That year Penny was suspended from membership. Undaunted, she sued the members of the executive board demanding that they account for money from the treasury. One officer countersued for $1,180,000 in a libel action. When it was finally settled, out of court, Penny was again a member of the union, and is now a vice-president and executive secretary. In 1966 she came to New York where she led a strike by the famous Rockettes, the first in their history, against Radio City Music Hall. It lasted twenty-seven days.

She lives in Los Angeles with her husband and their two daughters, neither named "Cookie."

"Blondie" an important AGVA leader today. N.Y. *Daily News*

In the costume she wore on opening night, March 13, 1911, in *The Pink Lady*.

HAZEL DAWN

Hazel Dawn was the kind of star Alice Faye used to portray in movie musicals of the 1930's. At the age of seventeen she had Broadway at her feet. There were stage door Johnnies wearing Inverness capes and carrying long stemmed roses. The still popular the "Beautiful Lady Waltz" was "her" song and across the street from the New Amsterdam Theatre, where she was playing, Murray's Restaurant proclaimed a new drink in her honor—the Pink Lady Cocktail. Overnight she had become known as "The Pink Lady," the title of her hit musical.

Success, however, is sometimes harder to overcome than failure. Her acclaim in the title role of that Ziegfeld production was so great that she was never able to shake the public image that was forged and she remained typecast in the minds of theatregoers throughout her career.

Ironically, Hazel has never had a Pink Lady, nor any other alcoholic beverage. She was born a Mormon and, although she admits to having a few cups of coffee and tea, has remained faithful to her strict religious upbringing.

Her family took her to London where her sister, a promising singer, was to study voice. The impresario Paul Reubens discovered her and changed her name from Letout to Dawn.. She debuted in London in *Dear Little Denmark* in 1909.

In 1913 she was set for the lead in *The Little Café* but at the last minute she was replaced by the girl friend of producer Abraham L. Erlanger. All Broadway heard about the shabby trick that had been played on her and when she walked on stage opening night in a lesser role the audience gave her a five-minute ovation.

. Her bad experience with *Little Café* made her sign a movie contract with Famous Players. Some of her silent films are: *One of Our Girls* (1914), *Niobe* (1915), and *The Lone Wolf* (1917), in which the late Bert Lytell made his screen debut.

Three of Hazel's stage vehicles were considered at the time very racy and ran into considerable trouble with the censors which in the long run proved to be good publicity for the shows. They were *Up in Mabel's Room* (1919) with Enid Markey (like Hazel, a New Yorker and still a friend), *Gertie's Garter* (1921), and *The Demi-Virgin* (1921).

For over a decade Hazel Dawn was one of Broadway's top leading ladies. In 1916 she appeared with Elsie Janis, Leon Errol, Van & Schenck, and Marie Dressler in *The Century Girl*. It was produced by Flo Ziegfeld and had music by Irving Berlin and Victor Herbert. She introduced the song "Valencia" in *Great Temptations* (1916). In the cast of that show was a relatively unknown violinist-comic by the name of Jack Benny. In *Nifties of 1923* she did a parody on *Rain*. There were *Kèep Kool* (1924) and *Ziegfeld Follies of 1925,* which had as its ballerina a soon-to-be silent star named Lina Basquette (owner of the country's top kennel of Great Danes in Chalfonte, Pennsylvania).

In 1927 Hazel became Mrs. Charles Groehl. Her only Broadway appearance after that was in *Wonder Boy* which Jed Harris produced in 1931. The play came in with rave notices from its out-of-town tryouts and a huge advance sale but had been so oversold that when the curtain went up opening night Hazel says "it was like a cold wind swept that stage. I still can't understand what happened. It was my only flop."

The Groehl family moved to California in 1935. Her husband, a mining engineer, died in 1941. In 1947 Hazel returned to New York to launch her daughter as an actress under the name Hazel Dawn, Jr. After a brief but very promising career the girl married a doctor and now lives in a New York suburb with her husband and five sons. Hazel's other child, a son, is a commercial photographer in Florida.

From 1953 until she retired in 1964 "The Pink Lady" enjoyed another kind of stardom. She was undoubtedly the most popular receptionist in New York in her job with the J. Walter Thompson advertising agency's casting department. Her sympathetic encouragement and good advice to those waiting nervously for auditions is still legend among New York actors.

Hazel is still seen constantly by New York theatregoers but now she is one of them. "I try to see all the shows," she says. "I am really enjoying life and am able to do what I want. I can't think of any people I would rather be around than theatre people. I have many, many friends and my grandchildren and my health. I've been very lucky and I'm very grateful."

In her seventies, a grandmother, and still in the pink.

Weighing in after winning the Hialeah Park Inaugural Handicap, his third victory on January 7, 1944. *UPI*

TED ATKINSON

The jockey with over three thousand wins to his record was born in Toronto, Canada, in 1916. His full name is Theodore Francis. His father, a glass engraver, eventually settled the family in Brooklyn. Ted went through a succession of jobs selling papers, mowing lawns, and peddling flowers. Although Atkinson had little formal schooling, he read prodigiously and acquired considerable knowledge, which led to his being dubbed "The Professor" by his fellow riders. Before turning to the track he worked for a Brooklyn chemical plant, pasting labels on bottles for $8 a week, which he worked into $35 a week for packing bottles and doing odd jobs.

The 5 foot 2 inch 100-pounder progressed to chief bottle packer, only to be barred from the job by the union.

A truck driver for the firm introduced Ted to the late Silvia Cucci, a jockey, and Ted soon found himself at the Greentree Stable in Red Bank, New Jersey, as a valet. Before departing Brooklyn for Red Bank, however, Atkinson made a quick trip to the Van Cortlandt Park riding academy and formally introduced himself to his first horse.

A long apprenticeship followed in which Atkinson went through the daily chores of cleaning out stalls, walking, and breaking yearlings. He left Greentree because only experienced jockeys would ever ride its Thoroughbreds in competition.

Atkinson drifted to Ohio and after months of disappointment finally got a mount aboard Musical Jack. That was on May 18, 1938, at Beulah Park, Ohio. He admits to making every mistake in the book while guiding his horse to his first victory. But the triumph gave him some much-needed confidence and, by the year's end, he had piloted thirty-six winners.

The following year, still playing the "leaky roof" circuit, he met Martha Shanks, a North Randall, Ohio, farmgirl whose father was a harness horse enthusiast, and shortly thereafter (in 1940) they were married.

In 1940 Atkinson tried the New England circuit for the first time. He rode ninety-five winners that year and the following season he rode his first stakes winner, War Relic, in the Massachusetts Handicap at Suffolk Downs. Later in 1941, he was astride War Relic when the colt defeated Whirlaway in the Narragansett.

He made the big move to New York in 1943 and success on the major circuit came quickly. In 1944 he won his first national championship, riding 287 winners, the most he ever rode in a single season. Two years later he again captured the national title, with a 233 total. After this season Greentree Stable signed him to a contract as a regular rider, succeeding Eddie Arcaro, a position he maintained for eleven years.

Atkinson wore the pink and black silks while astride such outstanding campaigners as Straight Face, Hall of Fame, Tom Fool, Capot, and One Hitter.

One of Atkinson's biggest regrets is that Tom Fool, "the greatest horse I ever rode," was not sound enough to be a starter in the Kentucky Derby of 1952. The virus that sidelined the Horse of the Year in 1953 probably cost Atkinson a victory in the Derby which, strangely enough, is one of the few major American racing fixtures to have eluded him. In November of 1957 he was installed as one of the twelve present members of the Jockeys' Hall of Fame.

Ted's last race was in January, 1959, at Tropical Park. The jockey who ranks with Sir Gordon Richards, Johnny Longden, and Eddie Arcaro* as the only jockeys ever to ride three thousand winners, lives with his wife and two children in Palantine, Illinois. Since a back ailment caused his retirement, he has worked as a New York Patrol Judge from 1959 until 1960. During that time he was also Assistant Clerk of Scales and Assistant Paddock Judge and Entry Clerk. Since April of 1961 he has been State Steward at Chicago racetracks.

Riding a desk today. *Clifford May*

The idol of the bobby-soxers in 1940.

ARTIE SHAW

The *enfant terrible* of the swing era was born Abraham Isaac Arshawsky in 1910 in New York's Lower East Side, where his Jewish immigrant parents were in the dressmaking business. Straitened circumstances led to their moving to New Haven, Connecticut. He managed to save up enough money as a grocery store errand boy to buy a secondhand saxophone, with five free lessons. He took only two, and they constitute Shaw's entire formal musical education. Soon after he was booked with a young banjo player traveling the New Haven area, appearing on so-called "Amateur Night" shows. After this, followed his own four-man, $8-a-night Pan Novelty Orchestra, and a job with the Johnny Cavallaro Orchestra. He was fourteen years old. His first "professional" job was as first alto sax with the Olympia Theatre Orchestra in New Haven. The grind proved too much for him. He joined the Joe Cantor orchestra in Cleveland and left New Haven for good.

After a year with Joe Cantor, learning to arrange and orchestrate, and writing for other bands as well, he moved to Cleveland's top band, the Austin Wylie Orchestra, remaining for two years.

A job with his first "big name" band, Irving Aaronson's Commanders, came in Hollywood, at nineteen. From then on he moved from orchestra to orchestra—Andre Kostelanetz, Howard Barlow, Peter Van Steeden, Richard Himber, Red Nichols, Paul Whiteman, and Freddie Rich.

The break came in 1935 at a musicians' benefit at the Imperial Theatre in New York City. Shaw got together a small group to fill in between the big band performances. He composed a piece for clarinet, viola, cello, guitar, string bass, and drums entitled "Interlude in B Flat." The reaction was immediate and electric—from fellow musicians. But not from the general public. He formed a more orthodox band, which caught on, and won him a contract with RCA Victor. The record company changed his name from Art to Artie.

The first record was a swing version of Friml's "Indian Love Call," with Tony Pastor singing. Victor had more than a hit. The flip side happened to have "for quiet contrast" an old Cole Porter song that had not gone anywhere. The song: "Begin the Beguine." In 1939, he won the *Downbeat* title of "King of Swing," replacing Benny Goodman, and landed a radio contract with NBC to play on the Robert Benchley Old Gold program. However, the sponsor and station, deluged with angry protests over his interview comment that "all jitterbugs are morons," readily accepted his "voluntary resignation." At this time he made his two Hollywood pictures, *Dancing Co-Ed* with Lana Turner, and *Second Chorus* with Fred Astaire and Paulette Goddard.

At the very peak of his popularity and earning some $500,000 annually, he announced his retirement. (Shortly before, Shaw had been stricken with a usually fatal blood disease, granulocytopenia.)

The following year, he organized a band. His first new record was "Frenesi," an immediate hit.

He enlisted in the Navy in World War II, and toured the South Pacific with a band for two years entertaining the troops. Medically discharged because of "operational fatigue," he underwent analysis for a year and a half, and retired to Norwalk, Connecticut, and began to write. In 1952 his book *The Trouble With Cinderella* was published, which was fairly well received.

The following year he was called before Representative Velde's (Republican, Illinois) House Un-American Activities Committee and admitted to having been a "red dupe," and recounted three persons he had seen at Communist recruiting meetings in 1946.

In 1954 he organized the Gramercy Five, another combo that failed to find an audience. He claims he has not touched the clarinet since. He lived on the Costa Brava in Spain while writing three more books, one of which, *I Love You, I Hate You, Drop Dead,* was published in 1962. That same year, Victor Records, in commemoration of their twenty-fifth year of association, presented him with eight gold discs. The eight over-one-million records: "Dancing in the Dark," "Back Bay Shuffle," "Summit Ridge Drive," "Frenesi," "Nightmare" (his theme), "Traffic Jam," "Begin the Beguine," and "Stardust." Also, in 1964 he produced a rather fine motion picture, *Seance on a Wet Afternoon,* starring Kim Stanley. In addition to his Manhattan apartment, he lives in a twenty-two room mansion in Lakeville, Connecticut, and enjoys a financial independence arising from royalties on his recordings. There he shoots, reads, and writes.

Mr. Shaw's marital excursions have made considerable news. Among his eight wives were Lana Turner, Ava Gardner, Kathleen Winsor, and the present Evelyn Keyes.

The "King of Swing" in abdication.
Diana Keyt

In 1937.

DOLORES COSTELLO

The actress who was the daughter of one of America's greatest matinee idols, and the wife of another, was born in Pittsburgh, Pennsylvania, in 1906. Her mother was leading lady (on stage) to father Maurice Costello (he was also one of the earliest, most popular leading men of the silent screen). As children, she and her sister Helene played in many of their parents' plays. Dolores made her debut at the age of five playing a little boy. Both girls played child roles in their father's movies.

Despite their famous name, the Costello sisters did not seem able to break into movies when they became young ladies. Exasperated, they came to New York City, where Dolores had some success as a model. One of the artists she posed for was the famous James Montgomery Flagg. In 1924 the girls landed roles in the George White Scandals of that year. *Scandals* ran on Broadway for over a year, and then went on the road. In Chicago a talent scout for Warner Brothers spotted them. They were placed under contract and sent to Hollywood, where once again there seemed to be no parts for them. Then one day, John Barrymore saw Dolores emerge from a car at the studio. Barrymore had seen her years before on the Costello estate on Long Island when he came to visit her father, but she was only a child at the time. Even before Warner told him who she was, the Great Profile said he wanted her for his leading lady in *The Sea Beast*, a screen adaptation of *Moby Dick*. In addition to the sheer pleasure of being manhandled by the heartthrob of millions of women, it was a guarantee to stardom.

Barrymore and Costello, two of the period's greatest names in the American theatre, made the picture in 1926. Though Dolores' role was nonexistent in the classic, it was added to the screenplay to assure a love interest. Their scenes together were torrid, and in a short time they announced their engagement. The wedding had to wait until 1928 when his divorce from Michael Strange became final. Together they made the screen versions of *Manon Lescaut*

(1926) and *When a Man Loves* (1927). Her other silents included *A Million Bid* (1927), *Glorious Betsy* (1928), *Tenderloin* (1928), *Madonna of Avenue A* (1929), and *Glad Rag Doll* (1929).

She became much less active in pictures after her marriage. In 1932 their son John, Jr., was born, and the following year they had a girl, Dolores. In 1934 their marriage, which because of John's drinking was never very stable, broke up after Barrymore phoned his wife to say goodbye and good luck. Somehow she managed to maintain a semblance of dignity while her husband cavorted around the country with his protégée Elaine Barrie.* The Barrymores were divorced in 1935. Dolores received $163,000 in securities and $850 monthly alimony.

Her credits in sound pictures include *Show of Shows* (1929), *Breaking the Ice* (1931) with Bobby Breen,* *Yours for the Asking* (1936), *Little Lord Fauntleroy* (1936) with Freddie Bartholomew,* *Girls on Probation* (1938) with Ronald Reagan and Jane Bryan, *Whispering Enemies* (1939), *The Magnificent Ambersons* (1942), and *This Is the Army* (1943), her last.

In 1939 Dolores married Dr. John Vruwink, with whom she lived in New York City until their divorce in 1951. The same year she attempted a comeback on stage in *The Great Man*.

Before her father's death in 1950, he sued her for an increase in his allowance. In those days she also was supporting her sister, who had been hospitalized for some time; Helene died in 1957. After her second divorce Dolores moved to California where her daughter had her arrested on a drunk and disorderly conduct charge.

For a number of years now, the former actress has resided with her teenage grandson on a ranch in Del Mar, California. She is occasionally visited by her son, but otherwise has little contact with Hollywood. Visitors are greeted by an array of dogs, which herald their arrival.

In a rare interview, Dolores said, "Whenever I think of John, it is with great compassion."

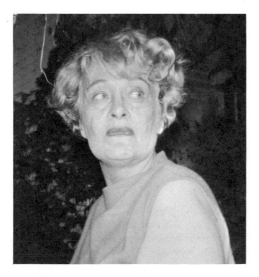

On her ranch in Del Mar, California.
Jon Virzi

107

In 1912, dancing "The Dying Swan" at the Metropolitan Opera House. Toscanini conducted.

ANNETTE KELLERMAN

The first woman to wear a one-piece bathing suit and to attempt to swim the English Channel was born in Australia in 1888.

Crippled by polio shortly after birth, Annette had to wear large steel braces about three times the weight of those used today. She was, however, determined not to allow her affliction to break her health or her spirit. Through exercise, perseverance, and sheer will power she learned to walk without the aid of braces or canes. Not content simply to be able to get around like others, Annette continued her strenuous exercises and by 1905 while astounded onlookers stood by she made a perfect dive off the pier at Ramsgate into the waters far below. After picking up a few local swimming awards she debuted at the Theatre Royal in Melbourne in a diving act, which was booked immediately for a London theatre. Audiences were amazed by the girl billed as "The Perfect Woman with the Form Divine."

The three main elements of her fantastically successful act were: (1) After the story of her childhood as a cripple was told the lady proceeded to go underwater and remained there for 2½ minutes, (2) It was the first successfully presented aquacade on stage, and (3) Her costume was a one-piece bathing suit, nothing short of a sensation at the time. Annette became the darling of the music halls.

Her United States tour got off to a well publicized start when in 1907 she was arrested by Boston police for daring to appear on Revere Beach wearing a one-piece bathing suit in plain view of decent citizens. Although many church and women's groups demanded that she be banned entirely, there were enough who felt otherwise to pack the theatres where she appeared.

In 1909 Annette made several attempts to swim the English Channel. Once she got over three quarters across before giving up, declaring that no woman had the "brute strength" required. Gertrude Ederle* proved her wrong in 1926.

Annette married James R. Sullivan in 1912, in Danbury, Connecticut. He managed and publicized her from then on.

In 1914 she was starred by Universal Pictures in *Neptune's Daughter,* a great box office success, which was followed by *Daughter of the Gods* in 1916. No stand-ins were needed. Portions of the films were used in *The Love Goddesses* in 1965, a movie made up of clips from the pictures of femme fatales from Theda Bara to Marilyn Monroe.

For the next fifteen years "The Diving Venus," another of her titles, made seven world tours on which she made a seventy-five foot dive into a forty-ton glass tank of water for paying customers from Shanghai to Buenos Aires. Her mail-order plan for beauty and health was advertised well into the thirties and was a great financial success in all the countries where she had appeared.

During World War II Annette and her husband, James R. Sullivan, spent a lot of time in Australia where she produced shows to entertain United States troops stationed in the South Pacific. She is probably best remembered during these years for her idea to have those at home send the Sunday funny papers to the boys overseas.

In 1949 M-G-M filmed Annette Kellerman's life story in color, starring Esther Williams. Made as a musical, *Million Dollar Mermaid* was a box office smash, and introduced the song "Baby, It's Cold Outside."

In 1956 the Sullivans revisited Australia to see the Olympic Games, and have lived there ever since. Their summers are spent in Sydney and they winter on the famed Gold Coast in Queensland, the surfer's paradise.

Although retired for forty years, "The Diving Venus" swims every day of her life. She is presently working for the Red Cross in aiding United States troops in Vietnam. In a recent letter to the States she said: "My past is past. The present keeps me very busy. I have continued to lecture, swim a half mile daily, do ballet practice, and I love to take long walks. We travel constantly."

Annette has never had a child. She is still married to James R. Sullivan who has never learned to swim a stroke.

Annette became a United States citizen in 1912 and spent much of the time since in this country, most of it in the Sullivan home in Pacific Palisades, before moving to Australia.

Now in her eighties, "The Diving Venus" swims every day. *Sydney Sun*

In 1936, in *It's Love Again.*

JESSIE MATTHEWS

Her pictures were the only successful musicals ever made outside of Hollywood until the Beatles did *A Hard Day's Night* (which was directed by an American) in 1964.

"Princess Personality," as a reviewer once called her, was born in London in 1907. At the age of ten she debuted on the English stage in the title role of *Bluebell in Fairyland.* Trained in classical ballet, Jessie was seriously considering an offer to dance with Anton Nolan when the great impresario Andre Charlot gave her a job in the chorus of his *Charlot's Revue of 1924.* She had been in *The Music Box Revue* the year before.

For awhile Jessie only danced in the show, but soon trouble developed with the understudy to Gertrude Lawrence, the star. The understudy's voice was poor and her temperament worse. Jessie got to understudy Miss Lawrence in London and on Broadway, and often was allowed to do one of her numbers.

In the next *Charlot Show* in 1926 Jessie was the star. She followed that with *Vanities of 1927* and *One Dam Thing After Another* the same year. In 1928 she did *Jordan* and *This Year of Grace.* Her musicals were light and silly and exactly what the public wanted in the lush twenties. In 1929 Jessie starred with the late Jack Buchanan and Tilly Losch (a resident of Manhattan's East Side) in *Wake Up and Dream.* Probably her best remembered stage show was *Evergreen* which she did in 1930. In 1931 and 1933 she was in *Hold My Hand* and *Sally Who?* respectively.

"The Dancing Divinity," another of her titles, began her picture career in 1933, a year in which she made *The Good Companions* with the late Edmund Gwenn, *There Goes the Bride,* and *Friday the 13th.* Some of her movies, including her best one, *Evergreen* (1935), played the Music Hall in New York City at a time when foreign films were little more than curiosity pieces that usually played the second half of double bills or grimy little art houses in Greenwich Village. Gaumont-British, which had experienced serious financial troubles at the time, signed Jessie, and was able to pay off all their debts with

110

her grosses. She made one picture after another for them. Some were not very good, but all were financially successful. Her credits include: *It's Love Again* (1936), in which she co-starred with Robert Young, *First a Girl* (1936), *Gangway* (1937), *Head Over Heels* (1937), and *Climbing High* (1939).

There was much talk of her coming to Hollywood. She seemed the perfect partner for Fred Astaire. The English studio, however, had a firm contract with her and refused to let her go. She says today that she worked so hard in those years she was not even aware that offers from Hollywood had been made. She never made a film outside of England.

Broadway had not seen her in quite some time when she signed to do *The Lady Comes Across* in 1941. England was being blitzed, her third marriage was on the rocks, and the overwork of many years caught up with her. Jessie had a complete and severe nervous breakdown and left the show before it came in. Broadway never saw her again, nor did any other audience for many years.

In the fifties Jessie began to do an occasional play. In 1955 she produced *The Policeman and the Lady* and in 1958 she toured Australia in several plays. The same year she surprised and delighted her fans all over the world as the mother in M-G-M's *Tom Thumb*. Not long after Jessie got the part of Mrs. Dale on England's most popular radio serial, "Mrs. Dale's Diary," heard five days a week over the B.B.C. Almost everyone agrees that Jessie added several dimensions to the "Mrs. Dale" character. It has become more popular than ever, since she took it over.

In 1965 Huntington Hartford's Gallery of Modern Art presented "A Tribute to Miss Jessie Matthews," including a retrospective showing of her motion pictures and a twice a day in person appearance of the actress-singer-dancer whose pert smile lightened the Depression for so many moviegoers.

Along with her radio work she finds time for an occasional cabaret appearance. Unmarried for many years now, Jessie lives in the Northwood section of London with her sister Rosie.

Still acclaimed by her English public. *Gallery of Modern Art*

"Blondie" and "Dagwood Bumstead" celebrate
Christmas in 1945. *CBS Radio*

ARTHUR LAKE

"Dagwood Bumstead" (as he was known to millions) was born in 1905 in
Corbin, Kentucky. He attended school for a while in Nashville, Tennessee, but
most of his boyhood was spent traveling with his family. His father and his
father's twin brother had an aerialist act called "The Flying Silverlakes." His
mother was a stage actress, known as Edith Goodwin. Although his parents
would not permit him to perform when they were playing circuses, Arthur and
his sister Florence became part of the act as soon as it switched to vaudeville
and was renamed "Family Affairs." They toured the South mostly until the
act broke up in southern California.

Arthur's last name was shortened to Lake by his producer, Carl Laemmle, Jr.,
when he went into movies. His first role was in *Jack and the Beanstalk* (1917),
after which he went into a number of Franklyn Farnum westerns. During the
twenties Arthur and Florence worked on the stage and in silents whenever there
were parts for adolescents. One of Arthur's best known pictures during that
period was *Skinner's Dress Suit* (1925).

In 1924 Arthur Lake began making *Sweet 16* comedies which typecast him as
a teen-ager, a part he played until he was into middle age. In 1928 he portrayed the title character in the silent version of *Harold Teen*. The following
year he had the juvenile lead in the color musical *On With the Show*, in which
he sang "Don't It Mean a Thing To You?" His first sound film was *Air
Circus* (1929).

Arthur and Florence made a musical short, *Glad to Beat You,* for Vitaphone
in 1934, but movie roles were few and he toured the vaudeville circuits in
order to earn a living between films. He had parts in *Silver Streak* (1934) with
Charles Starrett, *Orchids to You* (1935) with Jean Muir (the blacklisted
actress lives in Ossining, New York), and *Topper* (1937).

Arthur played the original role of Dagwood, and stayed with the series in
motion pictures, radio, and television. When Penny Singleton left the radio

version after seven years, Mrs. Lake, the former Patricia Van Cleve, took over the role and continued for the remaining five years the series was on the air. When it became a TV program in 1954, Blondie Bumstead was played by Pamela Britton for the short time it ran. It premiered in January and was dropped in December. In July of 1958 it commenced again, but this time it lasted four months.

The part of the pugnacious neighbor, Herb Woodley, was played by radio's original "Great Gildersleeve," Hal Peary (who lives in Redondo Beach, California).

When *Blondie* came along in the form of a movie in 1938, Arthur was very grateful. He has never complained about being so closely associated with the character that the public could not accept him as anything else. He was hired once for another picture by a producer he had convinced otherwise. Halfway through production they both agreed he had played the part as if it were the character Dagwood. After 1939, in the few movies he made which were not *Blondies* he played parts very much like creator Chic Young's character.

He used to entertain ideas of becoming a scenarist or director. The closest he came was when he made a travelogue on Guatemala in 1950. After the 1954 "Blondie" TV series was canceled, Arthur and his wife had a short-lived situation series called "Meet the Family." Naturally, Arthur played the dopey but likeable husband.

The Lakes, who have been married over thirty years, are the parents of two children. Their home is many times the size the Bumsteads occupied on Shadylane Avenue in the series. It is set on a short street in Santa Monica only a few yards from the Pacific Ocean. It was in Santa Monica that Arthur, following his retirement, opened a bar which lasted all of six weeks.

Along with his large earnings acquired during his heyday, the Lakes were well remembered in the will of Marion Davies who had a great affection for her niece—Arthur's wife. One of Patricia Lake's trinkets that would be beyond the Bumstead family budget is a $600,000 cabochon cut-star sapphire necklace.

"Dagwood" today. *Jon Virzi*

In the title role of *Tosca,* 1921.
Metropolitan Opera Company

MARIA JERITZA

One of the most talented and temperamental divas of this century was born in Brünn, Austria, in 1887.

When she debuted in 1910 as Elsa in *Lohengrin* at the Olmutz Opera House, it was under her real name, Mitzi Jedlicka. By 1912 word of her artistry had reached Emperor Franz Josef who attended a performance of *Die Fledermaus* at a summer resort—just to hear for himself. It is doubtful whether it was only the big, glorious voice of the soprano that brought the old man. Like most of her fans, he was taken as well by her beauty. Few opera singers at that time were beautiful. If one had a voice there was no need. Maria Jeritza not only had a great voice, but she was so lovely to look at she could have been a stage star without bothering to sing a note. Maria's personality was something else.

Her Metropolitan debut in 1921 was less than spectacular only because the vehicle she appeared in was the now virtually forgotten opera *The Dead City* by Erich Wolfgang Korngold. Though her personal notices were excellent, it was not until American fans heard her in such operas as *Carmen, The Girl of the Golden West,* and *Thaïs* that she became the popular star that she remained until her retirement from the Met in early 1932.

Jeritza was more than a great beauty with a superb voice. She was also a remarkable actress. Puccini asked her to sing the title role in the premiere of *Tosca.* It was she who first sang "Vissi d'arte" from a prone position, a tradition still followed by many of those essaying the role.

Her repertory was large and the salaries she commanded were huge. Fans threw flowers onto stages wherever she appeared. But while critics and public were wild about her those who appeared with Jeritza often were simply mad at her. The diva's behavior was outrageous. Whenever opera lovers or musicians discuss scene stealing and onstage tricks of the trade the name of Maria Jeritza is sure to be brought up. It is said that a Polish soprano who was the brunt of one of Maria's jokes during a performance in Vienna spat in her face in full view of the audience. Her followers seemed to adore her antics. Her contemporaries made no effort to hide the fact that they did not enjoy working with her. Her temper was nearly as impossible as her professional manners.

Those who did not have to suffer her unpredictable behavior were devoted admirers. Perhaps her greatest fans were those who composed the music she sang. Puccini adored her. The great impresario Max Reinhardt starred her in *Belle Hélene* in 1911 and the following year Richard Strauss asked her to create the title role in his *Ariadne auf Naxos.* Critics wrote of her "luminous intelligence," and "enthralling vitality."

After leaving the Metropolitan Jeritza continued to concertize for a number of years in the thirties and made occasional appearances throughout the country at concerts, and with small opera companies, with great success. It is unfortunate that she marred what would have been a nearly flawless career by appearing in the forties and early fifties when her voice was little more than a suggestion of what fans remembered or could hear on her old phonograph records.

At the end of her career Madame Jeritza appeared once more at the Metropolitan in the role of Rosalinde in *Die Fledermaus* in 1951. *The New York Times* music critic, Harold Schonberg, wrote: "The fabled creature made her entrance looking young, looking as though she had commanded the years to go away. And they crept away, ashamed to touch her."

In 1948 Jeritza married a millionaire manufacturer, Irving J. Seery, her present husband. Previously she had been married to Baron Leopold Popper De Podharagh, an Austrian industrialist; and the Hollywood director, Winfield Sheehan, who died in 1945. Her marriage to the Baron was dissolved in the twenties.

Mr. and Mrs. Seery live in a mansion enclosed by a tall brick wall on Elwood Street in Newark, New Jersey. She still attends the Metropolitan regularly.

In 1967 her homeland honored her with the Golden Ring of the City of Vienna, one of Austria's most coveted awards to artists. When the eighty-year-old prima donna arrived for the presentation her fans were again titillated by what one paper described as a moment in which "the gemutlichkeit was as thick as whipped cream." She looked remarkable and was as flamboyant in manner as ever.

At a recent reception in her honor at the Austrian Consulate in New York. *New York Times*

In 1939, the top male star on the RKO lot.

TIM HOLT

Tim Holt is probably the only movie star born in Beverly Hills. The year was 1918 and his father was Jack Holt, a leading man in the silent era and a successful character actor during the thirties and forties.

When Tim, whose real name is Charles, was ten years old he played his father as a boy in *The Vanishing Pioneer* (1928). His late father never encouraged him to go into movies and Tim did not seem a bit interested in doing so until he graduated from the Culver Military Academy. Up until then about his only mention of Hollywood was when people asked him about his girls and he would complain that whenever he took one home she lost interest in him and got a crush on his dad because he was a movie star.

After the Academy, he joined the Westwood Theatre Guild and got a part in a play produced by and starring Mae Clarke (who still makes an occasional appearance on television). Walter Wanger caught the show and signed him up. Tim's first role was the radio operator in *History Is Made at Night* (1937) with Jean Arthur and Charles Boyer.

His home lot put him in a series of westerns at a time most cowboy stars were middle-aged. He never looked particularly tough and could not sing a note. Still, in a very short time the volume of mail from fans addressed to "Tim Holt, R-K-O" was second only to the queen of the lot, Ginger Rogers. The horsemanship Tim had learned at military school was put to use in a string of oaters that were all money-makers. The only trouble the studio had with their young star was that leading ladies who looked as young as he were hard to come by.

Most of the pictures Holt made during those years are best forgotten. A few of the cheapies, western and otherwise, were: *The Renegade Ranger* (1938) with a young starlet named Rita Hayworth, *Spirit of Culver* (1939) with

Freddie Bartholomew,* *Come on Danger* (1941), *West of Tombstone* (1942) with Charles Starrett (now a resident of Laguna Beach, California), and *His Kind of Woman* (1951) with Jane Russell.

When he did manage to break out of the casting rut, however, it was to make a blockbuster. The two really good westerns he made were a couple of the greatest ever made by anybody: *Stagecoach* (1939) and *My Darling Clementine* (1946).

Tim and Terry Kilburn (unmarried and living with his mother in Santa Monica) were part of the *Swiss Family Robinson* (1940). Orson Welles used him in *The Magnificent Ambersons* (1942), which would have been a masterpiece had it been edited by the director rather than the front office. Tim and Bonita Granville (the wife of broadcasting millionaire Jack Wrather) were two of *Hitler's Children* in 1943, the first film to be advertised by a radio saturation campaign. The prize role of his career, however, came in 1948 when John Huston cast him as Curtin in one of the best pictures of all times, *The Treasure of Sierra Madre*.

In 1942 Tim enlisted in the Air Corps. He was discharged in 1945 as a major. He continued to make movies but that fresh boyish quality he had been able to project before the war was gone.

Holt's first two marriages ended in divorce. In 1950 he moved to Hurrah, Oklahoma, where he lives now with his third wife and their three children, Jack, Bryanna, and Jay. For a while he was the sales manager of a radio station in Oklahoma City and the host of a local TV program. Recently he joined Jamco, Inc., a multi-industry company, as an executive.

Meanwhile, back at his ranch in Hurrah, from where he commutes to his office daily, Tim keeps in shape by daily horseback rides. He by no means considers himself retired from films and wants to be ready when a part is offered him. His last movie was *The Time Machine* in 1960.

At his office in Oklahoma City, Oklahoma. *Cliff May*

A scene from one of their two-reelers made in 1922.

SMITH AND DALE

"Dr. Kronkeit and his patient," as they have been known to audiences for over 70 years, were born Joseph Seltzer and Charles Marks in New York City in 1884 and 1882 respectively. Smith was one of thirteen children and had to leave school at the age of twelve to help support his family. He and Dale met one day in 1898 when Dale was riding his bicycle north on Eldridge Street at the same time that Smith was cycling east on Delancey. They have always referred to their first encounter as "a smasher." After a voluble argument a local merchant who was watching with great amusement told them they reminded him of the famous comedy team Weber and Fields. Within two months the pair had worked up a routine doing a buck and wing dance.

Their first tour was of the so-called beer-hall circuit starting from the Chatham Club in Chinatown and ending at Tom Sharkey's on 14th Street. Their act consisted of their dancing while dressed in tattered pants and sweaters.

Dale's brother, who was the manager of the Palace Garden on 13th Street and Third Avenue, got them a job there. They took on the noted honky-tonk pianist Mike Bernard who stayed with them until 1901 when they formed a troupe with Jack Coleman, Johnny Lenhart, Frank Martin, and Will Lester called the Imperial Vaudeville and Comedy Company. They played the Catskills when the Borscht Belt was in its infancy, but most of their engagements were one night stands. It was during this period that they took on the names of Smith and Dale.

A printer had one hundred cards on hand for a team called Smith and Dale that had split before the job was finished. He offered them for only 25¢ each. Unable to resist such a bargain, they took the signs and became Smith and Dale.

In 1902 they joined the Avon Comedy Four with a skit called "The New School Teacher" which went over so well that it became a staple of their act for years. The group went on tour "playing every town in which the train stopped."

In 1914 the Four sailed for England where they were the first all-American act to play the Finsbury Park Empire.

In 1915 they created their classic skit, "A Hungarian Rhapsody." It was in this act that "Dr. Kronkeit" was first introduced. Some of their other popular routines were "S.S. Malaria," "Venetian Knights," "The Last National Bank," "False Alarm Fire Company," and "Real Estators."

In a career that has bridged the Spanish-American War with Vietnam, Smith and Dale have been in every phase of show business. They made silent two reelers, played vaudeville, burlesque, appeared in Broadway shows, revues, and were on radio and television. A few of their shows were *Why Worry* (1916) with Fanny Brice, *The Passing Show of 1919, 1920, and 1921, Mendel, Inc.* (1930), *Crazy Quilt* (1932), *The Sky's the Limit* (1935), *Summer Wives* (1936), *Laugh, Town, Laugh* (1942), and *Old Bucks and New Wings* (1962). On radio they guested with Kate Smith, Rudy Vallee, Ben Bernie, and Al Jolson, and Ed Sullivan had them on several times during the past fifteen years. When the Palace Theatre reverted to a two-a-day vaudeville policy in 1951, Smith and Dale were on the first bill. A few years later they were back at vaudeville's cathedral supporting Judy Garland.

Although in the past two decades, it is more their dated brand of humor that has limited their appearances than their advanced ages, the two have remained close friends. In 1962 when they were told that there was only one role open on a "Trials of O'Brien" TV segment they tossed a coin to see who would do it. Smith won. They are not only alert but actually want to work. Someone asked Smith not long ago if he ever intended to retire and was told: "Yes, every night when I go to bed." Most of their contemporaries have either died or are in complete retirement.

Smith, a widower, resides at the Actors Home in Englewood, New Jersey. Dale lives with his wife on Manhattan's West Fifty-fifth Street.

In 1948 the Lambs Club gave the pair a Golden Anniversary night in their honor and in 1967 they celebrated their seventieth year in show business by doing some of their old skits at the club.

The famous partners at a recent meeting at the Lambs Club. *New York Times*

The Number One box-office attraction in 1926 and 1927.

COLLEEN MOORE

The superstar of the silents was distinctive right from birth in Port Huron, Michigan, in 1902. She had one blue and one brown eye. Her real name was Kathleen Morrison. Her father was a successful engineer.

Colleen maintains that D. W. Griffith did not discover her and that she did not appear in *Intolerance* (1916) as a dancing girl, that they did not even meet until her career was well established. According to her, Griffith arranged for a screen test at the persuasion of her uncle, Walter Hovey, who was then city editor of the Chicago *Tribune*. Hovey was later immortalized by Ben Hecht and Charles MacArthur in their play and film *The Front Page*.

Colleen had a real flair for comedy. She began with *The Bad Boy* (1917) and then made *The Busher* (1919) with Tom Mix. She was with Mix in *Wilderness Trail* (1919) and opposite Sessue Hayakawa in *The Devil's Claim* (1920), opposite John Barrymore, then at the height of his career, in *The Lotus Eater* (1921) and in *Forsaking All Others* (1922) with Cullen Landis. The same year she made *The Ninth Commandment* with James Morrison.

Colleen hit her stride in flapper roles. She made *Flaming Youth* (1923) with Ben Lyon who was with her again in *Painted People* (1924), which had Clara Bow also in the cast. By the time of *The Perfect Flapper* (1924), her Dutch boy bob was the rage throughout the world and her salary was $12,500 a week. The same year she starred with Wallace Beery and Ben Lyon again in Edna Ferber's *So Big*. Her two best remembered vehicles were *Sally* (1925) with Leon Errol and *Irene* (1926). Both were adapted from Broadway hits and the latter had sequences in primitive technicolor and the hit song "Alice Blue Gown," which was played on the piano or organ in theatres running the film.

Along with talent and energy Colleen had the advice and assistance of John McCormack, a onetime studio press agent who became the production head of First National Pictures. She and McCormack were married the day after her twenty-first birthday.

Colleen's drawing power at the box office continued until the advent of sound. Her pictures such as *Ella Cinders* (1926), *It Must Be Love* (1926) with Mary Brian, *Naughty But Nice* (1927), *Orchids and Ermine* (1927), in which Mickey Rooney played an adult midget, and *Lilac Time* (1928) with Gary Cooper were well received. *Lilac Time* had sound effects and a synchronized musical score playing the lovely "Jeannine, I Dream of Lilac Time."

Colleen had a good voice and some meaty roles in a few of her talkies, but somehow it was just never the same. She and Neil Hamilton (the police commissioner on TV's "Batman") did *Why Be Good?* (1929) and a young actor named Fredric March was brought from Broadway to support her in *Footlights and Fools* in 1929. She scored in *The Power and the Glory* (1933) with the late Spencer Tracy and Helen Vincent. William C. deMille was associate producer and "Mickey" Neilan was director for the screen adaptation of *Social Register* (1934), which had been a Broadway vehicle for Lenore Ulric. However, it was a flop. Her final effort *The Scarlet Letter* (1934) was also a failure.

After divorcing McCormack in 1930 Colleen married Albert P. Scott, a New York stockbroker, in 1932. Two years later that marriage was also dissolved. From 1937 until his death in 1966 she was the wife of Homer P. Hargrave, a partner of the brokerage firm Merrill, Lynch, Pierce, Fenner & Smith. They lived together in Chicago where Colleen made quite a social splash. Her doll house on which she lavished over $435,000 over the years has been displayed for many charities. It was built in 1935 and is now on permanent loan to the Museum of Science and Industry in Chicago. Decorated by Hollywood set designer Harold W. Grieve, the house features running water and electric lights. Some of its furniture is carved from precious stones.

Colleen spends much of her time in Rome with trips to Chicago, Hollywood, and New York at least once a year. In 1968 she published her autobiography, *Silent Star,* in which she stated that if she had it all to do over again she would do exactly the same. A staunch Republican, Colleen is the godmother of Governor Ronald Reagan's daughter.

With Mervyn Le Roy today.

BARBARA ANN SCOTT

For a little Canadian girl who had a chronic ear ailment and was left fatherless at three, Barbara Ann did all right—she became a world skating queen.

When she was only ten years old the pert blonde won the Canadian Junior Championship. The year was 1939 and Barbara Ann was the youngest ever to win that gold medal. The next year she became the Junior Lady Champion of Canada. Four years later Barbara was crowned Senior Lady Champion of Canada, a title she was to hold from 1944 until 1948. In between there were other victories such as the North American Championship from 1945 to 1947 and the European Championships won in Davos, Switzerland, in 1947 and Praha, Czechoslovakia, in 1948. She took the World Championship in Stockholm, Sweden, in 1948 and again the next year in Switzerland. When in 1948 Barbara Ann Scott was proclaimed Ladies Figure Skating Champion at the Olympics no one was very surprised. Her score was 163.756.

Barbara found smoother skating on the ice than off. Her amateur career was colored by several well publicized controversies. In 1947 when she was training for the European competitions, the European skating authorities passed a rule allowing only Europeans to enter. The officers backed down after a public outcry of "sour grapes," but their fears were well founded because, of course, Barbara won that year and the next. Her other tussle with officialdom was when her home town of Ottawa gave her a welcome—60,000 cheering fans and a new Buick convertible with the license plate No. 47UI signifying her 1947 skating triumphs. Olympic chief Avery Brundage cited the gift as improper and demanded that she return it in order to maintain her amateur standing. After taking the 1948 Olympic title for Canada, however, she was given another car which, having decided to turn professional, she kept.

After turning professional she appeared in *Rose Marie* on the London stage and signed to headline Ice Capades of 1950 when it was still being produced by John H. Harris, a sports promoter with a reputation in the skating world for pettiness and personal abuse of employees. Harris was not able to hold names long. Sonja Henie* and Dick Button have skated for him, but for very short periods. When Arthur Wirtz asked her to star in his Hollywood Ice Revue she jumped at the lucrative offer as well as at the more pleasant atmosphere in his company. Barbara brightened that show for four highly successful seasons beginning in 1952.

During her last year with Wirtz Miss Scott met a Madison Square Garden press agent named Tommy King. They were married on September 17, 1955. After retiring, the Kings moved to Chicago where her husband is now an executive with the famous Merchandise Mart.

The Kings have no children, which has left Barbara with sufficient time to pursue sports and business activities. In the Chicago suburb of Glencoe she owns the Barbara Ann Scott Beauty Salon. She has changed sports and has developed into a top equestrienne. The Kings own two horses and Barbara shows them regularly in and around the Illinois-Wisconsin circuit. In 1966 she garnered sixty-four ribbons and twenty-one first places. She and her husband, once a professional basketball player, are avid golfers, and Mrs. King has been flying her own plane for several years. All this activity has kept her measurements and weight just the same as when she was setting attendance records in skating arenas everywhere.

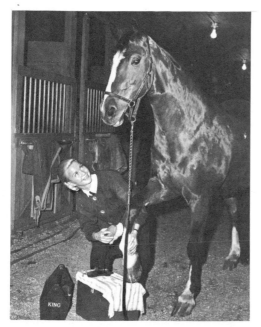

Grooming her bay gelding, Regal Tipper, who won twelve first-place ribbons in the past year.

Tarzan's son, with friend "Cheetah" in 1939.

JOHNNY SHEFFIELD

The world's most envied boy-actor was born in Pasadena, California, in 1931. His father was Reginald Sheffield, an English-born actor, who had played the title role in the 1923 silent film version of *David Copperfield*. The family claims a distant relationship to another John Sheffield, one of England's Poet Laureates, and to America's Benjamin Franklin.

Johnny weighed only four pounds at birth and was sickly during the first three years of his life, but his father was a firm believer in exercise and nourishing food and had his son as hale and hearty as any boy his age by the time he was five.

His first role was a plum. He was chosen to play the part of the grandson in the original company of *On Borrowed Time,* a play which began its out-of-town tryouts in Los Angeles before opening on Broadway in 1938. It starred the late character actor, Dudley Digges.

Metro-Goldwyn-Mayer let it be known that it was looking for a boy about seven years old who could not only act the part of a child brought up in the jungle, but one who could go through the grueling paces required of the part. Thanks to the exercises he had been used to since he could walk and the swimming he had learned at the same time, Johnny was hired. When his father told him that he was to play the role of Boy, the adopted son of Tarzan, Johnny yelled "Yip-eeee!" Along with his regular schooling and memorizing of lines for the pictures the young actor was given further swimming lessons by one of swimming's all-time greats, Johnny Weissmuller, who was also to play Tarzan in the films they made together.

In 1939 they made *Tarzan Finds a Son* and *Tarzan in Exile.* As all Tarzan fans know, Boy was found by the Ape Man when he survived a plane crash in the jungle. He was raised by the King of the Jungle and Jane, the King's mate. Some of the other romps Johnny had in the role on the back lot of the Culver City studio were *Tarzan's Secret Treasure* (1941), *Tarzan's New York Adventure* (1942), *Tarzan Triumphs* (1943), *Tarzan's Desert Mystery* (1943), *Tarzan and the Amazons* (1945) *Tarzan and the Leopard Woman* (1946), and *Tarzan and the Huntress* (1947).

Johnny made a few movies in which he appeared in something other than a loincloth: *Little Orvie, Lucky Cisco Kid,* both in 1940 (Duncan Renaldo who portrayed the Cisco Kid for so many years has retired to the Hope Ranch in Santa Barbara, California), and *Million Dollar Baby* (1941) with Priscilla Lane (now Mrs. Joseph A. Howard of Andover, Massachusetts).

After leaving the Tarzan series, Sheffield went to Allied Artists where he starred in his own series as Bomba, the Jungle Boy. The first film was made under that title in 1949. Some of his others were *Bomba and the Lost Volcano* (1950), *Bomba and the Jungle Girl* (1952), and *Bomba on Panther Island* (1953). The pictures did very well as low budget programmers which played mostly as the second half of double bills and as the Saturday matinee feature for kiddies, but when they were re-released for television a whole new generation discovered the character and the fan mail poured in.

In the mid-fifties, however, Sheffield left movies and enrolled at U.C.L.A., from which he was graduated with a B.A. in Business Administration. So completely did he divorce himself from his former profession that neither of the studios he worked for even had an address to forward his fan mail.

His earnings during the forties and early fifties had been well invested in real estate in Santa Monica, Pacific Palisades, and Malibu. Other than looking after his holdings Johnny does not do much these days besides play with his two sons and swim in the Pacific Ocean, which his Malibu home is set along.

"Boy" as a man—a rather pudgy one at that. *Jon Virzi*

"Spit" in the movie version of *Dead End,* in 1937.

LEO GORCEY

The leader of the Dead End Kids, East Side Kids, and Bowery Boys was born in New York City in 1917. His mother was Irish Catholic, his father Russian-Jewish, an actor, Bernard Gorcey, who played the role of Papa Cohen on Broadway during the twenties in *Abie's Irish Rose.*

Leo came by the accent that was to make him over one million dollars quite naturally during his boyhood in the Washington Heights section of New York City. It was somewhat more refined than the location of *Dead End,* but not much.

During the Depression, Gorcey considered himself lucky when he was able to work as an apprentice in his Uncle Rob's plumbing shop on 23rd Street for the weekly salary of $6. He complained to his father about being refused a raise. The elder Gorcey suggested that he try out for a part in the Sidney Kingsley play which was then being cast. There were a number of parts in *Dead End* for tough-talking young street hoodlums. This was the first time Leo had ever considered following his father's profession. He won the part of Spit who was more or less the leader. The others were Sidney Lumet (now a top Hollywood director), Huntz Hall (who commutes between New York and Florida, and does an occasional TV role. He has a son at Yale), Bernard Punsley (now a Beverly Hills obstetrician), Billy Halop (who works as a male nurse and lives in Pacific Palisades, California), Gabe Dell (a top Broadway comedian and member of Actors' Studio), and Bobby Jordan (who died in 1965). Leo's salary was originally $35. After several critics singled him out as being the best of the group he asked for a raise, which was refused. "There are hundreds of kids on the streets of New York who can play this role," the playwright told Leo. "Ya," answered Gorcey, "well, go out and find one." His next paycheck was for $50.

Samuel Goldwyn bought the screen rights and hired Gorcey and the others (with the exception of Lumet) to re-create their roles. The picture, directed by William Wyler, was released to rave reviews in 1937.

The kids were put under contract to Warner Brothers where they made some of their best pictures. They were with Humphrey Bogart in *Crime School*

126

(1938), Jimmy Cagney (retired on his farm in Martha's Vineyard) in *Angels With Dirty Faces* (1938), and Ronald Reagan in *Hell's Kitchen* (1939). In 1940 they went to Monogram Pictures where they remained until 1955, by which time it had been changed to Allied Artists Pictures. Some of the "B" features they turned out during those years were *Ghosts on the Loose* (1943), *Bowery Bombshell* (1946), *Bowery Battalion* (1951), and *Bowery to Bagdad* (1955). Leo received star billing over the others in most of the cheapies they made and always was able to command the largest salary. That he was admittedly "the worst actor of the bunch" amuses him greatly. At present there is a possibility of an animated cartoon series utilizing their voices. The project, which was initiated by Huntz Hall, is being discussed by them, but Leo's interest is strictly financial.

When Leo's father, who had played the role of the sweetshop owner "Louie" in many of their films, was killed in an auto accident in 1955, Leo called it quits, and has remained close to his ranch. His only effort of any consequence since then was a small part in *It's a Mad, Mad, Mad, Mad World* (1963).

Leo wrote a book, *Original Dead End Kid Presents Dead End Yells, Wedding Bells, Cockle Shells, and Crazy Spells,* which was published in 1967. It told mostly of his four unsuccessful and expensive marriages.

Leo has custody of his two children, a boy and a girl, who live with him and his mother on the ranch he has owned for many years in Los Molinos, California. The Brandy Lee Ranch has Herefords, pigs, and chickens, with Leo holding forth as gentleman farmer and local celebrity. Not only does he claim not to miss Hollywood, but maintains that he never liked it. Asked what he does with his time he said recently that he thoroughly enjoys his outdoor life and liquor.

His famous manner of speech is as pronounced as ever. Very little of Gorcey's personality has changed since he left Washington Heights for Hollywood and Broadway. When the New York boy who hadn't been to his home town in over twenty years visited Manhattan in 1968, his clothes were so outlandish he was refused service in a neighborhood bar. In his pictures, Spit might have gotten tough with the barkeeper. Nowadays he just makes a joke of it and goes on his way without bothering to show them the loaded revolver he keeps tucked inside his belt.

Huntz Hall, author, and Leo Gorcey (left to right) during Leo's first visit to New York City in over twenty years. *Diana Keyt*

In 1943, America's Number One child star.

MARGARET O'BRIEN

The 1944 special Academy Award winner was born Angela O'Brien in Los Angeles in 1937 to her Irish father and Spanish-Italian mother, dancer Gladys Flores. Her first movie was made for the U.S. government and had James Cagney as her co-star.

Metro-Goldwyn-Mayer put her under contract and she attended their Little Red Schoolhouse on the Culver City lot. The studio chose her parts carefully and Margaret played them for all they were worth. In 1941 she made *Babes in Arms* with Mickey Rooney and Judy Garland. The following year she really came into her own in *Journey for Margaret*.

Miss O'Brien was not funny like Jane Withers or pretty like Shirley Temple, but she had other qualities which she used with the skill of a veteran. Like all child actors she could cry on cue, and when the occasion called for it she could be unbearably cute. And when the scene did not allow for tears or cuteness Margaret, while other actors delivered their lines, could hold her own just by being so itsy-bitsy the audience couldn't take its eyes off her. She had a distinctive acting style which is still imitated today by moppets on television, particularly in commercials.

One of the most precocious children the screen has ever produced, she was published at eleven years of age. Her book was called *My Diary* which she not only wrote but illustrated. She guested on many radio variety shows of the day trading lines with such performers as Bing Crosby and Edgar Bergen. Bob Hope and other comedians had jokes about her. As the nation's top child star, she made numerous public appearances in which she did readings.

While her movie plots differed greatly, M-G-M found a formula which showed her off to the best advantage. Her big scenes usually were with men rather than women, and old men rather than boys. Van Johnson was all right to pose with for publicity pictures because she was too young to make the bobby soxers jealous, but character actors such as Lionel Barrymore, Wallace

Beery, Charles Laughton, Walter Brennan, and Edward G. Robinson were much preferred.

Though it lasted only a decade Margaret made a goodly number of films: *Madame Curie* (1943), *Jane Eyre* (1944) with Peggy Ann Garner, *Lost Angel* (1944), *Thousands Cheer* (1943), *Canterville Ghost* (1944), a memorable musical with Judy Garland and Tom Drake (who is now attempting to reactivate his career after a long bout with alcoholism), *Music for the Millions* (1944), *Our Vines Have Tender Grapes* (1945), *Bad Bascomb* (1946), *Three Wise Fools* (1946), *Tenth Avenue Angel* (1948), *Little Women* (1949), and *Her First Romance* (1951) which attempted to establish her as a teen-age star. The change of image never worked.

In 1955 in another try to reestablish her career, she made *Glory,* about which one critic said, "The only glory in this one can be found in the title." "Glory" was a horse.

Perhaps Margaret's most dramatic and best remembered scene took place in 1947 when her mother married orchestra leader Don Sylvio. Mrs. Sylvio said that her daughter "turned on the tears" and refused to kiss her new stepfather. The morning after, Margaret and her mother left together. There was a reconciliation but the marriage was doomed.

In 1958 *Life* did a cover story on her new career in television—she repeated her role of Beth in a musical version of "Little Women," with mostly good reviews, and starred in a "Studio One" production. Margaret's only picture in the last twelve years was *Heller in Pink Tights* (1960).

Since 1959 she has been married to Harold Robert Allen, Jr., a commercial artist with a Los Angeles advertising agency. They have no children. Margaret occasionally leaves Sherman Oaks to do stock versions of *Under the Yum Yum Tree, Barefoot in the Park, A Shot in the Dark,* and *A Thousand Clowns.*

Under California's Coogan Law most of Margaret's money was put in trust for her. In 1977 she will be able to spend the principal and interest of the $1,000,000 she earned during her childhood.

A big girl now. *Jon Virzi*

In 1935, still one of the world's greatest tenors.

GIOVANNI MARTINELLI

The great tenor from the Golden Age of Opera was the first of fourteen children born to a cabinetmaker in Montagnana, Italy, in 1885. He apprenticed in his father's trade and studied the clarinet. When he was drafted for three years into the Italian Army, his skill with the instrument landed him a cushy job in the band.

While in military service Martinelli and a friend used to imitate phonograph records. His friend would play an instrument and Giovanni would sing. By chance, a vocal coach heard him and took the young soldier to Milan where a group of operatic managers, after hearing him, decided on the spot to finance his training as soon as military service had ended. He made his debut in a Milan concert in 1910.

Early in Martinelli's career the great composer Giacomo Puccini heard of him and brought him to Rome where after an audition he was assigned the role of Dick Johnson in his *The Girl of the Golden West*. While in the Italian capital he met Arturo Toscanini and Guilio Gatti-Casazza. Both were to leave shortly for positions with the Metropolitan Opera Company in New York City —Toscanini as conductor, and Gatti-Casazza as general manager.

In 1913 Martinelli married Adele Previtali and together they sailed for the United States where his friends were to welcome him as an addition to the Metropolitan roster. He made his Met debut on November 20, 1913, in *La Bohème* in the part of Rodolfo.

It is a great tribute to his artistry that Martinelli was so well received by critics and fans, for at the time Enrico Caruso's well deserved reputation eclipsed all other tenors. Without developing a public or private rivalry between the two, Martinelli soon had a large and loyal following all his own. He and Caruso found they had much in common and developed a close friendship, which lasted until Caruso's death in 1921. Both Italians, both tenors from poor families, the two nearly had tragedy in common as well.

130

Caruso's last performance was in *La Juive,* which Martinelli performed three years later. Martinelli, after that final curtain, was stricken with typhoid fever, lingering near death for several days. His return to the Metropolitan a number of months later was one of the most memorable nights in the history of the now demolished house. Tickets were hawked at outrageous prices. When the curtain rose on *Pagliacci* every seat was filled and standing room had been sold out to capacity. Martinelli's entrance in the role of the clown brought thunderous applause, and with each aria the cheers grew, causing the production to be interrupted over and over again. When he stood before them at the final curtain Martinelli received a standing ovation from the audience, which was more than a welcome home to one of their favorites—his performance that night was one of the highlights of his career.

Although when he joined the Met he had a repertoire of only seven roles, by the time of his twenty-fifth anniversary with the house he was proficient in fifty-seven parts. He is credited with popularizing *Othello,* an opera which until then had been unsuccessful.

Martinelli's career is remarkable not only for its heights, but for its great length as well. When he left the Metropolitan at the end of the 1945–1946 season critics still marveled over his voice. At their peak most tenors have a rather short number of years. Giovanni's voice, however, was strong without a sign of a crack or quaver well into his fifties.

Even after leaving the Met he did not retire. In fact he has never actually left opera. He has performed in many roles during the past twenty years in cities all over the world and still turns out a recording now and then. As late as 1967 he essayed the role of Emperor Altoum in *Turandot* in Seattle.

Now a widower, Martinelli spends his summers on Lake Como ("to be near the home of Verdi"), other months he is in his luxurious hotel rooftop apartment half a block from Carnegie Hall. He attends Metropolitan performances and takes a keen interest in young singers, having several pupils in New York and London whom he coaches. He is the father of two girls and a boy but is the only musician in the family.

As he appears today. *Diana Keyt*

Dizzy Dean at the height of his career. *UPI*

DIZZY DEAN

The boy with the big right arm from the cotton fields of Arkansas who achieved fame as the zany big-league strikeout artist was born in Lucas, Arkansas, on January 16, 1911. He was one of five children of impoverished cotton-pickers. His mother, who died when he was three, named him Jay Hanna after Jay Gould, the fast-dealing Wall Street financier and the famous publisher Mark Hanna. At six, Diz changed his name to Jerome Herman to honor the father of his sick and dying friend. At six, along with his younger brother Paul (or "Daffy," who played with him on the Cardinal team), he was working in the fields, traveling with his brothers and his father from state to state. The boys learned to play baseball from their father, who had played third base professionally in Hartford, Connecticut. He had fashioned his own bats and balls for the boys out of scrap.

Diz joined the army at sixteen, and remained until nineteen, taking a job with the San Antonio Public Service, pitching for the team when he was not assisting reading gas meters. A St. Louis Cardinal scout who saw him play signed him on the spot, and he was shipped to St. Joseph in the Western League where his clowning kept the fans rolling in the aisles while he racked up 17 wins out of 25 starts.

He quickly moved up to the Texas League, in Houston. At an exhibition game against the Chicago White Sox, his great pitching antagonized the big leaguers, but his clowning was too much for the manager of the Sox, who kept screaming, "That dizzy kid is making fools of us." The name stuck. Before the year was out, the Cards brought him up to the major leagues. That was 1930. His first appearance during spring training in 1931 was as a relief pitcher, but as the season got under way he was returned to Houston, winning 26 out of 36 for the year. Following his return to Houston, he met his wife,

Patricia Nash, who has been with him ever since. Recalled by the Cards in 1932, Dizzy was paid $3,000, as he was in 1933. In 1934, he was increased to $7,500 as a result of his 30 wins, increased in 1935 to $18,500, and for 1936 and 1937 combined, $27,500.

On July 7, 1937, in the All-Star game in Washington, a line drive smashed into his left foot. In pain, Diz continued to pitch until he wrenched his arm, and was never the same.

Starting in 315 games, he won 150, and lost 83. He was averaging 22 wins yearly, and 1934, his best year, he took 30 games, losing only 7. However, following his injury, he won a mere 13, in 1937, and was sold in 1938 to the Chicago Cubs, winning 7 and losing 1 that year.

In 1940, after a brief return to the Texas League, he was recalled by the Cubs late in the season to win 3 out of 6. In 1941, he took a job as a broadcaster for the St. Louis games for the Falstaff Brewing Company as a result of having befriended the Falstaff president's invalid son years earlier. He was a great success, joking and clowning between innings and during the action. Some time later, when he came to New York to do the TV broadcast for the Yankees, his employers tried to teach him the king's English, but he continued to fracture it with lines like "he slud into second." In 1952, his life story was the basis for the movie *Pride of St. Louis,* and in the following year he was voted into the Baseball Hall of Fame. By 1958 Diz was ready to throw in the towel on his $62,500-a-year CBS broadcasting job on the big league's Game of the Week.

These days, when not golfing, he delights audiences at dinners with his hilarious malapropisms. He has put on weight, but it suits a man with oil and real-estate holdings in the Southwest. Diz no longer drops water bags from hotel windows. Not long ago, he was so outraged over an estimate he got from a floor-covering store in Phoenix, Arizona, where he was until recently living on his ranch, that he bought the company. He now lives with Pat in Wiggims, Mississippi, and still broadcasts, this time for the Atlanta Braves.

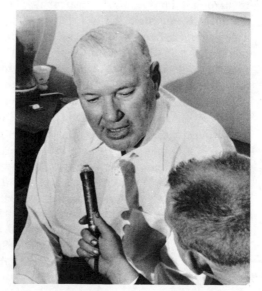

"Ole Diz" during a recent interview.
UPI

His antics in the fifties were watched on television by millions. *NBC TV*

PINKY LEE

The lisping comedian who became a household name through television during the fifties was born in St. Paul, Minnesota, in 1916. From the time he was five years old he was taking dancing, singing, and xylophone lessons. When he was thirteen Gus Edwards made him part of his famous "School Days" act which toured American vaudeville houses. Pinky had to leave when his voice began to change. Returning to school, he had written a serious essay, which he read aloud. The other kids howled with laughter. It was then that he realized just how funny his lisp made things sound. He claims that the impediment is inherited. All of his cousins lisp and have for generations.

By the time Pinky was old enough to go out on his own in vaudeville, the medium was in the doldrums. For a while he teamed up with another young man to do a sailor act. Their agent explained that the act lacked sex appeal. They hired a girl named Dotty. The agent suggested that Pinky, whose real name is Pinkus Leff, take the name Lee and that the act be called "Port, Lee [the two sides of a ship] and Dotty." From then on he was Pinky Lee.

During the thirties he accepted a job in burlesque from Harold Minsky. At first he felt that it was a great comedown, as he had played Loew's State and the Palace, but jobs were few and far between. Burlesque was something that performers came from. One didn't go into it unless one were on the way down. He toured the Eastern and Western Wheels (burlesque terms for circuits) for producer Milton "Be a Booster for Milton Schuster" Schuster.

In 1932 Pinky married Bebe Dancis. The ceremony was in court, after which they were wed at a religious ceremony in St. Paul, and twenty-five years later the Beverly Hills Chief of Police married them again. For this ceremony they were required to take blood tests.

By 1942 Pinky was getting top billing at Earl Carroll's Hollywood theatre-restaurant. He stayed on until 1946 and appeared in the movie *Earl Carroll Vanities* (1945). His first and by far his best was in 1943 when he played the burlesque "banana" in *Lady of Burlesque* with Barbara Stanwyck. Some of his other films were *Blonde Ransom* (1945), *That's My Gal* (1947), and *South Caliente* (1951) with Roy Rogers.

Pinky was an early, big hit on TV. His situation comedy series "Those Two" began on NBC-TV on November 27, 1951, which ran for two years. His first co-star was Martha Stewart who was later replaced by Vivian Blaine. After "Those Two" went off, Pinky switched to a kiddie format with equal success. Betty Jane Howarth was his companion on that program which ended when he collapsed on the air. Many reports called it a heart attack. The truth is, Pinky's sinuses had become so bad that they had poisoned his entire system. Following doctor's orders, he moved to Tucson, Arizona, where the climate improved the condition greatly. In 1966 he returned to Los Angeles and one of the biggest disappointments in his life when, after an expenditure of $183,000 by the producers, *Little World, Hello,* a musical in which he was to have starred, closed out of town. The book was based on the life of the late comedian Jimmy Savo and it was Savo's widow who prevented the show from continuing by exercising an option in the contract.

Pinky and his wife of thirty-five years live in a large, luxuriously furnished apartment in a new development in Culver City, California. They have two children and a grandson. None of whom lisp.

He would like to end his career with a Broadway show, something he has aspired to all his life. He considers himself semiretired, but will work when parts appeal to him, and only for short periods. In 1967 he went out for ten weeks with the Ann Corio show, *This Was Burlesque.*

Interviewed by the author during a recent trip to Manhattan. *Clifford May*

In 1937 "Our Gang" posed on the Hal Roach lot. From left to right: Carl "Alfalfa" Schweitzer, Billy "Buckwheat" Thomas, "Spanky" McFarland, Darla Hood, Porky Lee, and Baby Patsy.

DARLA HOOD

The distaff member of the screen's best remembered series of comedy shorts, *Our Gang,* was born in Leedy, Oklahoma, in 1931. Her father was the banker in their town of five hundred. Darla was an only child, whose mother was determined that her daughter was going to be a success in show business. When Darla was only three, Mrs. Hood enrolled her for dancing and singing lessons which were given in Oklahoma City, necessitating a 150-mile round trip once a week.

In 1935, Kathryn Duffy, Darla's coach, took her to New York City on a trip. One night they were dining at their hotel, the Edison, in Times Square, when the orchestra leader asked Darla if she would like to lead the band. The tot guided the group through a number, to the delight of the audience. Afterward Miss Duffy and Darla were joined by Joe Rivkin, a talent scout for Hal Roach Studios. They were looking for a "little sweetheart" for the mischievous boys in their *Our Gang* series. Darla was tested in New York, signed to a nine-year contract, and sent to Hollywood where she was joined by her mother. Mr. Hood commuted as much as possible from Leedy. From 1936 until 1945 Darla appeared in over 150 of the famous shorts.

The "Gang" was tutored on the Roach lot by Mrs. Alma Reubens, who recently died in Hollywood. When the series was sold to Metro-Goldwyn-Mayer they attended the famous "little red schoolhouse" on the M-G-M lot.

Although Darla holds happier memories of Hollywood than most child stars, she admits that being the only girl among a group of preadolescent boys was often quite lonely. While the boys were always nice to her, most of the games they played excluded girls and more often than not she was left alone with her dolls.

Few *Our Gang* pictures were made during World War II because of the shortage of film, which was reserved for feature pictures. By the time they were ready to revive them Darla was too mature for the role. In 1945 she left the group and enrolled at Fairfax High School in Hollywood from which she was graduated as an honor student. She planned to continue her studies at the University of Southern California but Ken Murray offered her vocal group, "The Enchanters," a job in his famous *Blackouts of 1949* which had a long run in Hollywood before it went to Broadway. In 1950 she started the first of four seasons as Murray's leading lady on his TV series. After that Darla made numerous appearances in nightclubs in Las Vegas, San Francisco, and New York.

In 1957 she became the wife of music publisher, José Granson. Darla has a stepdaughter, Robin (18), and two children of her own, Brett (10½) and Darla Jo (8). In 1963 they moved from Los Angeles to Englewood Cliffs, New Jersey. In September of this year they moved to North Hollywood, California.

Darla still receives a great deal of fan mail from children about as old as her own, who watch the series on television under the title of "The Little Rascals." They usually want an autographed photograph. She sends out old stills from the thirties because she has found that the kids are disappointed when they discover she is a grown woman. Nearly all want to know about the other members of the "Gang." Carl "Alfalfa" Schweitzer was killed January 12, 1959. "Buckwheat" Thomas has made a career of the United States Army. "Spanky" MacFarland is the secretary-companion to a Hollywood star. "Porky" Marlowe lives in Duluth, Minnesota.

Asked if her children are impressed that their mother is in the shorts they watch on TV she said, "They take great delight in calling me in from the kitchen to show me how my ruffled panties are showing under what I guess was the first miniskirt in the movies."

Darla works quite often on TV but is seldom seen. Most of her jobs are for dubbing or voice-over work. The best known is probably the Chicken-of-the Sea commercial in which she sings the mermaid jingle.

Author Richard Lamparski interviews the adult Darla Hood. *Clifford May*

A publicity picture of the 1930's.
Metro-Goldwyn-Mayer

RICARDO CORTEZ

A few years ago a book on motion pictures was published that announced with waspish glee that the great Latin lover of the silent screen was really Jake Stein, "a plain American." It is true that Ricardo Cortez's first name was Jacob, though his last name was Krantz. It is also true that he was not born in Spain but to Jewish parents in Vienna in 1899. However, he was anything but "plain."

Cortez came to Hollywood and clicked at a time when Rudolph Valentino was proving to be very difficult. Paramount had placed him on suspension and were looking for another actor with "bedroom eyes" who could replace him if he failed to return to the lot or, after his return, to be held over his head as a threat.

Rival studios were offering the swarthy sex appeal of the late Antonio Moreno and Ramon Novarro* to a public that could not seem to get enough of the dark, brooding virility these stars projected. Moreno, however, was older than the others and his career went back as far as 1913. Novarro got better parts than Cortez but Cortez lasted much longer than Moreno or Valentino and matured more gracefully than Novarro.

Some of the silents in which he had the ladies in raptures, both in the audience and on the screen: *Feet of Clay* (1920), *Sixty Cents an Hour* (1923), *The Spaniard* (1925), *The Swan* (1925), *The Eagle of the Sea* (1926), *The Sorrows of Satan* (1926) with Lya de Putti who choked to death on a chicken bone in 1931, and *The Private Life of Helen of Troy* (1927) with Maria Corda.

When Greta Garbo was brought to this country from Sweden by Metro-Goldwyn-Mayer they borrowed Cortez from Paramount to play opposite her in *The Torrent* (1926), her first American picture. It was the first and last time that anyone was billed over Greta Garbo in any film she made in America.

Cortez underwent more than the usual trauma suffered by all silent stars when talkies proved to be permanent. Not only was he like all the others unsure of how well his voice would record or match the image in the minds of his fans, but he was faced as well with a crisis in his personal life. His wife, the lovely Alma Reubens who had been a star in pictures before and after his career caught fire, was a hopeless drug addict. Cortez had tried his utmost to cure her of the habit. She died in 1931.

Cortez then concentrated on his career and changed his image. He emerged as the suave heavy and in very short time became the kind of man audiences love to hate. He was the head of the mob, the doctor who bilked old ladies, the lawyer who could get you out of any jam. He made dozens of movies during the thirties, among them *Big Business Girl* (1931), *Thirteen Women* (1932) with Irene Dunne,* *Torch Singer* (1933) opposite Claudette Colbert, *Wonder Bar* (1934), in which he made a fool out of Dolores Del Rio while Al Jolson's heart broke, *Secret Agent* (1935) with a young blonde who was about to become famous as Bette Davis, *The Walking Dead* (1936), in which he got his comeuppance from Boris Karloff whom he sent to the electric chair in the first reel, and *Broadway Bad* (1933) with Ginger Rogers and Joan Blondell.

He continued acting in movies into the forties with such features as *Free, Blonde and 21* (1940), *Romance of the Rio Grande* (1941), *Tomorrow We Live* (1942), and *Make Your Own Bed* (1944).

In 1948 Cortez (his brother Stanley Cortez is the cameraman who distinguished such films as *The Magnificent Ambersons* (1942) and *Night of the Hunter* (1955) with his cinematography) tried his hand at directing with *The Inside Story* starring William Lundigan. His last on-screen performance was in a small but memorable part in John Ford's *The Last Hurrah* (1958).

After he began to lose interest in acting, and it was clear that his career as a director was not developing, Ricardo Cortez began to take a serious interest in the stock market. Having done quite well manipulating his own holdings and those of several friends, he joined one of the top brokerage houses in New York where he has developed a large and grateful clientele as a customer's man.

Though the former Latin lover is retired from acting, he has not tired of actors. He can be found quite often at the Lambs Club exchanging stories with contemporaries.

Cortez resides just off Fifth Avenue in the East Seventies.

At a recent party with the character actress Ethel Griffies. *Warner Bros.-Seven Arts*

A typical Barnes pose, in 1941. *John Robbins*

BINNIE BARNES

No one ever shot a furtive glance or delivered a caustic comment as well as the actress who was born in London in 1905 with the name Gertrude Maude Barnes. She is of English-Italian descent. Her father was a bobby, and one of Mother's three husbands. Binnie was one of seventeen children in the family.

Her first job was as a milkmaid, which must have made quite an impression because she soon left it to learn nursing at London's Great Northern Hospital. She then became an assistant in a draper's shop but claims to retain a great fondness for cows. When she saw "Tex" McLeod doing a rope spinning act at the Cosmos Club, she got a job working with him. Together they toured South America for a year. By 1928 Binnie had gone out on her own billed as "Texas Binnie" Barnes. She twirled a rope and spun tales about the great cattle ranges of the West she had never seen.

In 1929 she began her stage career with the late Una O'Connor and Charles Laughton in Sean O'Casey's *Silver Tassie*. Her big break came when she got the part of Fanny, the cabaret singer, in Noel Coward's *Cavalcade*. Binnie was brought to Hollywood to repeat her performance in the film version, but the studio decided against her and gave the role to Isabel Jewel.

Miss Barnes returned to England and was cast as Catherine Howard in *The Private Life of Henry VIII* (1933). Charles Laughton won the Academy Award for his portrayal of the title role, and Binnie was seen for the first time by United States audiences. She was brought back to Hollywood, and this time they had work for her. Lots of work. She began with Universal in *There's Always Tomorrow* (1934), which starred Lois Wilson (on AFTRA's board, and a Manhattan resident). Binnie made twenty-six two-reel comedies in England with Stanley Lupino, father of Ida and a top comedian of his day, and *The Private Life of Don Juan* (1934) with Douglas Fairbanks, Sr., before moving permanently to the movie capital.

Whether menacing the hero or trying to break up a marriage, Binnie excelled at both brittle dialogue and looks fraught with vitriol. She managed to bring subtlety and nuance to some very heavy-handed scripts. During the thirties and forties she made *The Lady Is Willing* (1934) with the late Leslie Howard; *Diamond Jim* (1935), in which she played Lillian Russell; *Sutter's Gold* (1936); *The Adventures of Marco Polo* (1938); *Three Blind Mice* (1938) with Loretta Young (who resides in Manhattan, where she is a consultant to a fashion house); *The Divorce of Lady X* (1938) with Laurence Olivier; *Daytime Wife* (1939) with the late Linda Darnell and the late Tyrone Power; *Til We Meet Again* (1940); *The Man from Down Under* (1943); *The Hour Before the Dawn* with Veronica Lake* (1944); *It's in the Bag* (1945) with the late Fred Allen and Jack Benny; and *If Winter Comes* (1948). Her last pictures during this period were *Fugitive Lady* (1951) and *The Decameron Nights* (1952).

From 1931 until 1936 she was the wife of Samuel Joseph, an art dealer and publisher. In 1940 she married former U.C.L.A. All-American football hero Mike Frankovitch, who at the time was a sportscaster. The next year Binnie made the papers when she threatened to sue Columbia Pictures Corporation after being duped by director Alexander Hall into doing a scene in black lace bra and panties for *This Thing Called Love*. According to Binnie, she had been assured that she would be seen on the screen in silhouette. Her new husband was most annoyed, but they both wished that Binnie had let the whole thing drop when newspapers around the country printed a still from the scene showing Binnie in her unmentionables. Twenty years later Mike Frankovitch was one of the production heads of Columbia. They released Binnie's last and only picture in many years, *The Trouble with Angels* (1966). Binnie played a nun. A "Donna Reed Show" was her one excursion into TV in 1963.

The Frankovitchs adopted twins, who are now in the United States Army. The couple have a beautiful home on Hillcrest Drive in Beverly Hills. Binnie says she likes to work only once in a great while, and hasn't the time to miss acting because of all her duties as the wife of a studio executive. "I raise orchids," she said recently, "do gardening, and work on church projects. That's about it." Those are activities for when she is at home. A great deal of the time she travels with her husband, which she likes very much because of the theatre in New York and visits to London, her home town.

A nun in her last motion picture, 1966. *John Monte*

In *The Egg and I*, 1947. *Universal Pictures*

MARJORIE MAIN

In 1890 one of the finest character actresses this country ever produced was born in a small town in Indiana. Her father, a minister, took a dim view of actresses, but somehow his daughter managed to attend a dramatic school for a few years. She changed her name from Mary Tomlinson to Marjorie Main.

She traveled the country for a few years on the Chautauqua circuit, in vaudeville and stock companies. By the time she met and married Dr. Stanley L. Krebs in 1921 Marjorie had developed some excellent sketches and a solid reputation, in her profession. While not a star by any means, she played the Palace Theatre and could hold her own with some of the best scene stealers of the day.

Her psychologist husband and she toured the United States together. He gave lectures and she handled the details. In the mid-twenties the Krebs settled in New York City and Marjorie decided to try her luck in the theatre. In 1927 she was with Barbara Stanwyck and Hal Skelly in *Burlesque* and played Mae West's mother in *The Wicked Age*. Her real break came in 1933 when she got a large part in *Music in the Air*. It was the first of three stage vehicles which she was to repeat on screen. The film version (1934) was made with Gloria Swanson and the late Douglass Montgomery but Marjorie's part was far less important than it had been on stage. Her next play was the smash hit *Dead End* in 1935. She stayed on Broadway with it for over a year and did the film in 1937, playing the mother of a gangster (Humphrey Bogart). The scene in which she slaps his face and cries "Ya dirty yellow dog" was so moving that the studios gave her one role after another in which she lived in a tenement with her bad-boy son. Also in the picture was Wendy Barrie, now the hostess of a syndicated radio series.

Marjorie's last stage appearance was in *The Women* in 1936 and again Hollywood made use of her when it was filmed in 1939.

In over eighty films beginning with a bit part in *House Divided* (1932), Marjorie Main never gave a bad performance. She saved many a bad picture and made the good ones better. During the fourteen years she spent under contract to M-G-M such stars as Jeanette MacDonald and Nelson Eddy were delighted to have her liven up their vehicles, such as *Naughty Marietta* (1935). She worked with Barbara Stanwyck in *Stella Dallas* (1937) and supported Clark Gable in *Test Pilot* (1938) and *Honky Tonk* (1941). Ronald Reagan had Marjorie with him in *Angels Wash Their Faces* (1939) and one year later she made *I Take This Woman* with the late Spencer Tracy. Cinema societies still run *The Dark Command* (1940) for the memorable performance she delivered in it. In 1941 she appeared in her first color picture *Shepherd of the Hills*.

Some of Marjorie's other important roles were in *Meet Me in St. Louis* (1944), which also had Lucille Bremmer (now Mrs. Rodriguez of La Jolla, California) in the cast, *Murder He Says* (1945), *The Harvey Girls* (1946), *Summer Stock* (1950), *Rose Marie* (1954), and *Friendly Persuasion* (1956).

In *The Egg and I* (1947) she portrayed Ma Kettle and was nominated for an Academy Award, after which she commanded a salary as large as many stars. She and the late Percy Kilbride made such an endearing pair as the eccentric farm couple they were featured together in nine Ma and Pa Kettle films which in spite of their low budgets and rather raucous humor were some of the biggest money-makers Universal International studios ever made. Her last picture was *The Kettles on Old MacDonald's Farm* (1957).

Marjorie never remarried after the death of her husband in 1935 and is now retired. Although she entered a profession her father did not approve of, she has remained throughout her life deeply religious. She is a firm believer in the Moral Re-Armament movement. She does not smoke or drink and never has.

She is justifiably proud of her career, but seems quite content to spend her time these days enjoying her homes in Los Angeles and Palm Springs. Probably the least pretentious actress in Hollywood, Marjorie does her own cooking and housecleaning which she considers good for her, mentally and physically. It is certainly not for economic reasons. Hard work and frugality were imbued in her as a child and like her midwestern accent, they have never left her.

As she appears today—always smartly dressed. *Jon Virzi*

"The Toy Bulldog," 1920.

MICKEY WALKER

The Toy Bulldog, which is how he was known during his career in the ring, was born in Kereighhead, New Jersey, which is the Irish section of Elizabeth. Mickey attended Sacred Heart School through the eighth grade, which was the end of his formal education. He then became a pin boy at the Elks Club Bowling Alley in Elizabeth and moved from that to a boiler shop of the New Jersey Central Railroad.

His first fight was on Washington's Birthday in 1918 at the local Y.M.C.A. It became so fierce, it had to be stopped.

By 1924, Mickey was getting $20,000 to box Harry Greb at the Polo Grounds. From then on Mickey would have his most colorful and successful years, under the management of "Doc" Kearns, who had also been Jack Dempsey's manager. In 1925 they made a fifty-fifty deal with a handshake and never had a word of disagreement about money after that. Kearns was noted for being a tough bargainer and he had a great deal of money for the Bulldog. Together they spent it all. After Kearns took over, his first fight that year was $100,000 to defend his welterweight crown at the Polo Grounds against Dave Shade. Mickey won in fifteen rounds. In May of 1926 he lost the title to Pete Latzo in Scranton and a month later Joe Dundee KO'd Walker in the eighth round in New York. Mickey thought he was finished. Kearns thought otherwise. On December 26, 1926, Mickey met Tiger Flowers in Chicago for the Middleweight Championship, which Flowers had taken from Greb. The gate was $77,127, the largest Chicago had seen. Mickey won a decision. He got a $110,000 guarantee to fight British Middleweight champ Tommy Milligan in England. Walker took not only the fight with a ten-round knockout but a bet of $440,000 besides. He yearned for a crack at the heavyweight crown and after beating Wilson Yarbo in Cleveland, felt he deserved one. He knocked out Mike McTigue and took a ten-round decision from Paul Berlenbach. After making over a million dollars in a few years he was forced to take $10,000 to fight Tommy Loughran in 1929. Walker lost that one, but his finances were so low that he was happy for the money. In July of 1931 he battled Jack Sharkey in Ebbets Field. The gate was $238,831. A crowd of 33,156 people watched Mickey fight Sharkey, the 2 to 1 favorite, to a draw. King Levinsky followed in 1932, and decked him in the first round of their fight but Mickey won that one, and he then beat the Basque Paolino Uzcudun the same year. Mickey might have gotten the chance at the heavyweight crown he longed for if he hadn't lost a decision in Cleveland to Johnny Risko. Instead he fought the former champion, Max Schmeling,* in Long Island City in 1932. Kearns threw in the towel in the eighth round. Toward the end of 1933 he made a try at the Light Heavyweight title when he fought Maxie Rosenbloom. He lost by a close fifteen-round decision. Then he had a draw in his fight with Bob Godwin in 1934 and lost a ten-round decision to Young Corbett in August of that year. Kearns and Mickey parted company. Kearns had advised him to quit.

But the Toy Bulldog was broke again and so he made a few more tries. He had a draw, lost a decision, and won over a guy rated as a bum. Then he knocked out Paul Pirrone in Philadelphia. He made eight more tries in 1935 which was his last year. The finale to one of boxing's most colorful careers came with a KO from Eric Seeling in 1935.

In his seventeen-year career in the ring, Walker had 141 fights. No one ever complained about going away without their money's worth.

He was always a ladies' man and used to date such lovelies of the day as Lilyan Tashman and Norma Talmadge, both long dead. After he saw Somerset Maugham's *Moon and Sixpence,* he began to paint. His primitives were given a one-man show at a Manhattan art gallery in 1944 and *Esquire* Magazine published many of them in color in one of their issues that year. Mickey has tried to sell his life story to Hollywood on several occasions, without success. In 1967 he retired from his executive position with National Distillers Corporation and now receives a pension. He has four children by previous marriages, and ten grandchildren. Mickey works closely with the poverty program in New Jersey speaking before high school audiences on the art of boxing, refereeing bouts between the youngsters, and advising on recreational facilities.

The man who was twice a world champion, holding the Welterweight title from 1922 until 1926, and the Middleweight title from 1926 until 1931, now lives on East Fifty-second Street in Manhattan with his fourth wife.

Former champions (left to right): Tommy Loughran, Mickey Walker, Jack Dempsey, and Georges Carpentier reminisce at a recent party at the Gallery of Modern Art in New York City. *Paul Cordes*

The forties.

SONNY TUFTS

The actor whose name has become a joke was born into Boston society in 1911. Sonny's father was a banker. His great-uncle, Charles Tufts, was founder of Tufts College in Boston. The first Tufts arrived in the United States from England in 1638. Bowen Charleston Tufts, III, which is his real name, went to Phillips-Exeter and then broke with the tradition of his family by enrolling at Yale rather than Harvard. He was a member of the school's most exclusive and secret senior society, Skull & Bones, and a member of the famed singing group, The Wiffenpoofs. One of his classmates was Winthrop Rockefeller.

During his years at the university Tufts had altogether five different bands, which he led at Yale and neighboring colleges. Sonny was also the vocalist for each group. His best received, most often sung numbers were "Sweet Sue" and "Egyptian Ella." He spent six months studying voice in Paris before World War II broke out, and trained for another three years on his return and even had an audition at the Metropolitan.

In 1938 he landed a part in the musical *Who's Who* on Broadway, which he followed in 1939 with *Sing For Your Supper*. Sonny sang at supper clubs and hotels such as the Glass Hat, the Belmont Plaza, the Beachcomber, in Manhattan, and the Patio, in Palm Beach.

Lex Thompson, a millionaire sportsman who had been a year behind Sonny at Yale, suggested he try his luck in Hollywood and offered to back him financially. Tufts signed a contract with Thompson for a weekly salary in return for a percentage of his future earnings. Another friend, Jack Donnelly who was a Hollywood hotel manager, introduced him to Joe Egli, Paramount's casting director. Sonny screen-tested in a scene from the Charles Boyer film *Love Affair* in which he felt uncomfortable and played the whole thing as a gag. The result was a Paramount contract and a role in *So Proudly We Hail* (1943), in which he played Kansas under Mark Sandrich's direction.

College football injuries kept him out of the war and there was a great shortage of younger leading men because of the draft. Tufts was 6 feet 4 inches with

146

blonde hair and blue eyes. He caught on as a well-meaning but fumbling big guy and never changed his image. The films in which he appeared were *Government Girl* (1943) with Olivia de Haviland, *I Love a Soldier* (1944) with Paulette Goddard, *Here Come the Waves* (1944), *Bring on the Girls* (1945), *Miss Susie Slagle's* (1946), *Swell Guy* (1947), and *The Seven Year Itch* (1954). In the late forties as the stars returned to Hollywood and younger men came up Tufts was nearly finished.

In 1950 several ladies accused him of having bitten them in the thigh. One, the dancer-stripper Barbara Gray Atkins, sued him for $25,000. Two weeks later dancer Marjorie Von sued him for $26,500 in a similar action. Miss Von claimed a three-inch contusion. There were more arrests for drunkenness. Once he was found by police unconscious on the sidewalk, being nursed by a shapely blonde.

In 1951 the former Barbara Dare, a Spanish dancer Tufts had married in 1938, sued him for divorce. They had been separated for two years.

In 1963 Sonny played the father of Doug McClure in the TV show "The Virginian." Seventeen years ago he had played the McClure role in the movie version starring Joel McCrea.

Tufts has made two hard tries at a comeback. The first was in 1955 when he got the male lead in *Ankles Aweigh,* a musical with Betty and Jane Kean. Just before the Boston opening, he was dropped because his part "just didn't come off." In 1959, after staying sober for a year, he lost the part of Jim Bowie that he wanted so badly in John Wayne's *The Alamo.*

In 1966 he was a "trivia guest" on a TV special. The same year he was a guest on the Merv Griffin Show. As he walked on comedienne Totie Fields suggested that he sit down before he fell over, and the band played "Show Me the Way to Go Home." After taking a lot of kidding, he said to one of the guests, "You're really a young Sonny Tufts." It got a big laugh except from the actor he said it to—Tab Hunter.

Sonny is unmarried and lives in Hollywood. He says he made and spent over $2,000,000 and had a lot of fun doing it.

The sixties. *Jon Virzi*

A publicity still from 1928.

FAY WRAY

The girl King Kong took such a shine to was born on her father's ranch, "Wrayland," in Alberta, Canada, in 1907. While still a small child, she moved with her parents to Los Angeles, and attended Hollywood High School where she took part in the annual Hollywood Pilgrimage Play.

The first time Fay tried to get into the movies her mother accompanied her to the casting office of Century studios. She was refused rather curtly. Just as they were leaving the lot a producer spotted the teen-ager and offered her a small part in a comedy. She continued to do bits and extra work until Erich von Stroheim picked her from a line of bathing beauties in 1926 to star in his lavish production, *The Wedding March*. It was a choppy but memorable silent film with some splendid photography. It was released in 1928 and Fay became a star.

Fay had no faith in her career in talkies. When she made *The Texan* with Gary Cooper in 1930 they both thought they had no future in the medium. The same year she co-starred with Richard Arlen in *Sea God,* and then appeared with Ronald Colman as her leading man in *The Unholy Garden* (1931). In 1933 she was seen in such thrillers as *Vampire Bat* and *Mystery of the Wax Museum* with Glenda Farrell. Her co-stars, Joseph Schildkraut, and Leo Carrillo in *Viva Villa* (1934) are dead, as is Constance Bennett who headed the cast of *The Affairs of Cellini* which Fay did in 1934 with Fredric March. The next year she went to England where she starred in two films, *Alias Bulldog Drummond* and *The Clairvoyant* with the late Claude Rains. Her pictures were mostly programmers after that. In 1936 she was in *They Met in a Taxi* and *Roaming Lady*. In 1937 she starred in *Murder in Greenwich Village* and *It Happened in Hollywood*. Toward the end of her career she was reduced to playing in such "B" films as *Smashing the Spy Ring* (1939), *Navy Secrets* (1939), and *The Wildcat Bus* (1940).

Fay Wray was assured of movie immortality the day she accepted the role in *King Kong* (1933), although she claims she had no idea of the plot when the contract was signed. The superb special effects and fine photography made believable the story of a mammoth gorilla who falls in love with a pretty redhead. It is one of the largest grossing pictures in cinema history and has been revived by R.K.O. over and over again. In one theatre in Africa it played over twenty years.

Fay never succeeded on Broadway despite her valiant efforts as an actress and playwright. Her first try was in 1931 in *The Brown Danube* and again the same year her first husband John Monk Saunders, wrote *Nikki* for her. It was sold to the movies, but the late Helen Chandler got the role. In 1939, a year after her divorce from Saunders, Fay collaborated with Sinclair Lewis on *Angela Is 21*, but it never made it to Broadway. Her last play was *Golden Wings* in 1941.

In 1942 Fay married the scenarist Robert Riskin who wrote *It Happened One Night*. There was a rumor of a serious romance with Howard Hughes but the Riskin marriage squashed the speculation. Upon this second venture into matrimony, Fay announced that she was retiring from the screen. Not until after Riskin's death in 1955 did she accept another part.

Part of the reason for her reactivated career in the fifties was the sale of *King Kong* to television. Once again she was "a name" to young people who were not even born when the picture was originally shown. Her comeback was less than sensational. She did a few TV programs and played Jane Powell's mother in *Small Town Girl* (1953). Her last film was *Hell on Frisco Bay* in 1955.

In the past few years Hollywood's most menaced lady has spent a lot of time traveling. She has never remarried and lives alone in her home on Tigertail Road in the Brentwood section of Los Angeles. It hangs over a cliff and has a spectacular view of the city. The fan mail still pours in from around the world where *King Kong* is still being shown in theatres and on TV. Most of it is from adolescent boys.

In her Brentwood home. *Jon Virzi*

A publicity shot from 1939.

ANDY DEVINE

The gravel-voiced comedian was born in 1905 in Flagstaff, Arizona. His grandfather was Admiral James Harmon Ward, one of the founders of Annapolis and a tutor of Admiral Dewey. Andy's father was the owner of a hotel. While at Santa Clara University, he made quite a name as a football player. He also attended Arizona Teachers College for awhile. After leaving school he played pro football for a time and was also a lifeguard, telephone lineman, and news photographer.

Andy came to Hollywood in 1925 with the purpose of becoming a movie actor. His first job was as an extra in *The Collegians* (1927). He was doing quite well as a featured player, with such credits as *Red Lips* (1928) and *Hot Stuff* (1929), when the talkies came in. Most people in Hollywood, including Andy, felt that he had no career in sound films because of his very peculiar voice, which he has had since childhood. He had been playing with a curtain rod pretending it was a horn, when he fell, driving the rod through the roof of his mouth. For a full year he couldn't speak at all. When he finally did talk it was a duotoned sound with more than a slight wheeze. In 1931, however, he got a comedy part in *The Spirit of Notre Dame*. The raspy quality of his voice coupled with his girth and natural comic ability enhanced his effect. From then on his voice was a very valuable trademark.

Most of Devine's pictures were made during his seventeen years under contract to Universal. Some of those from the thirties and forties were *All Quiet on the Western Front* (1930), *Tom Brown of Culver* (1932) with Tom Brown (who resides in Sherman Oaks, California), *Dr. Bull* (1933) with Will Rogers, *Gift of Gab* (1934) with Edmund Lowe (now a resident of the Motion Picture Country Hospital), *Chinatown Squad* (1935) with Valerie Hobson (married to John Dennis Profumo, the central figure in the international scandal), *Coronado* (1935) with Johnny Downs, *Way Down East* (1935) with Rochelle Hudson (who is a realtor in Los Angeles), *Romeo and Juliet* (1936), in which he played Peter, *A Star Is Born* (1937), *In Old Chicago* (1938) with Alice

Faye, and *Stagecoach* (1939), probably his best role. Andy was a frequent guest on Jack Benny's radio program, usually featured in the "Buck Benny Rides Again" skits. In the early forties he was a regular on "Al Pierce and His Gang" and did many guest stints on "Lum 'n' Abner."* He continued with pictures, appearing in *Ali Baba and the Forty Thieves* (1944) and *Sudan* (1945). He became less active thereafter turning out such clinkers as *Michigan Kid* (1947) and *Ranchero* (1948). In 1951 he made *The Red Badge of Courage*.

For six years beginning in 1951 Andy played Guy Madison's sidekick Jingles on the "Wild Bill Hickok" TV series. He wisely accepted a meager salary while insisting on a 10 percent share of the gross. It turned out to be most profitable role he ever played.

In 1957 Andy made his stage debut playing "Cap'n Andy" in Guy Lombardo's production of *Show Boat* at Jones Beach, repeating the role in 1958 at the St. Louis Municipal Opera House. Andy had his own TV series "Andy's Gang," which was syndicated in 1956 and 1957. In 1966 he was seen on five episodes of "Flipper." In 1967 he did *My Three Angels* at the Cherry County Playhouse in Traverse City, Michigan.

His last features have been *The Man Who Shot Liberty Valance* (1962), *How The West Was Won* (1962), *Zebra in the Kitchen* (1965), and *The Ballad of Josie* (1967) with Doris Day. It was so bad it played as the second half of double bills.

For a few years he was the honorary mayor of Van Nuys, California, where he had bought a five-acre ranch at a time when the whole area looked like a location for one of his westerns. Today he spends most of his hours in his home in Newport Beach, California. Unlike many of the old residents of the San Fernando Valley, Andy doesn't complain about the shopping centers and apartment houses that have been built everywhere. Whenever anyone asks about them he laughs and says he can't say much since most of the land they are built on was sold by him.

The comedian has been married since 1933 to Dorothy Irene House. Their two sons, Denny and Tod, appeared with their father in *Canyon Passage* (1946).

A judge in his last movie, *The Ballad of Josie. Universal Pictures*

In the 1930's, his was one of the best known voices on radio and phonograph records. *NBC Radio*

MORTON DOWNEY

Although he was known variously throughout his long career as "The Golden Voiced Irish Tenor," "The Irish Troubadour," and "The Irish Nightingale" among others., Morton Downey was not from Ireland at all, having been born in 1902, in Wallingford, Connecticut. His father, who had been born in Ireland, was Wallingford's fire chief and a tavern keeper.

Downey began singing in small clubs and smokers to supplement his wages as a candy butcher on the New Haven Railroad. But his first professional appearance, at the age of nineteen, was in a little theatre in Sheridan, where he was picked out by a talent scout for Paul Whiteman. He thus became the first band vocalist per se, for until then all singers were expected also to play an instrument. The step was so unheard of that he was given a dummy saxophone in order to look like a bona fide member of the orchestra. He left the band in 1926 when he was signed by Ziegfeld for *Palm Beach Nights* in Florida.

Following this he went on his own to London, singing at the Kit Kat Club and at the Café de Paris. From London he went to Paris, Berlin, and the French Riviera, gaining an international reputation.

Upon his return to New York City, he opened his successful Delmonico Club, where he entertained and hosted the café society of the day.

Hollywood beckoned in 1929, and he made *Syncopation*, in which he sang the hit song "I'll Always Be in Love with You" to his co-star Barbara Bennett (of the famous acting family including father Richard and sisters Constance and Joan) whom he married on completion of the picture. He made another film that year, *Mother's Boy*. His only other film was made in 1930, *Lucky in Love*. Movies, however, did not seem to be suitable for him. For one thing he tended to be heavy, which seemed to make him an unlikely romantic lead. Radio on the other hand offered him his greatest success, and when he was signed by CBS in the early thirties he competed favorably with the champs of the day. He sang successively for Camel, Woodbury, and Pall Mall, and at the peak of his career he received as many as 95,000 fan letters a week, earning, with theatre and nightclub appearances, as much as $250,000 a year.

During the New York World's Fair of 1939–40, he was the featured singer at Billy Rose's famous Aquacade. The following year he was signed by the Coca Cola Company for a daily radio program, singing with the Raymond Paige Orchestra. Thus began a lucrative association. He was soon to become president and director of the Coca Cola Bottling Company of New Haven (only one of his many business affiliations over the years, for Downey is or has been on the boards of such organizations as the Coronado Publishing Company, the American News Company, the Federal Bank and Trust Company, part owner of Sortilege, and many others).

His first TV appearance was in 1947, and two years later he had his own show on NBC, sponsored by a carpet company. In 1952 he was again sponsored by Coca Cola, which signed him to an exclusive five-year contract covering all radio and TV appearances.

His marriage to Barbara Bennett ended in divorce in 1941 after twelve years of home life and five children. After a bitter court dispute he won custody of the children. The battle was renewed in 1951, shortly after his marriage to heiress Margaret Boyce Thompson Schulze, the daughter of Margaret Schulze Biddle. However, Barbara, who in the interim had remarried, lost again. Barbara died in 1958. Three years later Margaret's first marriage to Prince Hohenlohe of Poland was annulled by the Catholic Church, and Downey and she were married in a religious ceremony. Following breast surgery, she died in 1964 at the age of forty-two, twenty years younger than her husband.

In recent years, his professional activity has been nil. The professional Irishman is much closer to the horsey set than to his former colleagues in show business. Morton has not remarried and lives on a large estate in Wallingford, Connecticut.

The widower in his Connecticut home. N. Y. *Daily News*

Circa 1932.

GENE AUSTIN

The man who offhandedly recorded "My Blue Heaven"—one of the biggest selling records of all time—was born in Gainsville, Texas, in 1900 and raised in Louisiana.

Gene had been knocking about in vaudeville and making phonograph records since 1923, but when he walked into a studio and cut "My Blue Heaven" on September 14, 1927, he was still a pretty obscure performer. It had no special arrangement and no elaborate accompaniment. What is more, radio had at that time come into its own and was the medium from which new stars were merging. The record business was in serious trouble. In spite of all these obstacles, the song hit and hit big—for 7,000,000 copies, and it provided him with the first gold record ever awarded. It is now in The Smithsonian Institution. It was over twenty years before Bing Crosby's "White Christmas" pushed it from first place as the biggest-selling record of all time.

Today's generation mostly knows Gene as the man associated with "My Blue Heaven," but he didn't stop there. He went on to perform such standards as: "Five Foot Two, Eyes of Blue," "Ramona," "When My Sugar Walks Down the Street," "Those Wedding Bells Are Breaking Up That Old Gang of Mine," "That Lonesome Road," "How Come You Do Me Like You Do, Do, Do," and "Sleepy Time Gal."

Austin caused less swooning than Vallee, Crosby, and Columbo, who followed him and to some degree copied his style. (His weight problem worked against him in personal appearances.) He sang regularly on radio during the thirties, but he never really clicked on the air, and by 1937 when he became the regular vocalist on the "Joe Penner Show" the recording business had been in the doldrums for some time.

Gene took it philosophically. He was still able to sell songs and his royalties were huge—his records, altogether, have sold over 87,000,000 copies. He made brief appearances in such pictures as *Gift of Gab* (1934), *Sadie McKee* (1934) with Joan Crawford, and *Klondike Annie* (1936). In the latter he wrote a song at the request of the star, Mae West, who told him she wanted something "Chineseie and yet sexy." What he came up with was one of her greatest numbers, "I'm an Occidental Woman in an Oriental Mood for Love." He also made a series of one-reelers for RKO.

In the late thirties when he was traveling the country making personal appearances his advance man was the colorful promoter, Colonel Tom Parker, who twenty years later hit it big managing another southern boy by the name of Elvis Presley.

Gene likes to travel and gamble which is what he has been doing since he went into semiretirement in 1940, making occasional club appearances. It may account also for the fact that he has gone through four wives. Fortunately, many of his songs have become standards and he can afford the extravagance that he is known for. In 1947 he located in Las Vegas which is still more or less his home base, although the only house he has there is an elaborate trailer named "My Blue Heaven." Also, for a few years, he had a gambling casino by that name.

In 1957 NBC presented a one hour dramatization of Austin's life in which the star was played by George Grizzard. There has been talk of a movie on him, but nothing firm.

In 1962 Gene headed the ticket in the Nevada gubernatorial elections, with Jimmy Durante's old partner, Eddie Jackson, as a running mate. They were defeated by the late Rex Bell, former cowboy star who was married to Clara Bow. Before that, Gene had campaigned in Louisiana for another singer-composer, his friend, Jimmy "You are My Sunshine" Davis, who was elected governor.

The man who once sent RCA Victor stock soaring by his string of hits can still be persuaded to sing a little at clubs in Las Vegas and New Orleans. Now a grandfather and well off through his royalties, though still traveling and gambling around the country, Gene is often kidded about the incongruity of his life, considering that his first and biggest hit was about the coziest song ever written. He just laughs and repeats what he has been saying for years, "I never want to nest anywhere."

The crooner of "Yes, Sir, That's My Baby" surrounded by current admirers in a Las Vegas nightclub. *Bernie Foyer*

In 1926, one of the most promising stars under contract to the director Thomas Ince, who was killed mysteriously aboard William Randolph Hearst's yacht.

JACQUELINE LOGAN

The smoky-eyed beauty of the silent screen was born in Corsicana, Texas, in 1904. Her father was a popular architect and her mother, who had a brief career in opera, did vocal coaching.

She was taken to Colorado Springs for her health where she took courses in journalism from future baseball commissioner Ford Frick (now one of her Westchester County neighbors). Her mother continued giving voice lessons. One of her pupils was Lowell Thomas.

Jacqueline set off to an uncle in Chicago, presumably for college. Instead she got a job dancing in the stage production of a local theatre, lying about her age. Her uncle was furious, resulting in her being let go. Again she lied and traveled to New York City with a theatrical troupe, landing a small part in *Flora Dora,* a Broadway musical of 1920. She was seen by Flo Ziegfeld who offered her a job dancing on his famous Ziegfeld Roof, replacing Billie Dove who had just gotten a Hollywood contract. There were also many modeling jobs including the prestigious Dobbs Girl in Alfred Cheney Johnston photographs and a Johnny Hines' comedy short. Soon she was given a screen test, which she made with another unknown named Ben Lyon (married to Bebe Daniels*).

In 1921 Associated Producers put her opposite Monte Blue in *The Perfect Crime,* which included a lovely blonde child actress named Jane Peters, later known as Carole Lombard. In 1921 she supported Mabel Normand in *Molly O* and had superstar Thomas Meighan as her leading man in *White and Unmarried.* Milton Sills protected her in *Burning Sands* (1922) and Ricardo Cortez was with her in *Sixty Cents an Hour* (1923). Leatrice Joy* headed the cast of their C. B. De Mille film *Java Head* (1923). In 1925 she played opposite the late Richard Dix in *A Man Must Live* and the following year Jacqueline and William Powell made *White Mice* in New York and Cuba. She and the late Louise Fazenda were in *Footloose Widows* in 1926, the next year she co-starred with Richard Arlen* in *Blood Ship.* Her other leading men, all of whom are deceased, were Lionel Barrymore, John Barrymore, Antonio Moreno, and Lon Chaney, Sr.

C. B. De Mille chose Miss Logan for the coveted role of Mary Magdalene in the religious classic, *The King of Kings,* which holds the record for audiences. It alone has been shown somewhere in the world every day since it was first released in 1927. Dubbed voices have been added. Not only does the film now carry the voice of the lady who played the silent part but the major editing also was done by Jacqueline before the talkie version was released.

Jacqueline never really made it in the new medium. She was a member of the all-star cast of the early musical *Show of Shows* (1929), after making several early and successful sound films for Columbia.

She went to England and received good notices for stage performances, such as in *Smoky Cell*. Her English picture *Middle Watch* was given a Command Performance and she was signed by British International to write and direct. When *Knock-Out* (1931), which she wrote, and *Strictly Business* (1931), which she wrote and directed, were hits, she returned to Hollywood hoping to continue her career behind the camera. Harry Cohn, production head of Columbia Pictures at that time, admitted they were good films but was unwilling to sign a female to direct. Jacqueline appeared in a few Broadway plays such as *Merrily We Roll Along* and *Two Strange Women* before she married in 1934 and retired completely.

She has been living in Westchester County ever since but she and her industrialist husband were divorced in 1947. Her winters are spent in Florida where she visits with her old friends Lila Lee* and Dorothy Dalton. The rest of the year Jacqueline and her prize Great Dane from the Lina Basquette Kennels are to be found in Bedford Hills, New York. All of her time is devoted to what she feels are her civic duties: "I am concerned about the One Worlders and the Treason Traders who are disrupting the Constitution and selling us down the river. It isn't easy to be a patriotic dissenter. It helps to be a member of the John Birch Society."

Today a fighter for right-wing political causes. *Ing-John*

Doing her theme song from Dohnán-
yi's "Children's Suite," 1931. *NBC*

IREENE WICKER: "The Singing Lady"

The petite radio pioneer was born in Quincy, Illinois. She studied journalism, drama, and mythology at the Universities of Florida and Illinois. Thereafter she settled down in Chicago which at that time was the center of radio in the United States, and married a business executive. After having two children, a boy and a girl, Ireene went into radio.

She began her broadcasts for children over WGN in Chicago in 1931. In six months the program was picked up by the Blue Network. (At that time NBC had a Red and a Blue Network, the latter becoming ABC after the Justice Department forced the split.) Her first sponsor, and the one that stayed with her for many years, was Kellogg cereals. Someone in the company's advertising agency suggested that she have a title and they hit on "The Singing Lady." At that time in radio, titles were very popular. Many artists dropped theirs, such as Lanny Ross,* who was billed for a time as "The Troubadour of the Moon." Ireene, however, was as well known for her title as for her real name throughout all her years on radio.

Her name was originally spelled Irene, but when she was about to go into radio an astrologer told her that by adding an "e" she would reap great rewards.

A generation of children and many adults who refuse to admit it were mesmerized by the lady who told them of princes, dragons, Indians, and animals that spoke. Ireene took her material from the classics, folklore, history, and well-known fairy stories. They were usually instructive and had a moral, but were always beautifully told. More times than not the programs would contain portions which were sung by Miss Wicker. On the network for over twenty years, "The Singing Lady" won every major award in broadcasting, including the coveted Peabody Award.

Then in 1950 at the height of the McCarthy hysteria, a Right Wing newsletter ran an article stating that Ireene Wicker had once signed a petition sponsoring Benjamin Davis, a New York Communist politician. And in case that did not prove that "The Singing Lady" had been subverting the minds of American children for two decades, they accused Miss Wicker of having loaned her home in 1945 to aid the refugees of Spain who had fled Franco.

Ireene's lawyer obtained a court order to examine the petition in question which contained over thirty thousand names. Her name was not included. As for the Spanish refugees, what *Counterattack,* the publication that had brought the charges, neglected to mention when accusing her of aiding the Loyalist cause in Spain was the fact that her home was opened as a benefit for any child in or out of Spain who was in need. Lest there still be doubts, Miss Wicker's counsel reminded *Counterattack* that in 1939, at the time of the Hitler-Stalin Pact, she signed the necessary paper for her only son, Walter, to join the RCAF. The boy was underage and needed his parent's consent. He was killed in action in 1942.

The reply of the paper that had set out to rid the arts of subversives was: "*Counterattack* wishes to repeat that we did not call Miss Wicker or any other person mentioned in the report a Communist or a Communist sympathizer."

Suddenly, in spite of conclusive proof to the contrary, one of radio's most popular performers was "controversial." The TV show she had signed to do was canceled. Three years later she had another one on ABC television, but it did not last long.

Ireene divorced her first husband in 1936. Five years later she married the director and owner of one of the most successful and prestigious art galleries in the country, Victor Hammer. Her daughter is married and lives in Connecticut. The Hammers travel a great deal. In 1966 Ireene toured Asia and Europe. Much of their winters are spent in Palm Beach, Florida. They live in a palatial co-op on Fifth Avenue overlooking Central Park. It is filled with priceless art, and their toy poodle.

She does a program on Sunday mornings over WNYC in New York.

Beneath a $450,000 Renoir in her Manhattan apartment. *Diana Keyt*

In 1947, in *Out of the Blue*.

ANN DVORAK

Ann McKim (her real name) was born in New York City in 1912 to Anna Lehr, a well known stage actress of the time, and Sam McKim, then a director at the old Biograph Studios. Ann's early schooling was at St. Catherine's Convent in Manhattan. Later she attended Page School for Girls in Los Angeles. In 1920 her parents were divorced, and Ann stayed with her brother. It was fourteen years before she saw or heard from her father again. By that time she had changed her name to Dvorak, which was her mother's maiden name. (She had used Anna Lehr for a short time, but gave it up when she signed a contract with R.K.O.)

During an interview in 1934 Miss Dvorak said that she would like very much to see her father again, but had no idea where he was. She asked readers to send her any information they might have, resulting in six immediate replies from men claiming to be her father. A seventh letter turned out to be the real Sam McKim. He was living in Philadelphia, and seldom went to the movies.

Ann's first jobs in Hollywood were as a chorus girl in early musicals. For a while she was a dance coach at M-G-M. After Page School she had written, directed, and acted in a few plays, but her only ambition was to be an actress. Her friend Joan Crawford introduced her to Howard Hughes who was looking for a girl to play in his production of *Scarface* (1932). Hughes put her under contract at $250 a week. After the picture was made he sold her contract to Warner Brothers. At first she had no objection. Then while making *Three on a Match* she discovered that the child actor Buster Phelps was earning twice her salary. She demanded a raise, which was refused because they had paid Hughes a goodly profit on her contract. She had recently eloped with the British actor Leslie Fenton, and now they went to Europe together, leaving Warners to think it over. When she returned a year later, it was with a boost in salary and the respect of almost every contract player in Hollywood.

Whether it was revenge or just poor judgment, the studio either gave her bad parts or bad pictures, or both. In film after film either she was over-shadowed by superstars or saddled with a hopeless plot. Although Bette Davis' performances in the two films she made with Ann, *Three on a Match* (1932) and *Housewife* (1934), seem ludicrous today, Miss Davis came away with all the attention. Even her leading man, the late Paul Muni, in *Scarface* and *Dr. Socrates* (1935), seems dated on the TV "Late Show" while Ann's underplay-ing and controlled intensity prove her a far better actress than believed. She made believable lines that most actresses would have choked on in clinkers such as *Away to Love* (1933) with Maurice Chevalier and *Murder in the Clouds* (1934) with Lyle Talbot. She supported Jimmy Cagney in *The Crowd Roars* (1932) and *G-Men* (1935). Some of her other leading men were Dick Powell, Errol Flynn, David Manners,* Pat O'Brien, Rudy Vallee, Douglas Fairbanks, Jr., and the late Richard Barthelmess.

In 1940 Ann went to England to be near her husband, and stayed on in London through the blitz. While there she made *This Was Paris* (1942) with Ben Lyon, *Escape to Danger* (1944), and *Squadron Leader X* (1942). Ann was divorced in 1944, and returned to Hollywood. In 1947 she married dancer Igor de Navrotsky. The marriage ended in divorce four years later.

In 1948 Ann starred on Broadway in *The Respectful Prostitute,* which ran for 314 performances before it went on the road. Her postwar movies were not much better than those she made while under contract. In 1947 she was in *The Affairs of Bel Ami* and with Henry Fonda in *The Long Night.* Her screen career ended in 1951 with *I Was An American Spy* and *Secret of Convict Lake.*

With her third husband, architect Nicholas Wade, she changed her primary residence from Malibu to Honolulu in 1959. Her husband had planned to live in Italy where he had designed several theatres. (Ann agreed, providing they spend two weeks in Hawaii before deciding!) Much of their time is spent traveling in Europe and the Orient, with long stays in their Malibu house. The Wades have no children. They are avid bibliophiles, and have a large and very valuable collection of first editions dating back as far as 1703.

At home today.

One of Hollywood's top leading men in the forties.

DENNIS MORGAN

The Hollywood leading man of the 1940's was born in 1910 in Prentice, Wisconsin, of Swedish parents. He acted in Marshfield High School plays and sang in the Glee Club. While attending Carroll College in Waukeska, Wisconsin, he was a member of the football team. At both the Wisconsin Conservatory of Music in Milwaukee and the American Conservatory in Chicago he studied voice. During his Chicago days he roomed with another hopeful, John Carroll (who is involved in a construction company in Slidell, Louisiana).

Morgan's first break came when he got a job singing at the Palmer Hotel in Chicago. After that he was for a time a radio announcer on station WTMJ and did a couple of seasons in stock. While traveling with an operatic group, for which he sang *Faust* and *Carmen* he came to the attention of the late Mary Garden who arranged for him to have a screen test at Metro-Goldwyn-Mayer. He was placed under contract and sent to the Culver City lot.

For two years he did absolutely nothing, but continued to draw a very good salary. Finally, they decided to have him sing "A Pretty Girl Is Like a Melody" in the now famous finale of *The Great Ziegfeld* (1936). Dennis was amazed at the premiere when he saw himself on the screen mouthing words that another voice was singing. Without his knowledge the studio had Allan Jones's voice dubbed in.

Morgan left M-G-M and went to Paramount where he was usually cast as a heavy, wearing a mustache. He then went to Warner Brothers where he fared no better, although they did drop his real name, Stanley Morner, for Dennis Morgan. Some of his films were made under the name Richard Stanley. The Burbank studio put him into one "B" film after another until Sam Wood took a chance on him for *Kitty Foyle*.

Dennis had heard that the director was looking for someone to play the part of a society snob. When he went to see Wood at RKO, he was offered the part of the young intern but flatly refused to play anything but the rich boy. Finally he got the role and Warners agreed to loan him out for the picture.

It was a tremendous success and a great boost to his career. His co-star Ginger Rogers won an Academy Award for her performance in the title role in 1940.

He returned to his home lot in triumph and was rewarded with some plum roles in such movies as *God Is My Co-Pilot* (1945) and *My Wild Irish Rose* (1947). When he was not working on a picture he was making personal appearance tours in which he sang the songs from some of his films. His film credits include *Waterfront* (1939), *Bad Men of Missouri* (1941), *The Hard Way* (1942), a memorable feature with Ida Lupino and Joan Leslie,* *Captains of the Clouds* (1942), *Thank Your Lucky Stars* (1943), *Christmas in Connecticut* (1945) with Barbara Stanwyck, *My Wild Irish Rose* (1947), *To the Victor* (1948), and *The Lady Takes a Sailor* (1949) with Jane Wyman. Probably his best remembered role was as the Red Shadow in *The Desert Song* (1943) with Irene Manning (living in Los Altos Hills, California, with her husband, missile scientist Maxwell W. Hunter II).

He was teamed with Jack Carson in several films, notably *Two Guys From Milwaukee* (1946). They were close friends off the screen and remained so until Carson died in 1963. Morgan had tried to join the comedian's vaudeville act during his period in Chicago.

When his movie career seemed over in the 1950's Morgan did quite a lot of television work. He was seen on NBC's "Star Stage," CBS's "Stage 7," and ABC's "Crossroads." He played a prominent role in the TV version of "Stage Door." In 1960 he had his own series for a short time, "21 Beacon Street." From time to time over the past decade he has been seen in low budget feature films such as *Uranium Boom* (1956) and *Rogue's Gallery* (1967).

Morgan has been married for many years to his high school sweetheart, Lillian Vedder. Most of his time is taken up with his extensive business holdings. Always very astute on money matters, Dennis had his last Warner Brothers contract written so that he received a salary of $25,000 a year until 1966 rather than pay huge taxes for a few years during his heyday.

A successful businessman today. *Paramount Pictures*

"Painting the Clouds with Sunshine" from the part-color "talkie" *Gold Diggers of Broadway* (1929), also featuring Nick Lucas.

ANN PENNINGTON

"The Dimpled Doll of Broadway" was born in Wilmington, Delaware, in 1893. When she was still a child her father, an executive with the Victor Talking Machine Company, moved the family to Camden, New Jersey, where one of Ann's neighbors was a girl who became one of Broadway's greatest comediennes, Rae Dooley (who lives with her husband, actor-director Eddie Dowling, in East Hampton, Long Island).

The famous pouting smile was first flashed at audiences in *The Red Widow* in 1911. The next year she appeared in Chicago in *A Polish Wedding*. By 1913 "Penny," as her friends call her, was in the Ziegfeld Follies. Her long dark hair and big brown eyes were so effective the great showman signed her again for the *Follies of 1914*, which had as its stars W. C. Fields and Mae Murray. In 1916 Ann again was in Ziegfeld's famous revue along with Marion Davies and Fanny Brice, who became her best friend. When Brice's racketeer husband, Nick Arnstein (who lives in Los Angeles where he draws a check every week for the use of his name in *Funny Girl*), was in trouble Penny came to the rescue with $20,000 in jewels, which were hocked for bail money.

She starred briefly in *Miss 1917*, a musical that ran only forty-eight performances in spite of a score by Jerome Kern and Victor Herbert. Ann's rehearsal pianist was a young man named George Gershwin.

In 1918 Ann Pennington was back in the Follies sharing billing with Will Rogers, Marilyn Miller, and Eddie Cantor.

The deliciously cute little dancer found time to make a few movies for Famous Players. A couple were *Susie Snowflakes* (1916) and *Sunshine Nan* (1918).

Another Broadway impresario of the era, George White, induced Ann to star in his *Scandals of 1919*, and then again in 1920 and 1921. In 1932 she starred in *Jack and Jill*, but the following year was back with Flo Ziegfeld for his *Follies*. George White won her back and she showed her famous dimpled knees in the *Scandals* of 1926 and 1928.

In 1930 Ann was one of *The New Yorkers* along with Fred Waring, and Clayton, Jackson, and Durante. The following year she was seen on Broadway in two shows, *Broadway Personalities* and *Everybody's Welcome,* both less than a smash hit. Demand for her services had begun to wane. In 1936 she was seen in M-G-M's *The Great Ziegfeld* in a small part, in which she played herself.

By 1937 the girl who had been photographed by Steichen, praised by George Jean Nathan, and squired by Jack Dempsey was the headliner of a second rate Broadway nightclub known as the Paradise. Her next booking, the same year, advertised her act as a "striptease." Although what she did was a few of her old dance routines, Ann permitted the show to be promoted otherwise. The trade papers shook their heads sadly, but admitted that "Penny" was still quite a little hoofer.

George Jessel showcased Ann in his *Little Old New York* show at the 1939 World's Fair. After that she toured in 1942 in *Hellzapoppin* and *The Student Prince* in 1943. That was it.

Since her retirement the "Dimpled Doll" has tried living in Florida and Hollywood, but always ends up back in Manhattan. Always, in fact, in hotels smack in the middle of the theatre district. Unmarried, after many well publicized romances with well known men, Ann lives alone. Her pastime is horse racing and when they're running "Penny" can be found at the nearest track just about every day.

She was one of those stars as greatly loved by her profession as by her fans. Her punctuality and good disposition were nearly as legendary on the Great White Way as her legs. She no longer gives interviews: "I see my contemporaries on TV sometimes and I think 'but how could you?' We're so old now. Young people do not know us and it must depress those who remember. I'd rather be thought of as the way I used to be."

Someone once asked Ann Pennington what was her favorite thing that had been written for her. She replied that it wasn't a song or a skit, but a line— "Pay to the order of Ann Pennington."

The radiant smile is unchanged. *Jon Virzi*

In 1929, with Universal Pictures.

LAURA LA PLANTE

The blue-eyed blonde who was for a number of years the top female star on the Universal lot, was born in St. Louis, Missouri, in 1904. At fifteen she began playing bit parts in Christie Comedies. In 1920 she was given what seemed at the time to be her big break when she won the part of the daughter in the "Bringing Up Father" series. The only trouble was that the series flopped and Laura returned to walk-ons. Not until she played with Charles Ray in *The Old Swimmin' Hole* (1921) did the producers begin to take notice of her all-American good looks and flair for light comedy.

Most of her pictures were made during her long contract with Universal. At first they cast her as Tom Mix's leading lady and opposite William Desmond in his serials *Perils of the Yukon* (1922) and *Around the World in Eighteen Days* (1923).

What makes Laura's success tale so extraordinary is that at the time it was more desirable to be the exotic than it was to be the girl-next-door.

Her two most outstanding films were the spooky classic *The Cat and the Canary* (1927) and the part talkie *Show Boat* (1929), for which she dyed her hair brunette to play the role of Magnolia. Other films were *Smoldering Fires* (1924) with the late Pauline Frederick, *Teasers* (1925), *Silk Stocking* (1927), *Scandal* (1929), *The King of Jazz* (1930) with the late Paul Whiteman, and *Lonely Wives* (1931).

Why Laura La Plante did not continue long in talkies is a mystery. Her voice proved to be as pleasant as her appearance and *Show Boat* was a blockbuster. But in 1932 she went to Europe. In Riga, Latvia, Laura divorced her first husband, director William Seiter, whom she had married in 1926. (Seiter's widow, silent star Marion Nixon, lives in Beverly Hills.) Shortly after, she became the wife of producer Irving Asher in Paris. Their wedding was witnessed by New York City's ex-mayor Jimmy Walker and his wife, Betty Compton, on June 19, 1934.

The Ashers made their home in London for the next ten years and Laura did an occasional play there, but no films. After returning to Hollywood in the forties, Asher continued to produce motion pictures. They lived in Beverly Hills. The only hint of a movie comeback for her was in 1943 when Myrna Loy announced that she wanted out of her Metro-Goldwyn-Mayer contract. Laura was seriously considered for the role of Nora Charles in the *Thin Man* series. But she did not make a screen appearance until 1956 when she accepted the role of Betty Hutton's mother in *Spring Reunion*. Fans and critics alike agreed that the only thing wrong with her return was that she looked too young for the part. The same year teamed with silent star Aileen Pringle she debuted on television in a dramatization of a suffragette's race for the presidency of the United States at the turn of the century. It was called "She Also Ran" and was produced for "Bell Telephone Time."

In the past year the Ashers have spent nearly all their time in their home in Palm Desert, a resort community not far from Palm Springs. (Anna Q. Nilsson, the silent star, lives fairly nearby in the senior citizen project of Sun City.) Both their children were born in England. Tony, who is an executive with a Los Angeles advertising agency, finds time to write songs. One of his efforts hit the best seller charts around the country and was chosen by Broadcast Music, Inc. as one of their Ten Best of 1966. It was called "Wouldn't It Be Nice?" and was performed by the Beach Boys. His sister, Jill, is the assistant creative director at the same agency and is married to a lawyer. Laura is not yet a grandmother.

Laura swears that she does not miss making movies and has no plans at present for appearing in a new one. She likes living in the desert and is trying to adapt herself to sand blown in her house by thirty to forty mile per hour winds.

At her swimming pool in Palm Desert, California.

In 1930, with First National Pictures.

BILLIE DOVE

In New York City in 1903, one of the most beautiful ladies of the silent screen was born. Her name was Lillian Bohny. She was educated in private schools in Manhattan. When she was only fourteen James Montgomery Flagg sketched her, calling her one of the most beautiful girls in America. She did a great deal of modeling for artists and photographers and at fifteen was hired by Florenz Ziegfeld although she could neither sing nor dance. Ned Wayburn taught her the rudiments of being a showgirl. The showman paid her more than any of the other girls in his Midnight Revue on the Amsterdam Roof, just to sit in a hoop and dazzle everyone. She did little more in his production of *Sally* in 1921.

Cosmopolitan Studios gave her a bit part. She appeared briefly in *Get Rich Quick Wallingford* and *At the Stage Door*. She left for Hollywood and was replaced in Ziegfeld's roof show by Jacqueline Logan. Right away Billie landed a featured role in the Constance Talmadge* vehicle, *Polly of the Follies* (1922). Much of her early success has been attributed to Christie Cabanne who saw her potential as a leading lady.

Billie Dove was the first actress ever to receive a color screen test. It landed her the part opposite Douglas Fairbanks, Sr., in *The Black Pirate* (1926). She had "a peaches and cream complexion," which came over beautifully even in black and white.

From 1923 until 1929 the star was married to director Irving Willat. The marriage ended in divorce.

Along with those films in which she played Tom Mix's leading lady, Billie made *Country Girl* (1922), *All the Brothers Were Valiant* (1923), which was directed by her husband and co-starred Lon Chaney, *The Folly of Vanity* (1925), *The Lone Wolf Returns* (1926), *The Tender Hour* (1927) with Ben

168

Lyon as her co-star and George Fitzmaurice as director, *Heart of a Follies Girl* (1918), and *Her Private Life* (1929).

Billie's voice was passable and she was able to continue in pictures after sound arrived. Some of her early talkies were *A Night at Susies* (1930) with Douglas Fairbanks, Jr., *The Age for Love* (1931), which was produced by Howard Hughes, and *Cock of the Air* (1932) with Chester Morris.

In 1930 at a Hollywood party someone pointed out to Billie a young millionaire producer named Howard Hughes. Billie says the initial impression he made on her was that his clothes were very sloppy. At the time, Hughes was making headlines by spending millions of dollars on *Hell's Angels,* junking the first version and spending millions more on a second. Hughes was intrigued by the luscious star who, unlike most actresses at the party, had not thrown herself at him. He began to send her dozens of white roses and extravagant presents. Part of his courting was done in an airplane he flew himself. Finally the two began dating and within weeks were the talk of Hollywood. Hughes announced that he would produce her future films. Billie stated recently that she found him much too erratic to take seriously for a long period of time. At the height of their affair he would disappear for days without warning or explanation.

The girl whose Hollywood career really began with *Polly of the Follies* ended her years as an actress with *Blondie of the Follies* (1932), which starred Marion Davies and Robert Montgomery.

In 1933 Billie married multimillionaire Robert Kenaston. They live in a beautiful home in Pacific Palisades close to Zeppo Marx. Their children Robert Alan and adopted Gail are married. Billie's retirement upon her marriage was complete except for a small part in *Diamond Head* in 1962, in which she played a nurse.

Mrs. Billie Dove Kenaston in front of her California home. *Jon Virzi*

During a radio broadcast in the late thirties on NBC. *Metronome Magazine*

HORACE HEIDT

The popular orchestra leader of yesterday was born in Alameda, California, in 1901. For the first thirty years of his life nearly everything went wrong. His mother bought him a piano, but he hated to practice. While a student at the Culver Military Academy, he finally became interested in a musical career. He attempted to join the Culver Jazz Band but was rejected. The late "Red" Nichols auditioned also and made it.

While at the University of California, he promptly fractured his back during a football game and was told he was finished in that sport forever. While recuperating Horace heard Guy Lombardo on the radio and decided to form a group of his own.

Horace Heidt and his Musical Knights played one night stands at theatres and hotels up and down the West Coast. Between engagements Heidt worked in a real estate office and as a service station attendant. There were many "Knights" during those years since the orchestra had to be disbanded over and over due to a lack of bookings. Finally, they got a national tour for the Fanchon Marco circuit of theatres.

By 1930 Heidt and his men had arrived at the legendary Palace Theatre in Manhattan. The emcee was Ken Murray and although they were second to last on the bill, just playing the Palace was a big boost to Heidt's career. Next they went to Paris and the Riviera and rested on past laurels. When they returned the following year they had rehearsed so little that their second Palace engagement was a complete flop.

But Heidt hit his stride in radio. His first success in the medium came in 1932 with "Answers by the Dancers," a show of dance music mixed with informal interviews from the Drake Hotel in Chicago. Two years later he came up with "Treasure Chest," one of the first giveaway programs in which couples from the audience who were celebrating their wedding anniversary competed for prizes. In 1935 he changed the format to include couples who were about to be married and brides and grooms fresh from the altar. The title was changed to "Anniversary Night with Horace Heidt" and was so popular the National Broadcasting Company carried it on both their Red and Blue networks on Saturday nights. His "Pot o' Gold" show which began in 1938 was the first to give away large amounts of money and was an overnight sensation. The Musical Knights supplied the music and there were big-name guests, but the real appeal was the long-distance call to somebody somewhere in the United States who just might win the "Pot o' Gold." The gimmick worked so well that movie-theatre owners complained that it cut attendance. The movies grabbed the title and made a feature about it in 1941 starring Paulette Goddard* and James Stewart. Everyone thought it would go on forever, but the Federal Communications Commission declared it in violation of its rules and eventually forced it off the air.

Heidt started many successful careers. A few who admit that their association boosted them professionally are: Art Carney, Dick Contino, the King Sisters, Gordon MacRae, Al Hirt, Frankie Carle, and Alvino Rey.

Heidt utilized his knack for discovery on radio, television, and on the road in his "Youth Opportunity Program." Boys and girls with no experience whatever were given a chance not only to perform before an audience, but to act as stage manager, publicist, or advance man. Many of the top paid people in the entertainment industry today acknowledge the training they got as part of the company that toured the nation from 1948 until 1953.

In 1953 Horace decided to devote all of his time to the real estate holdings he had been acquiring in southern California during his lucrative years in show business. His twin boys, Jack and Jerry, are respectively: the youngest vice president in the history of California's Union Bank, and the operator of a real estate business in Los Angeles. Horace, Jr., is a student at Stanford University and Hildegard is studying art.

Heidt is the resident landlord of a 170-unit apartment complex in the San Fernando Valley, which has proved so profitable that he is planning others. His neighbors (among them silent stars Eva Novak and Chester Conklin*) like him so well that he is now mayor of Van Nuys, California.

His Honor the Mayor beside a miniature Van Nuys Street.

As a cavalry officer in 1937.

JOHN BOLES

The popular leading man of the 1930's was born into an old southern family in Greenville, Texas, in 1900. His father was a prosperous banker and cotton broker. John went to the University of Texas with the intention of studying medicine, but performed in student theatrical productions.

John, who was something of a linguist, shipped out to France in 1914 as a volunteer with United States Intelligence, returning as a lieutenant. While in France he had become seriously interested in show business. After singing at the Y.M.C.A. canteen, several ranking officers suggested that he try it for a living. He returned to Texas briefly after the war but left for Paris where he studied with Jean de Reszki and Oscar Seagle.

When he came back to the United States he lived in Manhattan, and supported himself by giving French lessons at a girls' school. Every extra penny went to vocal lessons.

His first show was *Moonlight* which opened at the Longacre Theatre in 1923, followed with *Little Jessie James* (1923) with Miriam Hopkins. He also played opposite the late Gerald Farrar in the diva's only operetta. Another of his Broadway efforts was *Mercenary Mary* in 1925.

While appearing in *Kitty's Kisses* (1926) he caught the attention of the superstar of the silents, Gloria Swanson. She was looking for a leading man to play opposite her in *The Love of Sunya*. The movie was made at the old Cosmopolitan Studios on Manhattan's 122nd Street. On March 12, 1927, his was the first feature to play at the famous Roxy Theatre. For a decade afterward John Boles was one of the most popular leading men in motion pictures.

Boles had several very advantageous qualities. He was not a pretty boy so that men didn't resent him, and women found him believable and attractive. He was a reliable and untemperamental actor and could play a well-bred, intelligent man without appearing to be a stuffed shirt. When talkies came in he was more popular than ever, since many silent stars could not speak very well, much less sing like him. Musicals were definitely the thing and John played opposite Bebe Daniels* in *Rio Rita,* the picture that reactivated her career in 1929. The following year he introduced the song "It Happened in Monterey" in the lavish *King of Jazz,* and starred in the first sound version of *The Desert Song* (1929).

Female stars of the time loved working with a man whose ego would not clash with theirs. Some of the ladies who requested his services in their films were Barbara Stanwyck, Kay Francis, Joan Bennett, Lillian Harvey, Loretta Young, Rosalind Russell, Irene Dunne,* and Vivienne Segal.

John made many pictures during the thirties. A few examples of his best work are *Back Street* (1932), *Age of Innocence* (1934), *Music in the Air* (1934) with Gloria Swanson and the late Douglass Montgomery, *Craig's Wife* (1936), *Child of Manhattan* (1933) with the late Nancy Carroll, *A Message to Garcia* (1936), and the classic *Stella Dallas* (1937).

By the 1940's he was reduced to working for Monogram in such low-quality films as *Boy of Mine* (1941) and *Between Us Girls* (1942).

He did some stage work after the movies had no roles for him. In 1940 he starred in a revival of *Show Boat* in Los Angeles with Guy Kibbee, Helen Morgan, Norma Terris, and Paul Robeson. His return to Broadway in 1943 as Mary Martin's leading man in *One Touch of Venus* was a great success. His stage presence and voice were far from rusty. In the presentation houses he sang such favorites as "The Desert Song," "Waiting at the Gate for Katie," and "Rio Rita." In 1950 he was Gertrude Niesen's leading man in *Gentlemen Prefer Blondes* in Los Angeles and other cities. His last film was *Babes in Bagdad* (1952) which he made with Paulette Goddard.*

He has been married for the past forty years to the former Marceline Dobbs. They have two grown daughters, Frances Marceline and Janet. Although he does not have much interest in working anymore, he is still represented by the William Morris Agency.

The Boles divide their time between their homes in Los Angeles and Texas. The money he made during the thirties and forties was wisely invested in real estate which has made him a very rich man. John has one of the largest collections of swing music in Hollywood.

A distinguished realtor today. *Jon Virzi*

The original "It" girl at the height of her fame.

AILEEN PRINGLE

The original "It" girl of the silent screen was born to well-to-do parents in San Francisco in 1895. Under her real name, Bisbee, she attended Miss Murison's School in her native city, Madames of the Sacred Heart in Paris, and the McKenzie School in London. While in England she met and married Sir Charles Pringle who sometime later became Governor General of the Bahamas. Against the wishes of her husband and parents she debuted in the West End in *The Bracelet* in 1915. George Arliss saw her and later gave her a role in his play *The Green Goddess* on Broadway. Aileen made films long before she landed a Hollywood contract in 1922. As far back as 1920 she appeared in a movie called *Honor Bound,* made on a low budget in Fort Lauderdale, Florida, with an unknown mustached Italian actor named Rudolph Valentino.

Elinor Glyn, author of the popular Ruthenian romantic novels of the time, was asked who in America possessed the quality she had defined in her book *It.* She replied: "Antonio Moreno, Aileen Pringle, and Rex the Wonder Horse." While Aileen did not do *It* and Clara Bow capitalized on the publicity from the picture, it was she who was chosen by Miss Glyn to portray the Queen opposite Conrad Nagel (who lives on Manhattan's West Fifty-seventh Street) in *Three Weeks* (1924). The same year she and John Gilbert starred in another Glyn epic *His Hour.* Some other Pringle silents were *Souls For Sale* (1923), *The Christian* (1923), *Soul Mates* (1926), *Tea For Three* (1927), *Beau Broadway* (1928), and *A Single Man* (1929).

Aileen and her husband agreed to a very friendly separation after her decision to become an actress. Although they were not divorced for over twenty years, they never again lived together. Her only other marriage, to writer James Cain, in the forties, lasted eleven months.

Another of her titles was the "Darling of the Intelligentsia," and it was not always bestowed as a compliment. Aileen saw far more of writers than stars and her parties were attended by such names as H. L. Mencken, who was one of her more serious admirers, Joseph Hergesheimer, and Rupert Hughes. Until his death in 1966 her closest friend was Carl Van Vechten, author of *Nigger*

Heaven. She told all who would listen that she found the Hollywood intellectual climate suffocating and the natural climate boring, she thought little of Hollywood movies and the shop girls and merchants who starred in and produced them. The studio publicity department called her "highly uncooperative." She found Irving Thalberg "sneaky" and many of the other powers at M-G-M "vulgar." Aileen Pringle's career was ruined not by the advent of sound or bad pictures but by herself. Hedda Hopper thought the only explanation was her behavior. She could and should have been a major talkie star. Her voice was excellent and chic middle-aged stars such as Ruth Chatterton and Ina Claire were all the rage in the thirties. Instead Aileen continued for the whole decade making one atrocious picture after another. Her series with Lew Cody at M-G-M was bad but nothing to compare with her later sound films such as *Are These Our Children* (1931), *Piccadilly Jim* (1936), *Thanks for Listening* (1937) with Pinky Tomlin, and *John Meade's Woman* (1937), in which her part consisted of being pushed into a swimming pool while wearing an evening gown. Its star, Francine Larrimore, lives a few blocks away from Aileen today.

Although she says she wants to act again, her attitude has changed very little. Since her last film she has not worked professionally, though in 1959 she was asked to read for a part in the William Inge play, *A Loss of Roses.* When told that they were looking for a Nita Naldi type she asked them why they didn't simply hire Nita Naldi, who was living at the time.

After the death of her mother fifteen years ago, Aileen moved from her large Spanish house in Santa Monica, close to silent star Mary Miles Minter, to a small apartment in Manhattan on East Fifty-seventh Street.

She is still a sophisticated, beautifully dressed woman. She reads a great deal, sees most of the plays and movies, and is very active socially when her back, which has for years been a source of great pain to her, is well. One of her areas of knowledge is food. She is a superb cook and considers herself a gourmet. Many a waiter has been startled to hear the former star order her own meal and that of her male escort who "had no palate."

In Manhattan recently. *Jon Virzi*

Her voice and diction helped make her a star in her first "talkie," *The Awful Truth,* in 1929.

INA CLAIRE

When people complain that the theatre is not what it used to be they usually mean that there are no Ina Claire vehicles or Ina Claires around to act in them.

The actress, who was throughout her career the epitome of the well-heeled, well-bred woman, was born Ina Fagan in Washington, D.C., in 1895. With her mother as a chaperone she debuted in vaudeville at the age of twelve. In 1909 she opened in New York with an impersonation of the great Scottish entertainer, Sir Harry Lauder, that brought the house down. It also brought a lot of attention to the svelt teen-ager by producers of legitimate shows. In 1911 Ina appeared in *Jumping Jupiter* on Broadway and followed it with *The Quaker Girl.* In 1913 she starred in the London company of the Broadway smash *The Girl from Utah.* She played the part that had been originated by Julia Sanderson (Frank Crummit, Julia's husband and co-star, is dead, and Julia lives quietly in a Springfield, Massachusetts, hotel, gives no interviews, and permits no photographs).

Flo Ziegfeld featured Ina in his *Follies of* 1915 and 1916, but it was her role in *Polly With a Past* in 1917 that firmly established Ina Claire as one of the brightest comediennes in the country.

In 1919 she married critic James Whittaker, and had enormous success that same year in *The Gold-Diggers.* Ina and Whittaker were divorced in 1925.

Some of the drawing-room comedy-drama plays in which she dazzled audiences were: *Bluebeard's Eighth Wife* (1921), *The Awful Truth* (1922), *Grounds for Divorce* (1924), and *The Last of Mrs. Cheyney* (1925).

No one ever delivered a witty line on stage better than Ina Claire, but, unlike most actresses, when the occasion arose for a retort she did not need a playwright around to give her dialogue. During her brief (from 1929 to 1931) marriage to the silent screen idol, John Gilbert, a reporter asked her how it felt being married to a celebrity. "Why don't you ask my husband?" was Mrs. Gilbert's reply.

In 1929 she joined the parade of stage stars to Hollywood to replace the many silent stars whose voices made them unsuitable for sound pictures. She clicked right from the beginning and enjoyed great success in *Rebound* (1931), *Royal Family of Broadway* (1931), and *The Greeks Had a Name for It* (1932). But the stage remained Ina's first love and when S. N. Behrman wrote *Biography* (1932) for her she rushed back to the great White Way and her greatest triumph. Throughout the thirties she was seen in such plays as *End of Summer* (1936) with Osgood Perkins, father of the actor Tony Perkins, and *Once is Enough* (1938). Her two final pictures were *Ninotchka* (1939), in which she held her own with Great Garbo, and *Claudia* (1943) with Olga Baclanova.

After her marriage in 1939 to attorney William R. Wallace, Ina grew less and less interested in working. She did *The Fatal Weakness* on Broadway in 1946, but her kind of parts were simply not being written or at least produced.

Ina Claire is best remembered as the beautifully groomed sophisticate men desired and women envied. Year after year her name appeared on the "Ten Best Dressed" list.

If it was Ina Claire's intention to retire on a hit she did very well for herself. In 1954 she bid adieu to Broadway after a highly successful run in T. S. Eliot's *The Confidential Clerk*. One critic called her "a line drawing of the Twenties . . . delectable beyond belief."

For a while the Wallaces maintained a huge estate in Hillsborough, near San Francisco. Several years ago they gave it up and moved to an apartment on Nob Hill where Ina holds court to California society and a smattering of her old friends from the theatre. The lady who introduced the shingle bob hairdo to American women in 1929 as well as many clothing styles is equally imaginative in the decor of her home. Friends who have visited with her say that the flat on Sacramento Street could easily serve as the setting for one of Ina's urbane comedies.

She will not read scripts or discuss her career with reporters. The life of a matron seems to suit the former star very nicely. From outward appearances Ina Claire is very happy. If she has any problems at all they are certain to be elegant ones.

Still *soignée,* at a recent display of theatrical memorabilia in San Francisco. *San Francisco Chronicle*

All sweetness and light, the early thirties.

JANET GAYNOR

The actress who won the first Academy Award for Best Actress was born Laura Gainor in Philadelphia, Pennsylvania, in 1906. Her early years were spent in the city of brotherly love and Melbourne, Florida. By the time she was old enough to attend high school her family had moved to San Francisco.

After graduation in 1924 Janet pestered her mother and stepfather until they brought her to Hollywood. At first she worked as an extra in shorts and westerns. Then Winifield R. Sheenan gave her a contract with Fox Studios. Her first feature was *The Johnstown Flood* (1926), in which she played a very sweet little country girl beset by a number of tragedies but always brave, true, and, of course, pretty. This was essentially the character she played throughout her career in films.

On the night of May 16, 1929, at a dinner in the Hollywood Roosevelt Hotel, Janet received the first Oscar in history. The practice at the time was to give awards for several rather than just one performance. Her statuette was for her roles in *Sunrise* (1927), *Seventh Heaven* (1927), co-starring Charles Farrell, and *Street Angel* (1928).

When she wed attorney Lydell Peck in 1932 the couple was flooded with fan mail telling them that their marriage could not possibly work out, and urging Janet to wait until Charles Farrell's marriage to silent star Virginia Valli broke up, which they felt was unavoidable. The Pecks were divorced in 1934. The Farrells are still together.

Janet made such tear-jerkers as *Adorable* (1933), *Paddy, the Next Best Thing* (1933), *Change of Heart* (1934), *Carolina* (1934) with Lionel Barrymore and Warner Baxter, *Servant's Entrance* (1934) with Lew Ayres, *The Farmer Takes a Wife* (1935) with Henry Fonda, and *Small Town Girl* (1936) with Robert Taylor. One of her best talkies was *State Fair* (1933) with Will Rogers and Stepin Fetchit.*

David O. Selznick cast her in *A Star Is Born* opposite Fredric March. It was a smashing success that gave her another Oscar nomination in 1937, and it still holds up as one of the best pictures of its kind ever made. The musical version with Judy Garland made years later suffered greatly by comparison.

In 1938 after completion of *Young in Heart,* which along with *Seventh Heaven* is her favorite film, Janet announced that she was retiring from motion pictures. A year later she married Gilbert Adrian, Hollywood's most famous and successful designer. Their son, Robin, was born in 1940. Much of her time in retirement was spent with her husband on their two-hundred-acre ranch in Brazil.

In 1951 she and Farrell were co-starred once again in *Seventh Heaven* over Lux Radio Theatre. Two years later she appeared on a segment of TV's "Medallion Theatre" in a soap opera plot called "Dear Cynthia." Later in the 1950's she did a few more TV programs such as "General Electric Theatre" and "Robert Montgomery Presents." Her last movie was *Bernardine* (1957), which was Pat Boone's film debut. After Adrian died in 1959 Janet appeared on Broadway for a short time in the play *Midnight Sun.* It was unsuccessful and after that, rather than return to the Brazilian ranch she found "desolate now," she did a great deal of traveling.

In 1964 at the age of fifty-eight Janet Gaynor married Paul Gregory, a producer many years her junior, with whom she had been partners in several of his plays. Although Gregory is active in Hollywood, Janet denies any plans for a comeback either in television or motion pictures. Her demure manner on celluloid hid her true nature as an astute businesswoman. The year before her retirement she made $252,583, which made her the highest paid actress in Hollywood at the time. She admitted to having saved over $1,000,000.

Still active on the Hollywood social scene. *Jon Virzi*

Crooning in 1946.

DICK HAYMES

The troubled troubadour of the forties was born in the Argentine in 1918 to a cattle rancher of Scotch-Irish descent and an American girl who after running away from her Santa Barbara home had toured Europe as a singer and dancer. After his parents separated in the twenties, Dick went to school in Switzerland part of the year and spent the other part with his mother Marguerite who ran a dress shop in Rio de Janeiro. In his late teens they lived in Paris and London for a few years before Dick came to Hollywood in the thirties. His first trip to the movie capital was during his summer vacation from Loyola University in Montreal. After his band, The Katzenjammers, failed he joined Johnny Johnston's band as a vocalist at $25 a week. He also did short stints with the Bunny Berrigan, Harry James, and Tommy Dorsey orchestras. His top salary during that period was $50 a week. He sang on radio, did one-night stands, and worked as an extra in westerns to earn a living. In 1938 he had a small part in *Dramatic School* which starred Luise Rainer.*

It was not until 1943 that Dick Haymes hit the big time. Bookers and agents knew him by a growing reputation for a smooth, romantic delivery of love ballads, but the public had hardly heard of him when someone took a chance and showcased him in Manhattan's Martinique. It was the time of the crooners and Dick was one of the very best. The recording companies offered him their best songs. Twentieth Century-Fox signed him to a fat contract. His recordings of "Little White Lies" sold 2,250,000 copies. A Frank Sinatra disc has yet to achieve a million sale.

Hollywood was churning out big, colorful musicals and Dick clicked from the very beginning. His handsome features and "dreamy" voice were featured in *DuBarry Was A Lady* (1943), *Irish Eyes Are Smiling* (1944) with June Haver (who is retired in the San Fernando Valley with her husband, Fred MacMurray), *Diamond Horseshoe* (1945) with Betty Grable, *Do You Love Me?* (1946) with Jeanne Crain (who lives in Newport Beach, California, with her husband Paul Brinkman and her six children), *One Touch of Venus*

(1948), and *Up in Central Park* (1948) with Deanna Durbin, and *St. Benny the Dip* (1951). Dick's greatest hit was *State Fair* (1945), the only musical Rodgers and Hammerstein ever wrote for the screen. In it he introduced two songs which have become standards, "That's For Me" and "It Might as Well Be Spring."

His studio built a "boy next door" image for him. He had all the things at the time associated with movie stars: a pretty wife (Joanne Dru) who was also an actress, a private plane, several cars, his own radio program, and screaming teen-age girls following him wherever he went. He experienced his first bad publicity when it was revealed that he had avoided the draft by claiming an exemption as a citizen of a neutral country. He thereby forfeited his right to become a United States citizen. His first wife Edith Harper had their marriage annulled in 1938 after a few weeks. Following his split up with Joanne Dru, Dick married Nora Eddington who was previously married to Errol Flynn. In 1953 Dick married Rita Hayworth, and was nearly deported when he followed "The Love Goddess" to Hawaii without permission from the immigration people. Mrs. Haymes number 5 was Frances Makris who was followed by singer Fran Jeffries. Dick nearly made a comeback in nightclubs with Miss Jeffries. His reviews were excellent but about the time the bookings started, the marriage began to disintegrate. She married his best friend, director Richard Quine. Although Dick and Fran, by whom he has a daughter, keep in touch, Quine and Dick have not spoken since the divorce.

In 1960 with debts of nearly $500,000 Haymes declared bankruptcy. His last movie was *All Ashore* in 1953. During his marriage to Rita Hayworth their furniture was repossessed for nonpayment and their landlord sued him. In 1964 he moved to Ireland and became a citizen shortly thereafter. He and his seventh wife, model Wendy Smith, keep a small apartment in a London suburb but spend most of their time in Dublin when Dick is not on tour playing clubs in Africa, England, and Australia.

With Mrs. Haymes at their London wedding reception. *London Daily Express*

181

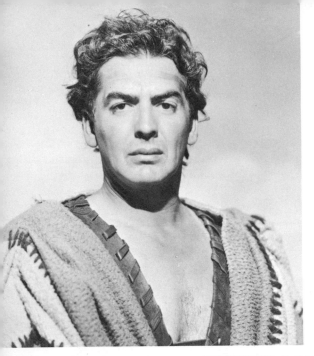

In *Samson and Delilah* (1949), under Cecil B. De Mille's direction.

VICTOR MATURE

The most famous Hollywood glamour boy of the early forties was an only child, born in 1916 in Louisville, Kentucky, of immigrant parents. His mother was French; his father, a scissors grinder, Austrian. He was wild and rebellious as a youth, quitting school at the age of fifteen. For a number of years he worked at various jobs, his most successful being a candy salesman. Later he ran a restaurant, lost $600 and sold out and headed for Hollywood.

He was twenty years old when he arrived. Supporting himself with such odd jobs as lawn mowing and dish washing, he started out in small roles at the Pasadena Playhouse, gradually rose to leads, doing some 150 parts in all. Then, in 1939, Frank Ross, vice-president of the Hal Roach Studios at the time, saw him in the Ben Hecht play *To Quito and Back* and signed him to a seven-year contract with options. His first screen appearance was in the small role of a gangster in *The Housekeeper's Daughter* (1939) starring Joan Bennett. Thirty thousand fan letters poured into the studio after his debut, and he was given the leads in *One Million B.C.* and *Captain Caution*. That same year, 1940, saw him in *No, No Nanette,* starring Anna Neagle.

In 1940, he accepted the role of the "hunk of man" in *Lady in the Dark,* starring Gertrude Lawrence. (The play was to catapult another comparative unknown to stardom, Danny Kaye.)

He appeared in *The Shanghai Gesture* (1941) playing Dr. Omar, chief aid to Madame Gin Sling—The Hayes' Office substitute for Madame Goddamn. Ona Munson played the nefarious Madame. Also in the cast were Gene Tierney and Walter Huston. With his Broadway success, his salary was upped from $450 to $1,750 per week. Later he did *I Wake Up Screaming* with Betty Grable and *My Gal Sal* with Rita Hayworth, both for Twentieth Century-Fox, who by then had bought up half his contract.

In 1942, he surprised all by joining the Coast Guard, seeing fourteen months of active duty before he was put into the branch's revue, *Tars and Spars,* which played film-vaudeville houses across the country. He was to spend almost four years in the Coast Guard.

After the war Fox signed him to a new contract giving him $3,000 a week. This was the period of his best films: John Ford's *My Darling Clementine* (1946), in which he played Doc Holliday to Henry Fonda's Wyatt Earp, *Kiss of Death* (1947) with Richard Widmark (making an auspicious film debut), and *The Cry of the City* (1948).

In 1949 De Mille borrowed him for *Samson and Delilah,* co-starring Hedy Lamarr. Other super productions came in 1953 when he did *The Robe,* and *Demétrius and the Gladiators* (1954). (Both were produced by Frank Ross.)

When his contract with Fox expired in 1954, Mature free-lanced, making adventure pictures—*Shark-fighters, Zarak*—and substandard spectacles—*The Tartars* and *Hannibal.* Usually made abroad, they were on a salary-percentage basis (as was indeed his TV series, *The Big Circus,* of which, in addition to his salary of $175,000, he owned 10 percent), and despite their poor quality he made a lot of money. Mature's last screen appearance was *After the Fox* (1966), playing an egotistical middle-age movie star reduced to playing in cheap Italian spectacles. He was never better. His income must have afforded him all the satisfaction he needed, for he never really took his career seriously.

The Beefcake King now lives on a ranch near San Diego, with his fourth wife, Britisher Joy Urwick (twenty years his junior) whom he married in 1959. Mature plays golf and lives like a country gentleman, going to Hollywood only on business (he has varied interests in real estate and such things) and to visit friends. "I had a ball there when I was younger—but what do I want with it now?" he says. "I guess I've grown up."

On a recent visit to Italy. *United Artists*

In the silent version of *Romeo and Juliet*.

BEVERLY BAYNE

The distaff side of the screen's first "love team" was born Beverly Pearl Bain in Minneapolis, Minesota, in 1895. At the age of eight her family moved to Chicago. She was in her third week as a freshman at Hyde Park High School when she and a friend, Grace Taylor, decided to visit the Essanay Studios. Chicago was then the center of motion picture production and the girls were intrigued with the glamour of the new medium. A director was struck with her dark beauty and offered her a role in *The Loan Shark* (1912). Her friend, a blonde, got nothing more than a tour since in the early stages of moving pictures blondes did not photograph well. The cameras made everyone look older, so leading ladies were nearly always in their teens. Asked about her salary requirements, Beverly, who was at the time receiving a weekly allowance of 25¢ said, "How about $35 or maybe $30, but at least $25." She was paid $25 at first, then raised to $35 and within six months was making $350.

Beverly starred in over 500 movies before she retired. Many were one and two reelers. She was teamed with another Essanay player, Francis X. Bushman. They were an immediate success and continued for several years as a team. Although they were married in 1918 it was kept secret from the public. At that time any star who was known to be married was washed up as a romantic actor. They starred together in such photoplays as *Under Royal Patronage* (1914), *One Wonderful Night* (1914), *The Diplomat Service* (1916), and *Social Quicksands* (1918). One of their starrers, *Ladies' World* (1911) had a young lady named Gloria Swanson who was later signed by Essanay. Their greatest triumph was the first movie version of *Romeo and Juliet* (1916) which made them superstars. The duo commanded huge salaries and formed their own company, Quality Pictures. When Louis B. Mayer headed Metro Pictures he induced them to star in a serial *The Great Secret* (1917), paying them $15,000, a colossal sum at the time. After their marriage was revealed, Bushman's career continued (he had been married once before), but Beverly spent more time at home.

The Bushman-Bayne marriage ended in a bitter divorce in 1924. They had one son, Richard Stanbury Bushman. Neither the wife nor the son ever saw or heard from the actor thereafter. In 1941 the son had his name changed legally to Richard Bayne. The father died in 1966, the son, in 1967.

Beverly Bayne made movies after her divorce but never again was a star of the magnitude she achieved with Bushman. In 1925 she was seen in *Graustark*. She did very well on the vaudeville circuits during the twenties, touring mostly for Keith-Orpheum, and in 1927 she starred in *The Road to Rome* on stage which she followed with *Once in a Lifetime* (1931), *As Husbands Go* (1932), and *The Shining Hour* (1934). Her last movie was *Seven Keys to Baldpate* in 1935 with Gene Raymond. In the thirties she also did some radio work and magazine writing on diets and beauty aids.

In 1942 she portrayed Phyllis Thaxter's mother in *Claudia* in the Chicago company. In 1946 she and Jean Parker were seen in the short-lived play *Loco* on Broadway.

Her second husband Charles Hvass, a New York manufacturer of road-building equipment, whom she married in 1937, died in 1953, and she has not remarried.

In 1956 Beverly and her son, who had never married, moved from their home in Pleasantville, New York, to Scottsdale, Arizona, which she always refers to as "The West's most Western Town." She lives there alone today near her long-time friend, Reta Berry, the widow of Wallace Berry, whom she knew fifty years ago at the Essanay Studios. Beverly travels occasionally to Hollywood where she visits with Mary Pickford and Buddy Rogers at Pickfair and to Florida to see her old friend, Olga Petrova, who lives in Clearwater. Another Floridian, one of the screen's earliest Tarzans, is Gene Polar, a resident of Hollywood.

After the death of her son Beverly seriously considered a return to the stage or a try at television, but she claims that she just cannot bring herself to leave Scottsdale.

Two former silent stars meet in Florida: Olga Petrova (left) and Beverly Bayne. *Clearwater Sun*

In a 1928 publicity shot.

CLAIRE WINDSOR

In an era when it was taboo for film stars to be married the blonde actress featured her infant son in most of her publicity.

She was born in 1897 in Cawker City, Kansas, and educated at schools in Topeka and Seattle. After a year of marriage to William Bowes, Claire left him and moved to Los Angeles, where, to support her little boy, she took a job at $5 a day as an extra at Lasky Studios. She considered herself very lucky if the casting director used her three days a week.

She was introduced one day to Lois Weber. The female producer-director-writer was at that time, in 1920, one of the most respected star-makers in Hollywood. She was looking for a girl like Claire for *What Do Men Want?* When rushes of her proved successful, Claire was offered a contract for $150 a week for the first year with a raise to $350 for the second.

Her name was changed from Clara Viola Cronk to Claire Windsor. "They called me Claire," says Miss Windsor, "because I was so fair, and Windsor because I was patrician."

In 1922 Claire was chosen as a Wampas Baby Star, roughly equivalent to our Deb Star Ball of today.

Claire worked for nearly every major lot until the end of the silent era. Going from First National to Tiffany, Fox, M-G-M, Paramount, Universal, and Goldwyn, she made such movies as *The Blot* (1921) opposite the late Louis Calhern, and in a great boost to her career teamed with one of the leading male actors of the time, Bert Lytell, imported from Broadway where he was already well established as a star, in *Born Rich* (1924), which had Doris Kenyon (retired and living in Beverly Hills) in the cast. She then made *Souls for Sables* (1925), *Money Talks* (1926) with the late Owen Moore, *Dance Madness* (1926), *The Claw* (1927), and *Bugle Call* (1927) with the top child star of the day, Jackie Coogan (who makes an occasional TV appearance and lives in the San Fernando Valley).

In 1925 Claire Windsor and Bert Lytell were married. The liaison lasted two years. (Lytell died in 1954. He had been the Shepherd of the Lambs Club and President Emeritus of Actors Equity.) Claire was one of the many silent stars who could not make the transition from silents to sound, and after her divorce, she made several attempts at a comeback in the new cinema, but they were hardly first class efforts. Mayfair Pictures released *Sister to Judas* (1933), in which she played with John Harron. The following year she and Johnny Mack Brown made *Cross Streets* for Invincible.

Most of the former star's money is invested in Los Angeles real estate. She lives in one of her own apartment buildings on Orange Drive in the heart of Hollywood. Claire has never remarried and claims she does not wish to work again. Having visited movie and TV sets in the past years she feels that the tension is much greater than in her day. Her son, Bill, works in the planning department of the Douglas Aircraft Company in Santa Monica.

She says, "I am very busy with creating oil paintings and designing my own clothes, which I also make."

In 1966 the star who has lived quietly for so long was again in the news when Lita Grey published one of the most tasteless tomes in the annals of Hollywood, *My Life With Chaplin*. She named Claire Windsor as one of her former husband's women. Miss Windsor's reply to the insinuation was "I have not read Lita Grey's book. Had she asked me I would have told her that I thought Chaplin was a great artist. He helped to start my career by taking me out about four or five times, which gave me nice publicity. I doubt I will ever read it. I'm too busy."

At an interview with the author.
Clifford May

With "Asta" and Myrna Loy in *Another Thin Man*, 1939.

WILLIAM POWELL

Myrna Loy's celluloid husband was born William Horatio Powell in Pittsburgh, Pennsylvania, in 1892.

After receiving many compliments for his performance in a Christmas school play Powell was hooked on acting. Thanks to money lent him by a wealthy aunt he was able to go to the American Academy of Dramatic Art in New York City, where his classmates were Edward G. Robinson and the late Joseph Schildkraut.

From 1912 until 1916 he appeared on Broadway and in touring companies in such plays as *The Ne'er Do Well* and *Within the Law*. During the long run of the latter he met and married a member of the cast, Eileen Wilson, in 1915. They were divorced in 1931. He had a full year's run in the musical *Going Up* in 1917, which was followed by several flops and then a season in stock. When Samuel Goldwyn offered him a part in *Sherlock Holmes* (1922), Powell was delighted at the chance to play with the great John Barrymore, who had the title role, and Carol Dempster.

In 1923 William was with Jetta Goudal in *The Bright Shawl*. In most of his silent films, as during his stage career, Powell was cast as the heavy. Some of those he menaced were the late Clara Bow in *My Lady's Lips* (1925), Lois Wilson (Gloria Swanson's closest friend and a Manhattan resident) in *The Great Gatsby* (1926), Evelyn Brent in *Love's Greatest Mistake* (1927), and Doris Kenyon in *Interference* (1928).

His years on the stage had given Powell a fine, distinctive voice which was put to good use in early sound pictures, delivering retorts and wisecracks as a detective or an attorney. It was his portrayal of Philo Vance in *The Canary Murder Case* (1929) with Louise Brooks (unmarried and living in Rochester, New York) that set his new image of the dapper and very clever gentleman. While making *Man of the World* (1931) with Wynne Gibson he met and married Carole Lombard. They were divorced two years later.

Evelyn Knapp (now Mrs. Snyder of Beverly Hills) was his leading lady in

High Pressure (1932). Gangster John Dillinger came out of hiding to see Powell and Myrna Loy in *Manhattan Melodrama* (1934) and was shot down by federal agents outside the theatre. The same year Powell was teamed with Myrna Loy in *The Thin Man,* which earned him a nomination for an Oscar— five more Nick and Nora Charles pictures were to follow and six others in which Powell and Loy were co-starred. She was Mrs. Charles in all the *Thin Man* pictures but one, which he made with the late Elissa Landi. Many of their fans believed they were actually husband and wife, or at least in love. They were and still are good friends.

The real love of Powell's life in those days was Jean Harlow, whose untimely death in 1937 sent him into a long period of deep depression. They made *Libelled Lady* together in 1936.

Powell portrayed Flo Ziegfeld in *The Great Ziegfeld* (1936), for which he received another Oscar nomination and in *Ziegfeld Follies* (1946). In between there were: *My Man Godfrey* (1936), *The Baroness and the Butler* (1938), *I Love You Again* (1940) with Edmund Lowe (for some time now a patient at the Motion Picture Country Hospital), and *The Youngest Profession* (1943). In 1947 he received his third Academy Award nomination for his brilliant performance as Clarence Day in *Life with Father.* The same year he co-starred with Ella Raines (the wife of Major Robin Olds, head of the Air Force Academy in Colorado) in *The Senator Was Indiscreet.* Then he made *Mr. Peabody and the Mermaid* (1948) and *How to Marry a Millionaire* (1953). His last film and one of his best was *Mr. Roberts* (1955), in which he played the ship's doctor.

Since 1940 Powell has been married to Diana Lewis, a former actress. Although he hates to stir from his beautiful home in Palm Springs, a good part in a picture would get him back to Hollywood. He certainly does not have to work as the money he made during the era of low taxes was well invested. Powell has an only child William, Jr., by his first wife. A number of years ago the actor successfully underwent a series of serious and delicate operations for cancer.

In Palm Springs. *Jon Virzi*

In 1933, a weekly feature on the "Eddie Cantor Show." *NBC*

RUBINOFF

The man who was once the best known violinist in America was born in Grodno, Russia, in 1896. At the age of five he was playing the balalaika so well that the town's music master offered to give him free lessons. His parents, who had wanted him to become a barber, invested the equivalent of $3 in a small violin and within a few years their son won a scholarship to the Warsaw Conservatory. After graduating he came to this country and settled with his family in Pittsburgh.

His professional career began in the steel capital's Cameraphone Theatre in 1912. He worked fairly steadily during the next fifteen years, but was less than a "name" when he managed to get a week's booking at the Paramount Theatre in Manhattan. Rudy Vallee, who prided himself on being able to spot undiscovered talent, took Rubinoff under his wing. Within a short time (1931) he was signed as the featured soloist on "The Eddie Cantor Show," the most popular variety show on radio, heard weekly on NBC. Overnight Rubinoff's name became a household word (he never used his first name—David—professionally).

Although he had been in this country since he was fifteen years old, Rubinoff never lost his heavy Slavic accent. He practically never uttered a word on the air. Once the red light over the control booth went out, however, he was anything but shy. His aggressiveness with the ladies led him into court on more than one occasion. In 1937 Peggy Garcia, a hat check girl whom the violinist had met in a Harlem nightclub, sued him for $500,000 in a breach of promise action. The tabloids played up testimony about the great musician's lavender pajamas and quoted Miss Garcia as stating that "Dave is a great petter." The plaintiff lost sympathy when it was disclosed that she had been married when she was twelve years old. Another time in 1943 the widower of a lady who had been acquainted with Rubinoff sued for alienation of affection.

In 1937, a year before his near fatal illness, he was applauded by 225,000 people in Chicago's Grant Park. During his career four Presidents complimented him on his performances. He shared billing with Al Jolson, Jack Benny, Jimmy Durante, and Maurice Chevalier. Near death in a Detroit hospital he looked back on a full and financially successful life. Rubinoff survived, but by the time his recovery was complete his box office appeal began to fade.

For a man who had made as much as $250,000 a year in the middle of the Great Depression his activities during these past years must have been a bitter pill. The brochure he sends out from his Detroit office lists his recent engagements at such places as the Romulus, Michigan Kiwanis Club, and the local high school of Ashland, Ohio. His repertoire is more varied than most jukeboxes. He might begin the evening with the "Warsaw Concerto," seque into "Fly Me to the Moon," and conclude the program by playing the themes from the most popular TV commercials.

Rubinoff took himself much more seriously than did his fellow musicians. Actually, he was a good violinist but nowhere near the caliber of a Heifitz or Menuhin. What he can rightfully be proud of, if he would admit it, is that his commercial approach to the classics on radio programs with a vaudeville format introduced a great many people to music they would never have heard ordinarily.

In 1962 he announced dramatically after a concert in Plattsburg, New York, that he was retiring.

Until 1965 Rubinoff had occupied an apartment in a second-class hotel in downtown Detroit. When he decided to move to another location in Detroit, he attempted to take the paneling from the living room walls and the plumbing from the bathroom. The management objected and he was again in court and in the papers. Before a settlement was reached someone reminded the court that the maestro had always been "high strung."

Five years after his retirement he was still playing. Thanks to his son, Lieutenant Rubin Rubinoff, who was stationed in Korea with the United States Army in the summer of 1967, the aging artist entertained the troops with his own composition, "Fiddlin' the Fiddle," in Seoul, Korea.

The maestro today with his Stradivarius, insured for $100,000, which he purchased in 1930.

In 1924, Carol portrayed Nancy Montague in *America*.

CAROL DEMPSTER

The lovely heroine of D. W. Griffith pictures was born in Duluth, Minnesota, in 1902. Her parents moved to Los Angeles when she was a baby. In the summer of 1915 Carol was a student at Ted Shawn's dancing school. Griffith was shooting his masterpiece *Intolerance* (1916) and called for some of the girls to perform as dancers. Carol was among them. He used her again when *The Greatest Thing in Life* opened at Clune's Auditorium in 1918. Griffith staged a live prologue to his picture for the Los Angeles opening in which Carol danced again. Although she does not remember him, the archives of the Museum of Modern Art show that Rodolpho di Valentina was also a player in that production. Of course he later became known the world over as Rudolph Valentino.

Griffith became quite smitten with the lovely brown-eyed girl and soon she replaced Lillian Gish in his affections, as well as in some of his films. In her autobiography Colleen Moore is rather bitchy about the relationship and dismisses Carol as a girl with "a thin, sharp face. . . . She couldn't act and he was unable to teach her to do so." Quite a few film buffs disagree. One is William K. Everson, one of the world's leading authorities on motion pictures. In one of his books he named her as one of a handful of silent stars who rank as all-time greats. Her acting he rated as "superb" and compared her performance favorably to Garbo in *Isn't Life Wonderful?* (1924).

Nearly all of Carol Dempster's efforts were under the direction of D. W. Griffith. Not all of them were commercially successful. It has been suggested that the director used the profits from his Lillian Gish films to finance those with Miss Dempster. Whatever his purpose, the Dempster vehicles hold up remarkably well today. Her films are *Scarlet Days* (1919), *The Girl Who Stayed Home* (1919), *Way Down East* (1920), in which she had only a bit part, *The Love Flower* (1920) with Richard Barthelmess, *Dream Street* (1921) with Tyrone Power, Sr., *One Exciting Night* (1922), *The White Rose* (1923) with Ivor Novello and the late Mae Marsh receiving top billing, *America* (1924) with Neil Hamilton who was with her again the next year in *Isn't Life Wonderful?*, *Sally of the Sawdust* (1925) with W. C. Fields and Alfred Lunt, *Sorrows of Satan* (1926) with the late Adolph Menjou and Lya de Putti, and *That Royal Girl* (1926) with W. C. Fields again and James Kirkwood. Carol had a part in a non-Griffith movie *Sherlock Holmes* (1920), which starred John Barrymore.

A great many people in Hollywood thought that Griffith and Carol would marry. One of them was Griffith. Instead Miss Dempster walked out of her contract which had three years left to run and announced her retirement. Rather than continue her acting career she chose to marry the wealthy young investment banker Edwin S. Larsen. Neither had been married before.

Since most of Carol's films were made in the East she was never really a part of the Hollywood community. Many of the greats of her era she has never even met. She frequently saw Charles Farrell and the late Virginia Valli during the winters, which the Larsens spend in their Palm Springs home. One of their closest friends is Lily Pons, who lives in Palm Springs most of the year. Occasionally Carol hears from Neil Hamilton who lives in Los Angeles.

From her retirement until 1965 Carol lived with her husband on their estate in Connecticut. They also maintained an apartment in Manhattan. Mr. Larsen has been retired since 1932 and in the years since then the couple has traveled extensively. In 1965 they sold their home and moved to La Jolla, California. They have no children.

Quite recently Carol said, "I just never think about my days in pictures. I am always very surprised that anyone remembers me. It was so long ago. So many of my movies were so sad. Maybe my fans would like to know that in real life Carol Dempster had a very happy ending."

At her La Jolla, California, home.
Clifford May

Punishing the parquet in 1938.

ELEANOR POWELL

The girl who was crowned the World's Greatest Female Tap Dancer in 1936 by the Dancing Masters of America was born in Springfield, Massachusetts, in 1913. Her mother, thinking that dancing lessons might help her daughter gain some poise and overcome her shyness, had enrolled her in a ballet class.

When she was only thirteen Gus Edwards saw her doing acrobatics on the beach at Atlantic City and asked her mother's permission to put her into the show he was producing at the Ritz Grill. In her late teens she went to New York determined to get into a Broadway show, but found that all of the jobs went to those who could tap. After some lessons from Jack Donahue and a lot of private practice she landed a spot in *Follow Through* in 1929. In 1931 she was in *Fine and Dandy,* and the following year Flo Ziegfeld gave her a part in *Hot Cha,* which starred Buddy Rogers (who lives with his wife Mary Pickford at Pickfair in Beverly Hills). While appearing in *At Home Abroad,* the Bea Lillie starrer, Eleanor suffered a collapse from overwork and had to withdraw completely after missing several performances, which she considered "worse than death."

When she was signed by Metro-Goldwyn-Mayer from her Casino de Paree engagement in 1935 Eleanor was still rather shy and certainly not pretty by Hollywood standards. Metro made her undergo extensive dental work, gave her voice lessons, and unleased its beauticians on the new contract player. It was a very glamorized Eleanor who tested for a featured role in *Broadway Melody of 1936.* The late Louis B. Mayer saw the test and gave her the lead. Playing a dual role, Eleanor did an imitation of Katharine Hepburn as well as a couple of dazzling tap numbers and emerged a brand new very big star. The studio rushed her into *Born to Dance* (1936) with Jimmy Stewart as her leading man and five hundred chorus boys to back her up in the finale. The next year they put her with Ilona Massey* and the late Nelson Eddy in *Rosalie* and with Robert Young in *Honolulu.*

As Ruby Keeler* became inactive, Miss Powell inherited her mantle, which meant that mothers around the country took their little girls to dance classes in hopes that they would become another Eleanor Powell. Some other pictures she brightened were *Broadway Melody of 1938* with Robert Taylor, *Broadway Melody of 1940* in which she held her own with George Murphy and Fred Astaire, *Lady Be Good* (1941), *Ship Ahoy* (1942), the original title of which was *I'll Take Manila*, *As Thousands Cheer* (1944), and *Sensations of 1945*.

At the height of her career Eleanor made as much as $125,000 a picture, adding huge sums from personal appearances at the Roxy, Loew's State, and Capitol, and London's Palladium. Eleanor made many appearances on radio variety programs and even cut some records for RCA for which she tapped out her numbers from *Broadway Melody of 1936* and *At Home Abroad* with Tommy Dorsey's orchestra backing her. Most of her routines she developed herself.

In 1938 she received her first and last unpleasant publicity when the late news hen Dorothy Kilgallen began her column, "Eleanor Powell's handsome male secretary can do most anything." The article ended with the young man's telephone number. Reached for comment, he said that there was nothing between them and that he only wanted to marry a little home girl. He did—Lynn Bari, followed by Judy Garland. His name was Sid Luft.

Eleanor retired shortly after her marriage to Glenn Ford in 1943. The only work she did after that was a TV series entitled "Faith Of Our Children" which ran for three years beginning in 1955. It was a religious series more like Sunday school, which won five Emmies and many other awards. In 1959 the Fords were divorced. Eleanor has not remarried.

In 1961, when she was forty-eight, her only child, Peter, talked her into a comeback. It was the kind that most performers only dream of. She looked great, and her dancing brought the house down at Las Vegas' Sahara and Manhattan's Latin Quarter. The act ran fifty-five minutes, during which she was assisted by four young men. It was however a very expensive production and few clubs could afford it. Then, too, Eleanor did not really care to continue, and wished to continue her church work. Formerly a Presbyterian, Eleanor is now a member of a religious group called The Symposium. As associate preacher she advocates their creed of "faith a-go go" and "love a-go go."

An associate preacher today. *Jon Virzi*

From *The Best Years of Our Lives.*

HAROLD RUSSELL

The only man to win two Academy Awards for one performance was born in Sydney, Nova Scotia, in 1914. When he was six, following the death of his father, a telegraph manager, the Russell family moved to Boston. He attended public schools there and in nearby Cambridge, graduating from high school in 1933. He then went to work for a chain store, where he soon became manager of the meat department.

Russell volunteered for paratroops service, qualifying as an instructor, and specialized in demolition and explosives. He had made more than 50 jumps before D-Day on June 6, 1944. While the Allied forces were invading Normandy, Russell, a master sergeant, was showing a group of inductees how to pull the fuse on a hand grenade, when it went off.

Harold recovered from the blast at Walter Reed Hospital, but he had lost both his hands. He was fitted for artificial limbs and hooks, and began to exercise and train for rehabilitation. He was selected by the Surgeon General to portray himself in a documentary film entitled *The Diary of a Sergeant,* which told how an amputee had overcome the loss of both hands. The twenty-minute movie was shown at military hospitals and war-bond rallies. It was at a rally in Hollywood that director William Wyler saw Russell in the short.

Wyler was under contract to producer Samuel Goldwyn to direct a motion picture from a story by McKinley Kantor entitled "Glory for Three." It concerned three servicemen and the problems they encountered on their return to civilian life. Dana Andrews played a flyer, Fredric March an army sergeant, and there was a third role of a spastic sailor. After Wyler saw Russell, he and Goldwyn decided to change the script and make the character an amputee.

The movie was made under the title *The Best Years of Our Lives,* and was a smash success financially and critically. Wyler insisted that Russell not be coached in acting, for he wanted a completely natural performance. None of the male cast wore makeup.

When Harold was nominated as the Best Supporting Actor of 1946 he had stiff competition from Claude Rains, Clifton Webb, William Demarest, and Charles Coburn. The Academy board members felt that he had practically no chance of winning, and voted to give him a special award on the evening of the Oscar presentations. His special award, "for bringing hope and courage to his fellow veterans," was presented to him by Shirley Temple. Russell was backstage receiving congratulations from the other nominees when someone pulled him back onstage and he learned that he had been voted the Best Supporting Actor as well.

Russell never seriously considered continuing a screen career. While touring the country for the picture, he received two offers of parts in other movies, but turned them down. In 1946 he married and returned to Boston, where he opened a public-relations office. He is a graduate of Boston University.

In 1949 his autobiography *Victory in My Hands* was published, and has been translated into twenty languages. At one point in the book he states his philosophy: "It is not what you have lost but what you have left that counts."

Russell was the National Commander of the AMVETS in 1949, 1950, and 1960. He is the only National Commander to serve three terms. He is now the president of Tag-A-Bag Company, and in 1962 was named by President Kennedy Vice-Chairman of the President's Committee on Hiring the Handicapped. President Johnson appointed him Chairman on April 18, 1964.

People often recognize Russell as he travels around the country on business trips and to lecture. He often runs into Hollywood people he knew during his time at Goldwyn Studios. Upon meeting new people he invariably extends his right hook which he feels puts people at their ease. "People accept your disability if you accept it," he says.

Russell divides his time between Washington, D.C., where he has offices as the Chairman of the President's Committee, and Wayland, Massachusetts, where he lives with his wife and two children Jerry and Adele Rita. On his mantle sit the envy of many actors—two Academy Awards.

Harold lends a "helping hand" to a fellow AMVET.

The Orchid Lady in 1925.

CORINNE GRIFFITH

"The Orchid Lady of the Screen" was born in Texarkana, Texas, in 1896. She was educated at the Sacred Heart Academy in New Orleans where she was chosen Queen of the Mardi Gras. After her picture appeared on the cover of rotogravure sections of newspapers around the country she was signed to a contract with Vitagraph Pictures. Her early films were made in the East so that when she arrived in Hollywood in the early twenties she was already a star. Very few of her contemporaries though had ever met her. Even in an era of great beauty Corinne was outstanding. Her delicate coloring and features earned her the title of "The Orchid Lady," and her beach house in Malibu was described as "orchidaceous." Five hundred movie editors throughout the country were polled, and voted her "The Most Beautiful Woman in the World."

Her silent pictures include *The Last Man* (1916), *Doctor Love* (1917), *Miss Ambition* (1918) with Betty Blythe (who is a resident of the Motion Picture Country Hospital in Woodland Hills, California), *Adventure Shop* (1919), *Human Collateral* (1920), *It Isn't Being Done This Season* (1921), *Received Payment* (1922), *Common Law* (1923), *Black Oxen* (1924), *Déclassé* (1925), *Mademoiselle Modiste* (1926), *The Lady in Ermine* (1927) with the late Francis X. Bushman, *The Garden of Eden* (1928), and *Saturday's Children* (1929). Her career was exceptionally long, but it ended with talkies. Her studio had so little faith in her that they paid off in full the remaining time left of her contract.

Miss Griffith, however, did not give up so easily. Even today she bridles when anyone refers to her as a "silent star." Although Corinne made several sound movies, none was a great success. In 1930 she made *Lilies of the Field* with John Loder (who lives in the San Luis province of Argentina) in Hollywood and then went to England where she did *Lily Christine* in 1932. In 1934 Radio Pictures gave her the female lead opposite Otto Kruger in *Crime Doctor* but she was released from her contract and paid off, with another actress replacing her. *The Mistress of the Close-up,* another of her titles, was so impossible over "her lighting" and "her scenes" (in what was supposed to be a man's picture), that the studio gave up on her.

After she was let go from the film, she toured in *Design For Living*. While away she rented her Beverly Hills home to Jeanette MacDonald whom she later sued for $1,018, claiming the singing star's dog ruined some of her furniture and draperies.

In 1936 Corinne married George "Wet Wash" Preston Marshall, owner of the Washington Redskins and a laundry empire. They lived in Washington, D.C., until 1958 when the marriage ended in divorce. While they were together Miss Griffith wrote six books, the two most popular being *My Life with the Redskins* (1944) and *Papa's Delicate Condition* (1952). Her first husband was actor-director Webster Campbell to whom she was married from 1920 until 1923 and her second was Walter Morosco, a producer who was her husband from 1933 to 1934.

Although the former star took a beating in the 1929 stock market crash, much of her $10,000-a-week salary was put into southern California real estate which has made her a millionairess many times over. She has bought, sold, and traded property until now she is one of the largest landowners in Beverly Hills.

Corinne had married Broadway dancer-singer Danny Scholl, who was then thirty-eight. After thirty-three days, during which Miss Griffith claims the marriage was never consummated, they went to court for a divorce. Scholl testified that he had married his wife believing that she was only fifty-two. He also complained that she bossed him constantly and preached Christian Science to him. When called to the stand the actress swore that she was only fifty-two, had never made a silent film, and that the real Corinne Griffith had died in the mid-thirties. She had only been her stand-in.

In spite of her age Corinne Griffith is never idle. She has according to her own count made over five hundred speeches on behalf of her pet project, the repeal of the personal income tax, which she refers to as "legalized thievery." In one of her early pictures she played a czarina. Her politics today are a bit right of the last czar.

Being interviewed after a recent robbery. *UPI*

Socking it to them on the Bob Hope radio program in the late forties. *NBC*

FRANKIE "SUGAR CHILE" ROBINSON

The pint-sized pianist who amazed and entertained millions during his short career in show business was born in 1940 and raised in Detroit, Michigan. When he was eighteen months old an aunt gave the Robinson family an old piano which was completely ignored until Frankie discovered that by touching the keys he could make sounds. His fingers were too short to reach from one key to another so he began striking the notes he wanted with his tiny fists. When a relative who knew something about music heard the child play he suggested that the elder Robinson listen to what his son could do. The father exclaimed, "I have and I can't stand it!"

Frankie had a natural talent for music and did not have to take lessons. When his parents showed no interest in a career for him friends and relatives started taking him to bars where he played for amazed customers. When some of the audience began dropping change on top of his piano, Mr. Robinson, who was an iceman, showed more appreciation for his son's talent. Stage shows were at that time common in large motion picture houses. The first theatre he was taken to for an audition dismissed the act because of Frankie's age. Phil Brestoff, in 1945 the musical director of the Michigan Theatre in Detroit, heard the boy by chance and put in a good word for him. Audiences confirmed his belief that the five-year-old was a real talent.

Although Frankie's biggest novelty lay in his youth, radio audiences were also enthusiastic. Overnight anyone hearing the name Frankie "Sugar Chile" Robinson knew that he was a preschool age Negro boy who could bang out boogie-woogie with the best of the professionals. He sat on more famous knees than anyone in America. Kate Smith, the Queen of network radio, had him on her show regularly. He was one of Danny Kaye's favorites. Bob Hope took

Frankie with him when he played the Palladium in London. True to show business tradition, "Sugar Chile" managed to steal the spotlight and sometimes the show from some of the most seasoned performers in the business. He was tiny, talented, and very cute.

One of Frankie's favorite stories about his days in the big time is when he was told that the King and Queen of England were in the audience and were looking forward to his act. He got so nervous he had a nosebleed right in the middle of it.

In 1946 at the age of six he had a contract with Metro-Goldwyn-Mayer and a $100,000 bank account. He appeared in *No Leave, No Love* (1946) with Van Johnson. This was his only movie. His managers felt he could make more money in personal appearances around the country. They were right and Frankie has no regrets. He said recently that in his time Negroes were hopelessly typecast in movies and besides, he enjoyed the excitement of a large audience.

The child prodigy dropped out of show business in the early fifties and settled down in Detroit. He and his father, who never delivered another cake of ice, own a grocery store in the Negro section of the motor city. The only time he plays the piano is at his parish church, but even that still draws a big crowd.

His only contact with his old profession is an occasional letter from one of the stars he has worked with. He swears he does not miss it a bit and has no regrets except for the fact that he suspects all the girls he dates are interested in his money. It had been put in trust and is now providing enough money from the interest alone for him to live on it. On top of that he has an investment in a therapeutic bath solution which is proving quite successful. Says Frankie, "I am a very happy man."

One thing about the boy wonder that has changed very little is his height. He is 4 feet 5 inches.

Behind the counter at his grocery store on St. Aubin Street, Detroit. *Detroit News*

Much sought after in the mid-thirties.

VIRGINIA BRUCE

The blonde star of the thirties was born in Minneapolis in 1910 with the name Helen Virginia Briggs. Her mother was an amateur golf champion of North Dakota for three years. Her insurance broker father, took the family to Fargo, North Dakota, where she attended high school, and thereafter was transferred to Los Angeles.

Virginia planned to attend U.C.L.A. but while touring a movie studio, director William Beaudine and his publicity man Harry Wurtzel saw her and Beaudine signed her to a personal contract at $25 a week. Her first film was with Madge Bellamy (who owns a scrapyard in Ontario, California, and lives under her real name Margaret Philpot). Virginia had a ·bit part as did Jean Harlow. Her second try was in the Helen Twelvetrees starrer *Blue Skies* (1929). Next came *Love Parade* (1929) with Jeanette MacDonald and Maurice Chevalier. Virginia had one line.

Through her friend Jack Harkrider, a designer of the Ziegfeld shows, she became one of the Goldwyn Girls in the Eddie Cantor picture *Whoopee,* the film that brought director Busby Berkeley to Hollywood in 1930. Harkrider helped get her a Broadway showgirl job in *Smiles,* which was produced by Flo Ziegfeld and starred Fred and Adele Astaire* in 1930, which was followed by another Ziegfeld production, *America's Sweetheart*. It lasted six months. She then departed for Hollywood to do a screen test at Metro-Goldwyn-Mayer with newcomer Robert Young. After a few small roles they put her in *Downstairs* (1932), which was written by and starred the great lover of the silent screen, John Gilbert. They fell madly in love during the shooting and were married as soon as it was completed. After the birth of their daughter Susan Ann in 1933 Virginia retired from the screen. One year later her retirement and her marriage ended. The Gilberts were divorced and she made *Jane Eyre* (1934). When he died in 1936 Gilbert left his ex-wife and their daughter the bulk of his $250,000 estate. In a flurry of activity Virginia appeared in fourteen movies in only sixteen months.

A partial list of her pictures are *Slightly Scarlet* (1930) with Evelyn Brent, *Mighty Barnum* (1934), in which she played Jenny Lind, *Metropolitan* (1935) opposite the late Lawrence Tibbett, *The Great Ziegfeld* (1936), in which she played Audrey Dane, *Women of Glamour* (1937) with Melvyn Douglas, *Let Freedom Ring* (1939) with Nelson Eddy, *The Invisible Woman* (1941) with John Barrymore, and *Careful, Soft Shoulders* (1942).

Virginia Bruce and J. Walter Rubin, the director-producer, first met when she arrived in Hollywood but they "didn't know it was love" until he directed her in *Bad Man of Brimstone* (1938). Upon completion of the picture the two were married on December 18, 1937. Virginia retired soon after, and her Metro contract expired. A son Christopher was born in 1941. Rubin died in 1942 leaving an estate of $50,000 in cash and securities.

In 1946 she married Ali Ipar, a twenty-three-year-old Turkish writer-producer who had just been inducted into the United States Army. She was then thirty-five. In 1947 he returned to visit his extremely wealthy father in Turkey and was denied reentry by the United States immigration authorities. A long legal battle ensued and he was finally readmitted in 1948. In 1951 her husband was called into the Turkish Army but Turkish law denies a commission to any Turk married to a foreigner. Virginia obligingly divorced him. He was discharged in 1952 and they were remarried. In the meantime Virginia and her children had lived with Ipar's family. In 1961 Ali was arrested in Turkey and spent nineteen months in prison, charged with a debt of over $3,000,000. While he was incarcerated his permanent resident visa expired which caused no end of trouble with the United States State Department.

With the exception of a film made in England in 1952 and *The Night Has a Thousand Eyes* (1948) with the late Gail Russell, she has remained retired. However, in 1960 she played Kim Novak's mother in *Strangers When We Meet*. Since then she has lived quietly in her beautiful home in Pacific Palisades, California.

As a southern California matron. *Jon Virzi*

The Hungarian beauty in 1923.

MITZI

The famous musical star whose real name was Marishka Hajos was born in Budapest, Hungary, in 1891. Shortly after she was able to talk the child began doing imitations of everyone and everything she came into contact with. From the age of four she appeared in Budapest theatres doing her imitations, singing and dancing under the billing of "the wonder child, Mitzi Hajos." She was taken to Vienna where her uncle secured a good manager who got her better billing and wages. Mitzi became so popular in Central Europe that the Emperor himself, Franz Josef, and Archduke Ferdinand, whose assassination touched off the First World War, came to see her on several occasions.

When she was only twelve years old she was brought to this country by the famous agent William Morris, who made a specialty of importing top European acts.

Morris presented her first in *The Barnyard Romeo* in 1910. That next year she was seen in *La Belle Paree* with Al Jolson, and toured in *The Spring Maid* in 1912. For her first few shows she hardly understood a word of what she was saying or singing.

Most of her vehicles were produced either by Henry W. Savage or J. J. Shubert. Savage felt that her last name should be dropped because it would never be mastered by Americans. It is correctly pronounced "Hoy-ousch." In such productions as *Her Little Highness* (1913) and *Pom-Pom* (1916) she was billed simply as Mitzi and it stuck. Her biggest hit was *Sari* in 1914 which introduced the famous "Sari Waltz." Jerome Kern wrote *Head Over Heels* for her in 1918. Sidney Greenstreet was her leading man in *Lady Billy* in 1920 and Stanley Lupino, father of Ida Lupino and a well known English stage star, was with her in *Naughty Riquette* in 1923. After *The Magic Ring* in 1926, Savage decided that the cost of musicals was prohibitive (*Ring* came in at $50,000. Minimum cost for a musical today is $600,000) and Mitzi went to the Shuberts. Her shows were light and airy with lots of music, singing, dancing, and an abundance of Mitzi. Arthur Treacher was with her in *Mad Cap* in 1928.

Another child star, Mitzi Green (wife of movie executive Joe Pevney and a resident of Newport Beach, California), was named for the Hungarian headliner after her parents had appeared in a Mitzi starrer.

By her own admission Mitzi never had much of a voice and has never had a lesson in her life but there was so much energy and personality packed into her 4 foot 10½ inch frame that she never had any trouble putting over a song. European stars were all the rage in those days and she was a particular favorite of the period.

In 1927 Mitzi became a Christian Scientist, with the usual fervor of a convert, and she neither smokes nor drinks.

In her entire career, which ended on Broadway with an unsuccessful revival of *Sari* in 1930, she missed but one performance; Mitzi, along with most of the audience, was unable to make it to the theatre in St. Joseph, Missouri, for a matinee because of a fierce snowstorm.

She was married to actor Boyd Marshall from 1920 until his death in 1950. They had no children. Following 1930, after leaving the stage she worked in the Shubert offices until 1952 when she was retired—"they made me quit. I just loved my work." In the spring of 1968 she moved from her Jackson Heights apartment into a home in Danbury, Connecticut. Mitzi sees many Broadway shows, particularly musicals. She comes into Manhattan at least once a week to have her hair done, see a matinee, and lunch at Schrafft's. She admits to missing her work in the theatre both on and behind the stage. "I'd work in a show tomorrow if I really felt the part was right for me, but listen, I'm no kid anymore and I know it." One aspect of show business that she does not long for is the attention of the public. "I just hate being stared at," she says in the still heavy Hungarian accent. "I know that's crazy for an actress and I never minded on the stage, of course, but on the streets and restaurants! It is something I never got used to. Now no one knows me and that's just fine."

Having a soda recently in Times Square, near the theatres where she once starred. *Diana Keyt*

In 1926, one of Paramount Pictures' most promising contract players.

ESTHER RALSTON

The actress known as "The American Venus" was born in Bar Harbor, Maine, in 1902. At two years old her parents worked her into their act, which played vaudeville, the Chautauqua circuit, carnivals, burlesque, and repertory companies. They were billed as "The Ralston Family"—featuring Baby Esther, "America's Youngest Juliet."

By 1916 the Ralstons had arrived in Hollywood where Esther became a bit player in Hoot Gibson and Tom Mix westerns. In 1920 she got a tiny part in *The Kid,* which launched the career of Jackie Coogan. In 1922, Coogan made *Oliver Twist* with Lon Chaney, and Esther got a bigger role. She continued in westerns until Jesse Lasky and Walter Wanger gave her the chance to play the role of Mrs. Darling in *Peter Pan* (1925). She was young but the producers wanted a child's idea of a mother. It is still considered one of the finest silents ever made.

The American Venus (1925) gave her her title. That year she married George Webb, a director-actor. A great boost was *A Kiss for Cinderella* (1926), in which she played the fairy godmother. The same year she made the silent classic *Old Ironsides* with Charles Farrell. B. P. Schulberg cast Esther and the late Clara Bow as leads in *Children of Divorce* (1927).

Josef von Sternberg used her in *The Case of Lena Smith* (1928), under whom she emerged a dramatic star.

Richard Dix and Esther debuted together in talkies with *Wheel of Life* (1929). In 1931 she was Lawrence Tibbett's leading lady in *The Prodigal*. She played London's Palladium and toured the provinces for a year, and made *After the Fall* (1933) with the late Basil Rathbone and *Rome Express* (1933) opposite Conrad Veidt.

In 1933 Esther returned to Hollywood where she and Webb were divorced, and she signed with Metro-Goldwyn-Mayer. The lady was uncooperative with production head Louis B. Mayer who admired her and so she was loaned out for pictures hardly calculated to boast her career. She suffered through thirteen for Universal, did *Black Beauty* (1933), for Monogram, and was even subjected to a Ken Maynard western, *Wheels of Destiny* (1934) at Republic. Her only important film for M-G-M during the contract was the Joan Crawford starrer *Sadie McKee* (1934). That year she married Will Morgan, a singer.

In 1936 she appeared in *Reunion* with the Dionne quintuplets for Fox and returned to her old lot, Paramount, for *Hollywood Blvd.* with Bob Cummings. It included cameo performances by her contemporaries from silent days. Esther's other movies in the late thirties were either undistinguished or just plain bad. Examples are *Girl from Mandalay* (1936) with Conrad Nagel and *Shadows of the Orient* (1937) opposite Regis Toomey.

Esther's last picture of consequence was *Tin Pan Alley* (1940), an Alice Faye musical in which she played the great vaudevillian, Nora Bayes.

Her second marriage ended in 1938, and the following year she married Ted Lloyd, a newspaper man. In 1941 and 1942 Esther played the title role in the radio soap opera "Woman of Courage." She went into retirement through the ensuing forties to raise her children. From 1950 until 1952 she toured the straw hat circuit. Esther was divorced again in 1954 and has not remarried.

In 1956 she went to work at B. Altman's department store branch in Manhasset, Long Island. She left in 1961, as head of the Boy's Shop, for a running part in "Our Five Daughters" on NBC-TV, until 1962. There were TV appearances on the "Kraft Theatre" and "Texaco Playhouse" until 1965 when Esther dropped in to visit her old friend, actor's agent, Marge Kerr. She accepted a job and has been there ever since as vice-president of the Kerr Talent Agency.

She commutes daily from an apartment overlooking Lake Oakland in Queens, New York, to her Manhattan office. Her spare time is devoted to writing her autobiography.

"The American Venus" in her Manhattan office. *Diana Keyt*